Family Affairs

In the decades between the close of the First World War and the end of the Thatcher era, English families faced unprecedented change and challenges. Technology transformed the housewife's lot. Attitudes shifted. In 1920 cohabitation, abortion, illegitimacy, divorce and homosexuality threatened family reputations; by 1990 they were commonplace.

Family Affairs explores the secret life of English families from 1920 to 1990. Mary Abbott takes the reader into her subjects' homes and hearts and provokes us to reflect on families past and speculate on families future. A product of intense original research of primary and secondary sources, this volume is an important contribution to the history of the family. Abbott has a talent for the telling vignette, the graphic detail and pungent phrase. This is an invaluable source for the student of family history as well as anyone interested in this perennially fascinating subject.

Mary Abbott teaches at the Anglia Polytechnic University in Cambridge. Her previous publications include *Family Ties: English Families 1540–1920* (Routledge 1993) and *Life Cycles in England 1560–1720: Cradle to Grave* (1996).

Family Affairs

A history of the family in
20th century England

Mary Abbott

Routledge
Taylor & Francis Group

LONDON AND NEW YORK

First published 2003
by Routledge
11 New Fetter Lane, London EC4P 4EE

Simultaneously published in the USA and Canada
by Routledge
29 West 35th Street, New York, NY 10001

Routledge is an imprint of the Taylor & Francis Group

© 2003 Mary Abbott

Typeset in Goudy Old Style by
BOOK NOW Ltd
Printed and bound in Great Britain by
MPG Books Ltd, Bodmin

British Library Cataloguing in Publication Data
A catalogue record for this book is available from the British Library

Library of Congress Cataloging in Publication Data
Abbott, Mary, 1942–
    Family affairs : a history of the family in 20th century Britain / Mary Abbott.
        p.   cm.
    Includes bibliographical references and index.
        1. Family–Great Britain–History–20th century. 2. Social change–Great
    Britain–History–20th century. I. Title: History of the family in 20th century Britain. II.
    Title.

    HQ613 .A2 2002
    306.85′0941′0904–dc21

                                                                    2002031681

ISBN 0-415-14586-4 (hbk)
ISBN 0-415-14587-2 (pbk)

Contents

Introduction

In 1920 decrees, commandments, laws and ordinances enshrined in the Old Testament books of Genesis and Exodus represented the dominant code of conduct in Britain:

- Honour thy father and mother
- If a man entice a maid . . . and lie with her, he shall surely endow her to be his wife
- Thy husband . . . shall rule over thee
- Thou shalt not commit adultery.

St Paul ranked abstinence above sexual gratification:

> It is good for a man not to touch a woman. Nevertheless to avoid fornication let every man have his own wife, and let every woman have her own husband . . . It is better to marry than to burn.

While there was power in the old morality, keeping up appearances paid dividends. As Phyllis James (born 1920), the child of an unhappy lower-middle-class couple, observed, when she was at school, the break up of a marriage 'was still regarded not only as a disgrace but as a social failure' and an economic catastrophe. For her mother, 'deeply religious, it would have been a sin'. 'I can't complain', 'I mustn't grumble' were the mantras of the married.

This regime did not go unchallenged. The literary lion H. G. Wells, born – into the lower-middle class – in 1866, campaigned against the 'haunting emphasis on sacrifice and discipline'. His heroes were the radical intellectuals – William Godwin (born 1756) and Percy Bysshe Shelley (born 1792). Wells addressed his liberating manifesto to men and to women without children. His own marriage was far from conventional. According to his own account, he and his wife Jane negotiated a *modus vivendi*. He was licensed as a 'casual lover' whose extramarital 'passades' were to be indulged. She had 'rooms of her own in Bloomsbury' where she inhabited 'the personality of Catherine Wells', a writer. While they were alive, Wells protected his lovers' reputations. The confessional postscript to his *Experiment in Autobiography* (1934) was not published for another fifty years. Even then it was expurgated. 'Courtesy and concern over litigation' led Wells's son and editor to suppress further material that was finally published in Andrea Lynn's *Shadow Lovers: The Last Affairs of H. G. Wells* in 2001. It is impossible to estimate how common discreet extramarital 'passades' were among the majority of men and women who did not choose to share their secrets with posterity.

The women and men of 2000 were less prisoners of gender – and biology – than the women and men of 1920. Thanks to Marie Stopes (born 1880), middle-class wives and indeed confident and solvent single women of the 1920s and 1930s had unprecedented control over their fertility. Painfully slowly, in the course of the following three or four decades, contraceptives became freely available to the majority of women in Britain. Legal abortions became common. As a result, a 'hasty exchange of bodily fluids' was much less likely to result in the birth of an unwanted child. By the end of the century the stigma and disabilities associated with births outside marriage had faded into insignificance. Men and women were increasingly inclined to stay together 'during pleasure'. George Bernard Shaw (born 1856), called H. G. Wells 'a spoiled child'. By the end of the century 'spoiled children' who rejected the traditional virtues of discipline and self-sacrifice abounded.

The evidence

The historian's task is forensic: identifying fragments and piecing them together, making educated guesses. Where I have had the choice, I have avoided sources tainted by hindsight. *Family Affairs* draws on articles and advertisements published in newspapers and magazines; entertainments, including anthologies of comic and curious verse; essays; letters; surveys compiled by social scientists; texts written for medical students (indeed on a variety of 'how-to' books); still and moving pictures; objects of all kinds; conversations with friends and, perhaps most of all, memoirs and biographies. Biographical writing biases the sample towards an articulate minority. However, many people, celebrated in later life, were brought up in 'ordinary' families: Phyllis or as she is better known P. D. James is an example.

I have fought shy of statistics. The distinguished social scientist Peter Townsend underlined the tension between the social scientist's anxiety 'to establish patterns, uniformities and systems of social action' and 'the uniqueness of each individual and each family'. The film-maker Derek Jarman was more emphatic: 'HAVE YOU EVER THOUGHT OF BECOMING A STATISTIC?' he asked.

We have to face up to the fact that images of family lives are much easier to recover than the realities. The criminal law demands proof 'beyond all reasonable doubt'; the civil law operates the far less testing 'balance of probability'. The evidence for the intimate life of families, even in recent times, is unsafe. Often we cannot approach the benchmark required in civil cases. Children grew up believing that families were meant to be happy – and pretended that they were. A boy whose mother was unable to resist the temptation to 'say something hard or hurtful' believed for a long time that his was the *only* unhappy family. And, in photographs, even his family looked happy. Memories are fallible. In the 1930s the unhappily married Mrs James 'was compulsorily admitted' to Fulbourne, the mental hospital that served Cambridge where her family lived in the 1930s. In adult life her daughter Phyllis could not remember precisely when that happened nor indeed 'how long it was before she came out again'.

Negotiating *Family Affairs*

Family Affairs begins with an exploration of bonds and barriers in family and society. In the chapters that follow families are set against a backdrop of the changing times they lived through. In the course of the three-score-years and ten between 1920 and 1990 machines inside the home and out of it made the household skills of making, mending, washing, cleaning and even cooking obsolete. In the Twenties the two-child family was already the norm in the expanding middle classes; by the 1990s parenthood had become a 'lifestyle choice'. The consequences were seismic.

But families have their own milestones and markers, tragedies and triumphs, births, matings, and deaths.

1   Cultural tribes

The Census of 1921 assigned households to one of five occupational classes. The professional person belonged to Class I; the unskilled manual worker to Class V. Life was more complicated than most social scientists' classifications suggest. The upper classes were not homogeneous. In October 1918 the shy but daring Virginia Woolf, born into the intellectual aristocracy of late-Victorian England in 1882, reflected on 'the gulf between respectable mummified humbug' of the Kensington she had been brought up in and 'life crude & impertinent' in the 'Bloomsbury' she helped to shape. In 'Bloomsbury' it was possible to mention both 'copulation' and W[ater] C[loset]s. Gait, dress, manners, accent even more than occupation or income were the cultural markers that distinguished 'them' from 'us'. In Lancashire in the 1930s women were divided into the hatted elite and the wearers of shawls – a shawl did double service as headgear and coat – and could accommodate a child in arms too. As a small girl, Phyllis Noble, a Londoner born in 1922, the daughter of a jobbing builder, recognised her mother's categories: 'rough', 'respectable' and 'posh'. As her son Alan (born 1934) recalled, Lilian Bennett, a Leeds butcher's wife, pigeonholed her acquaintances as 'better off', 'well off', 'refined', 'educated', 'ordinary' or 'common'. In the 1950s the Yorkshire broadcaster Wilfred Pickles (born 1904) contrasted 'good neighbourly fowk' with 'stuck-up fowk'. The examples of 'People Like Us' and, even more, of the people 'we' aspired to resemble were prime influences on conduct. The thumbnail sketch of Rosamond Lehmann (born 1901) that appeared in the Penguin edition of her novel *Dusty Answer* in 1936 exuded glamour.

> Her father was a Member of Parliament, a contributor to *Punch*, and also known as one of the best oarsmen in England. She is the wife of a well-known painter [Wogan Philipps], they spend much of their time in Wales, or in a country place not far from Oxford, he busy with his painting, she with her writing.

To Mrs Forster, a working man's wife living in Carlisle, the kind of life led by Mrs Dale, the suburban doctor's wife who shared her *Diary* with listeners in the 1940s and 1950s, was ideal.

By investing in a suitable nanny, a prep and public school education, wealthy parents could buy 'a little upper-middle-class child'. The grammar schools, paler imitations of public schools brought into the state system in the 1940s, 'learn[ed]' their pupils 'to be snobs', to quote a Yorkshire father's bitter verdict. Oxford or Cambridge could complete the transformation for a young man or woman who took polish well. Kathleen Raine (born 1908) was brought up in Ilford 'at the extreme boundary' of what she thought of as a 'makeshift suburb', where 'bricks and mortar met buttercup meadows'. Her schoolteacher father had learned 'educated English as a foreign language at Durham University'. His brothers were miners and among her cousins was 'the dirtiest baby' Kathleen Raine had ever seen, her bottom and legs 'were ingrained with dirt'. In 1926, the clever only child of ambitious parents, Raine went up to Girton, supported by a county scholarship and a college exhibition. She was entranced by what her contemporary Christopher Isherwood (born 1904) called the poshocracy. Returning from Cambridge to Ilford at the end of term was an 'extinction'. Raine's first husband, the son of a Methodist minister, came from a background not unlike her own. Her second, Charles Madge (born 1912), could trace his descent from a Norman knight who died within sight of Jerusalem in 1096. In marrying, she believed, they 'defied the ancestors'. Her final, unrequited, passion was for Gavin Maxwell (born 1914), whose grandfather was Duke of Northumberland.

In the course of time, humble origins acquired glamour. The architectural historian John Summerson (born 1904) was the son of 'a manufacturer of railway lines'. 'As a boy at Harrow School in the 1920s,' Summerson recalled, 'I did all I could to prevent *any*one from finding out that my grandfather was a common labourer'. A couple of generations on he would have made sure 'that *every*one knew'.' To his obituarists, however, his identity as a Harrovian remained paramount. Early in the 1990s Mark Hudson (born 1957) set out to explore his family roots. His father, Tom, born in a Durham mining village in 1922, had made a successful career in the art world – his *curriculum vitae* included one-man shows in London, senior posts in art schools in Britain and Canada. He had 'described so vividly the world of the old colliery houses' that his son was astonished to discover that he had in fact grown up in a house that was 'ultramodern for its time'. The family was a cut above the miners: the children were forbidden to speak 'pitmatic', the dialect of the colliery.

Writing in 1941, George Orwell (born 1903) identified 'the upward and downward extension of the middle class' as 'one of the most important developments in England during the past twenty years': 'It has happened on such a scale as to make the old' – Marxist – 'classification of society into capitalists, proletarians and petit-bourgeois (small property owners) almost obsolete'. Orwell discerned 'the germs of the future England' 'in the light-industry areas and along the arterial roads. In Slough, Dagenham, Barnet, Letchworth, Hayes'. He foresaw 'a rather restless cultureless life, centring around tinned food, *Picture Post*, the radio and the internal combustion engine. It is a civilization in which children grow up with an intimate knowledge of magnetos and in complete ignorance of the Bible'. Update the technology, find a substitute for the long-lamented *Picture Post* and you might conclude that he was not far from the mark.

Condemned out of their own mouths

Accents exposed the fine gradations of class and culture. In the schoolroom, Nancy Mitford (born 1904) ridiculed the 'refainments' of a governess's accent: 'ay lay on may ayderdown . . . tossing from sade to sade'. Between the wars the headmistress of her grammar school strove to 'fortify' Irene Thomas's 'Ls' – she trained her to say 'pencil' not 'pensoo' and 'milk' instead of 'meeook'. In 1960 Bronwen Pugh (born 1930), the daughter of a Welsh County Court judge and a former student of the Central School of Speech and Drama, married a significantly older man – Bill Astor (born 1907), educated at Eton and New College, Oxford. Pugh, by her own admission, 'was not upper class': 'My husband didn't like the way I said "round". He used to try to teach me to say "rauwnd".' When Bryan Gould (born 1939) arrived in Oxford in 1962, he encountered undergraduates a generation younger than Astor who spoke 'in the exaggerated upper class accents which [he] had only ever heard on radio comedy shows' at home in New Zealand. As Martin Amis (born 1949) explained to his sons, children of the 1980s, 'it used to be cool to be posh'. At Oxford Amis, schooled at grammars and crammers, learned to say 'lavatory', 'sofa', 'Mon*dee*' not 'Mon-day'.

The 'posh' belonged to a national village. Ordinary people went to local schools and had local loyalties and local speech. As Raymond Williams (born 1921) observed, 'You can talk about an Oxford or Cambridge accent, but go out into the working-class areas of Oxford and Cambridge and you won't hear either'. A working-class Cambridge man (men generally had stronger accents) would pronounce Hughes Hall 'whose haul'. Tom Driberg (born 1905) reported 'an interesting little class misunderstanding' that occurred at a bus stop in London in 1951. A young man with an 'Oxford' accent asked the cockney conductor how to get to Victoria: 'Tike yer dahnt' Chengcraws, gi'a number 'leven f' there'. It took the conductor three goes to make himself understood.

Cultural indoctrination started in infancy. Between the wars nanny-reared children acquired a stock of proverbs reeking of snobbery and chauvinism. They were taught to 'Leave something on your plate for the Duke of Rutland's son'. (The duke's family name was Manners – this pun had been circulating since the middle of the nineteenth century. It turns up in Robert Surtees's *Handley Cross*, published in 1843.) They were reminded that 'We don't like that girl from Tooting Bec' – the suburbs were not the habitat of the poshocrat – 'she washes her face and forgets her neck'. (As late as 1950 Enid Blyton (born 1897) described the 'unpleasant unwashed kind of smell' that wafted from a 'ragamuffin' to assault the nostrils of her 'Famous Five'.) Between the wars a farting child was 'talking German'.

Vocabulary was another give-away. The story goes that, when John Betjeman (born 1906) met his future mother-in-law for the first time, he set out to wind Lady Chetwode up with a sentence redolent of 'middle-classness': 'Well, I can't call you Mother, so I have to call you Auntie Star, but right now I have got to get my mac and my brolly ['gamp' would have done as well] and pop up to Town'. The magazine publisher Edward Hulton (born 1906) enlarged on the differences between posh and suburban usage:

In 1939 an inhabitant of Golders Green or Ealing would say, 'My cousin is an officer and he has phoned me that he is coming up to town.' An inhabitant of Mayfair would say, 'My cousin is a soldier and he has telephoned that he is coming up to London'.

During the Second World War the 'young officers' in the elite Brigade of Guards made fun of their opposite numbers in 'Line mobs' who 'put on a pair of slacks, got out the old bus, buzzed up to town and plucked a bird'. They did not 'telephone', they gave their friends a 'tinkle'. Words to describe what once would have been called the privy or the water closet were pitfalls. The artist Ben Nicholson (born 1894) was horrified to find a reference to a 'LAVATORY' – this he regarded as 'a damn fool Victorianism which pretends that you only wash your hands there'. He preferred 'WC' or, perhaps surprisingly, 'toilet'. Handwashing served as a long-lived proxy ·for urination. Asked by his host Christopher Soames (born 1920) whether he would like to wash his hands before lunch, Martin Amis's father Kingsley (born 1922) replied that he had 'washed them behind a bush on the way down'.

'Mr' and 'Esq' were snares for the unwary. In the mid-1950s, when Keith Thomas (born 1933) was a Fellow of All Souls, he 'received a note addressed to "Mr Thomas" . . . It began "Dear Thomas" and turned out to have been intended for one of the College Servants'. The sender, the 'eminent Socialist' G. D. H. Cole (born 1889), 'reproached' Keith Thomas for having opened it, pointing out that 'if the letter had been intended for [him] it would have been addressed to K. V. Thomas Esq . . . although it would still have begun "Dear Thomas"'.

Toffs were ridiculed too. 'Lord Haw-Haw', the nickname Jonah Barrington coined for William Joyce (born 1906) at the start of the war, was designed to evoke a man with a 'damit-get-out-of-my-way accent'. 'I imagine him with a receding chin, a questing nose, thin, yellow hair brushed back, a monocle, a vacant eye, a gardenia in his buttonhole. Rather like P. G. Wodehouse's Bertie Wooster'. In personifying Joyce's voice in this way, Barrington was pandering to the prejudices of his readers in the *Daily Express*: the intermittent Irish notes apart, Joyce sounded very much like a BBC newsreader of the 1930s. The BBC's wartime voices included Wilfred Pickles and J. B. Priestley (born 1894), whose speech proclaimed their Yorkshire origins. The war leader himself had an unashamedly upper-crust accent and pronounced 'Nazi' in the old-fashioned way – as it looked. Kingsley Amis guyed the delivery of the Oxford don Lord David Cecil (born 1902):

> Laze . . . laze and gentlemen, when we say a man looks like a poet . . . dough mean . . . looks like Chauthah . . . dough mean looks like *Theckthyum* [or something else, barely recognisable as 'Shakespeare']?

In *The Social Fetich*, published in 1908, Lady Grove had singled out 'week-end' as 'an expression that offends the fastidious'. She listed 'the actual possessions which are reserved solely for the use of middleclassdom': napkin-rings, fish-knives, tea-cosies. It was Alan Ross's paper 'Linguistic class-indicators in present-day English', published in *Neuphilogische mitteilungen* in 1954, that triggered a fresh and unprecedented explosion of media interest in U[pper class] and Non-U language. The Hon. Nancy Mitford (born 1904) weighed in. John Betjeman (born 1906), posh by marriage and adoption, offered verse advice on 'How to get on in society', a guide to the words lying in wait to ambush the *arriviste*: along with 'toilet', 'kiddies', 'lounge', 'couch', 'serviettes', 'doilies', 'cruet', 'sweet' (for 'pudding'), 'scones' (when rhymed with stones).

Professor Ross's demonstration that class-indicators changed over time was generally disregarded. The caveat was timely. Dennis Potter (born 1935) went up to Oxford in the 1950s determined to keep his Forest of Dean accent as a badge of his working-class roots. Potter was a trailblazer. In the 1960s, the Beatles helped to make regional accents fashionable – the broadcaster John Peel (born 1939) concealed his public school background by adopting a Scouse twang. By the end of the 1980s many privileged young people had adopted 'mockney, a faint but perceptible faux-plebeian accent'.

Talking dirty

Until the 1960s, an acquaintance with Latin was the hallmark of a gentleman – by birth or education. Not long after the end of the Second World War, Kingsley Amis observed a fellow academic in conversation with a man who had come to lay a carpet. His 'discourse included quotations from both Latin and Greek'. The Greek, 'as an obvious courtesy, he translated'. The Latin, 'as one gentleman to another', he 'left in the native state'. Men with a public or grammar school boy's grasp of Latin were licensed for entertainment unsuitable for ladies and the lower classes. Clement Egerton published his translation of *The Golden Lotus*, a Chinese novel of the twelfth century, in 1939. If the author had been English, Egerton observed,

> He would have avoided some subjects completely, skated over thin ice, and wrapped certain episodes in a mist of words. This he did not do. He allows himself no reticences. Whatever he has to say, he says in the plainest of language. This, of course, is frequently acutely embarrassing for the translator ... It could not all go into English, and the reader will therefore be exasperated to find occasional long passages in Latin. I am sorry about these, but there was nothing else to do.

Catullus's pungent verses about love, lust and loss were the schoolboys' favourite. As the *Spectator*'s reviewer pointed out, Robert Graves's pamphlet *Lars Porsena, or the future of swearing* (1927) was not 'for the squeamish'. Comparing Roman poets, 'Horace', said Graves, 'is my idea of a characteristically obscene man ... Catullus on the other hand is not obscene'. Graves (born 1895) cited the lines that graphically describe the love of the poet's life whoring on the streets and leave 'obscenity looking foolish'. In her biography of Angus Wilson (born 1913), published in 1995, Margaret Drabble (born 1935) quoted an anonymous young man from Bletchley, where the enemy codes were broken in the 1940s. He had been propositioned over the dinner table by a man using the 'immortally seductive words of Catullus "pedicabo et irrumabo"'. These she did not translate. Academic women achieved a kind of honorary manhood that armed them to confront strong language – by the mid-1990s Latin-literacy was a rarity among graduates under 40. A Note appended to the 'enlarged' fifth impression of *Lars Porsena* (1929) offered 'corrections and amplifications' sent in by readers. Mr Fred Hale of the Nelson Inn, Merryvale, Worcester, drew Graves' attention to rhyming slang. Even in a book that carried a health warning on its cover, it was deemed inappropriate to spell out the last stage in the equation 'Berk = Berkeley = Berkeley Hunt = . . .'.

Lewdness was by no means a prerogative of the 'educated'. Donald McGill (born 1875) was master of the saucy postcards that vulgar people sent each other when they went on day trips to the seaside. McGill was born and brought up middle class but he married into the music hall. His metier was the double entendre:

'Did you or did you not sleep with this woman?'
'Not a wink, my Lord.'

Frank Randle (born 1902) was the hero of the northern musical hall audience. In one routine he chalked an 'F' on a blackboard. His stooge persistently read it as 'K', setting up the rejoinder 'Why is it that every time I write "F" you see "K"?' His script was embellished with gestures that were regularly condemned by magistrates as 'disgusting, grossly vulgar, suggestive and obscene'. Randle's act did not travel well. Max Miller (born 1895) was the 'Cheekie Chappie' who delighted southern audiences with his *Blue Book*. He left the punchlines to the punters: 'When roses are red, they are ready for plucking. When girls are sixteen . . .'. When he peeled a banana, he counted: 'One skin, two skins, three skins . . . Here, lady, want a bite?'

'Auntie' BBC's *Green Book* of 1949 laid down the rules that reflected the proprieties observed in polite company, north to south, top to bottom. 'Programmes must at all costs be kept free of crudities, coarseness and innuendo'. Double entendres like 'winter draws on' were banned. 'God', 'Good God', 'My God', 'Blast', 'Hell', 'Damn', 'Bloody' – thirty-five years after Eliza Doolittle uttered it on stage – 'Gorblimey' and 'Ruddy' were expletives deleted from comedy scripts. Bright children learned to spell to penetrate the grown-up code: 'pas devants les enfants or Mrs H. is having a B-A-B-Y'.

Keeping it in the family

Language badged families as it badged classes and cultures. Private jokes, epitomes of shared recollections and family sillinesses were the stuff of family argots. Family expressions have a long documented history. 'The wig is wet' was Burney code for 'It can't be helped' in the 1760s. Glynnese, the patois of the great clan that William Ewart Gladstone (born 1809) married into, was preserved in a *Glossary* printed for private circulation in 1904. Glynnese infected the national pool of expressions: 'killing', as a measure of amusement; 'raving', as an index of enthusiasm; to 'sit upon', or squash; 'over the moon' for 'in prodigiously high spirits' – are – if we accept the *Glossary*'s word for it – escapees from Glynnese. Some people were protective of their intimate code. Fearing that she might die in childbirth, Vita Sackville-West (born 1892) wrote to her husband Harold Nicolson (born 1886) in 1914: 'If you marry again, which I expect you will, don't be just the same with her as you were with me; give her a place of her own, but don't let her take mine. Don't teach her our family expressions'. In the 1920s Nancy Mitford's little sisters Unity and Jessica 'made up a complete language called Boudledidge . . . into which [they] translated various dirty songs (for safe singing in front of grown-ups) and large chunks of the *Oxford Book of Verse*'.

Alan Clark (born 1928) included a glossary of his family's private slang in his published diary – their most graphic term was 'greywater', for diarrhoea. When, in the Eighties, Catherine Storr asked newspaper readers to share their family words for the embarrassing act of defecation, 'to pain' and 'to grunt' were among those offered. Expressions act as memorials to the obscure: as a boy, the sculptor John Skeaping (born 1901) lived next door to a Mrs Price, who was 'house proud to an extreme degree'. His own children habitually used 'to "Mrs Price" . . . to describe any meticulous cleaning or polishing'.

Remembering 'the time before you were born'

John Skeaping's story is an example of a memory inherited from 'the time before you were born'. In the 1930s Jim Copper (born 1882) made a 'Song Book' to preserve the words that he and his forebears had sung. In memory, the dead lived on. To her nieces and nephews born after the Second World War, Maureen McCarthy (1916–19) was 'a real person in their grandparents' house'.

Among the privileged, memories very often had a material dimension. The Shirleys' first recorded ancestor held land at Ettington in Warwickshire in 1086, the year of the Domesday Inquest: nine centuries later the estate was still in the family's possession. The eighth Duke of Wellington (born 1915) owned property in Belgium and Granada presented to the first duke (born 1769) in the lifetime of King George III. The pictures brought together in 1996 to celebrate the relationship between *The Artist and the Country House* had all come down in the family. More modest houses also preserved evidence of past generations. In Liverpool, the mercantile Mellys were in the habit of measuring children 'at various ages: their height, name and date [was] pencilled alongside'. Between the wars young George (born 1926) 'found it very strange to see [his] father's name next to the figures three feet six inches, and the date 12 October 1905, or [his] grandfather's in 1876 when he was only three feet two inches tall'. The working-class Nobles' front room was 'a proud exhibition of Gran and Granddad's past', the 'private museum' of working-class Londoners. In Bethnal Green tenancies were passed down the family. A woman born at the end of the nineteenth century was the third generation to live in the same house: 'My mother died in this room, my father died in this room, and so did my grandmother'.

Ephemera transmit memories. The poet George MacBeth (born 1932) lost both his parents before he was 20. When he read his mother's cookery book, he remembered 'on my tongue or my mind's tongue, the savour of almost forgotten dishes'. The green bowl his mother used for flowers, her crocodile handbag, the things his father had in his pockets when he was killed by a shell a decade earlier represented them. 'When my son was born, I put the things in his cradle and let his fingers touch them' – they formed 'a bridge between generations that never met'. The instinct to pass on keepsakes was still evident in the 1980s. Before Tim Parry, killed by a terrorist bomb, was buried, his father exchanged his son's signet ring for his own. He would wear Tim's ring for the rest of his life: 'Then I would want my son Dominic to wear it until the time is right for him to pass it on to his own son'.

Given names acted as cultural markers and embodied fragments of family history, secrets included. The name of Matthew White of Blagdon in Northumberland, who died in 1763, was handed down the generations of the Ridley kin who inherited his estate. Enoch Powell (born 1912) inherited his given name from his father and grandfather – it was both a family and a local badge: Enoch (said Aynuck) and Eli (said Aylie) were Black Country folk heroes. Panther, the middle name given to Anthony West (born 1914), was the pet name that his father H. G. Wells used for Anthony's mother Rebecca West. Tamzine, the name of a fishing boat that took part in the evacuation of Dunkirk in 1940, was bestowed, fifty years later, on the great-great-granddaughter of the boat's builder, Leonard Brockman.

Physical resemblances were prized badges. In the *Birthday Letters* (1998) he addressed to Sylvia Plath (born 1932), the poet Ted Hughes (born 1930) noted the way that their daughter's fingers 'remembered her mother's in everything they do'. Tony Benn (born 1925) was delighted to observe that his grandson's toes, like his own, were webbed. The intimate 'family sign' that linked David Leitch (born 1937) with his natural mother – who had given him up as a baby – and his son was a second toe 'distinctly longer than the so-called big or great toe'. Margaret Wheeler's daughter was accidentally swapped in the nursing home where she was born in November 1936. Mrs Wheeler catalogued the features that convinced her that the child she was rearing was not her own:

> I . . . knew Valerie was Blanche's child, the moment I saw the baby, Peter Rylatt. It was Valerie all over again. He had the same large head and heavy face. Peggy's head is small and so is her face; the same strongly marked eyebrows (Peggy's are weak) and the same scowl (Peggy can't scowl, all she can manage is a quick frown) the same thrust out lower lip and forward thrust of the lower jaw – Peggy has a beautiful mouth and chin, and the same shy smile that lights up and alters the whole face – (Peggy has a wide range of smiles – some of them with more than a spice of devilment quite lacking in Valerie's and Peter's), the same small well-shaped ears, flat to the head – (Peggy's ears and my other children's too, are, alas large, round and stick out like teapot handles). He also had the same plump, rounded firm little body and limbs as Valerie had (I saw him have his bath), while Peggy and my other three children were incorrigibly long and thin as babies, like skinned rabbits.

Family histories handed down the generations tend to melodrama with cast lists of martyrs, moral desperadoes, curiosities and comic turns. Stories of past prosperity or distinction acted as a spur to the ambitions of children born without material advantage. 'Sunken middle-class families', 'poor relations', victims of 'ill-health, bankruptcy, foolishness or any of the stray chances of life' saw education as a means of 'reclaiming' their social position.

Accounts of recent events are often composed of 'the same few exemplary episodes' told over and over again. Sybil Marshall (born 1913) described the process of anecdotal editing. 'Mum . . . has become a sort of fable to us' in which the 'side of her' that was 'such fun, such delight, so ludicrous', outweighs 'the difficult bitter old woman' of her last years. By the time he was born in 1922, the meanness of Kingsley Amis's grandmother was legendary:

> She would leave out two matches for the maids to light the gas with in the mornings: one match might plausibly break, so the reasoning was imagined, while more than one or two would be an invitation to some pyrotechnic revel. To save lavatory paper, Mater would cut up and hang up grocer's and similar bags on a hook, and one morning my Uncle . . . claimed to have cut his bottom on the lingering remains of a pear drop.

Like family expressions, family stories could escape into the public domain. Charis Frankenburg (born 1892) was one of the first Oxford women eligible to attend a degree ceremony. By 1921 she was a married woman with a 2-year-old son, Peter. In the middle of the ceremonial, 'he announced in such a loud voice that he had a nicer dressing-gown than the Vice-Chancellor's, *and* green pyjamas, that the Vice-Chancellor had him removed'. The episode became 'an Oxford story'. Years later Mrs Frankenburg was corrected by a stranger when she told the story and 'left out the green pyjamas'.

Family memories are legacy that some parents consciously hand on to their children. Charis Frankenburg was among the uncountable parents who systematically documented their children's lives. She kept a 'separate detailed diary' for each for her four children and filled albums with snapshots. Even at the end of the century, when photographs and home movies had come to dominate family archives, some families kept written records. Along with Tim's signet ring, future generations of the Parry family will inherit Colin Parry's account of his two small sons' doings and sayings. In June 1982 when builders were working on an extension to the Parrys' house, Tim

> fell into the wet concrete not once but twice. On the second occasion, we considered letting the wet concrete set on you so that we could put you in the garden as a garden gnome, complete with fishing rod, but because we love you, Mum washed you down.

Another time, 'sitting at breakfast', Tim told his mum that he had 'had pictures in his eyes' when he was asleep. Tim's tragic early death brought these stories to wider notice. Antonia Byatt (born 1936) described a perhaps commoner situation: 'When my father died I realized that what had died with him was his store of memories – his memories of his own father and mother, whom I hardly knew, my secondary or inherited memories'.

Keeping up appearances

Respectable families were anxious to 'keep up appearances': esteem and employment depended on it. 'Nosey parkers' who failed to observe the injunction 'mind your own business' were both despised and feared. Good neighbours did not pry, interfere or gossip. The neighbourly habit of turning a blind eye and a deaf ear to the goings-on next door shielded the hard-up and the abusive from exposure. For the sake of appearances, families that would scorn to tell an untruth were prepared to live lies.

Disabilities were kept secret. Donald McGill, master of the saucy seaside postcard, lost a foot as a result of an accident on the rugby field. This was something he kept quiet about. He did not limp even in his eighties and, when the housekeeper who looked after him in his old age came into a room while he was strapping on his artificial foot, it came as a shock to her and an embarrassment to him. Laurie Lee (born 1914) kept his epilepsy a secret from his daughter Jessy (born 1963) even after she had grown up.

Race and religion were sensitive issues. In 1923 Bet Powell was teaching at University College, Reading; she was engaged to marry her Irish-born colleague, E. R. Dodds. On her last night at home as a single woman she lay in bed listening to 'the continuous murmur of voices' from her parents' room:

> At last a door opened and Bet heard her mother's slippered feet padding softly along the corridor. 'Darling,' said an anxious small voice, 'Father [Father was an Anglican clergyman] says *Is he a Roman Catholic?*' 'No', said Bet sleepily, 'he's an atheist.' 'Oh, thank goodness! I must tell father; we couldn't sleep for worrying'.

Anti-semitism was rife bewteen the wars. Brought up as a Christian, in ignorance of her Jewish origins, Charis Barnett (born 1892) married Sydney Frankenburg, a leading member of the Jewish community in Salford. She was a prominent advocate of birth control. To the local Roman Catholic press she was 'an impertinent middle-class busybody' with a 'German-Jewish name'. In 1932 E. M. Forster (born 1879) transcribed what he called 'a good man's joke' into his Commonplace Book. The story went that Lord Birkenhead (born 1872) had said of Viscount Samuel (born 1870): 'When they circumcised that Jew they threw away the wrong bit'. When Lottchen Horsmeier's parents sent her from Germany to England in 1936 – she was 16 – she, understandably, reinvented herself as Jennifer Coates. Her children were brought up to conceal their Jewish heritage.

Jail sentences were kept secret, even when the prisoner had been convicted on a matter of principle. When Roy Jenkins's father was imprisoned for illicit assembly in 1926, the small son (born 1920) was told that 'he was on an extended tour of inspection of the coal mines of Germany'. 'The undesirable aspect was that I picked up the story almost surreptitiously through the chance remarks of others.' A generation later Trevor Grundy (born 1940) and his sister, brought up in a Fascist household, were trained by their mother to live in 'two worlds, this one and the one outside'. 'Special duties' explained the absence of their father, in prison from 1940 to 1944.

Though 'blubbing' at a sentimental film, opera or play was acceptable, even laudable, boys were encouraged to conceal emotion from an early age. In 1940 Anthony Quinton (born 1925) survived the sinking of *The City of Benares*, a ship ferrying children from England to the United States – of the twenty-three others in his lifeboat, fifteen died. When Quinton got back, his grandmother 'barely looked up from weeding the flowerbeds and remarked, "Good heavens, are you home already?"' Lucy Rothenstein was another child sent across the Atlantic for safekeeping: her American grandparents were struck by her phlegmatic bearing, but, she confessed, she was 'sadder' than they thought. Demonstrative families stood out. Across three generations fathers and sons in the Benn family exchanged 'big kisses' in public. Cledwyn Hughes's remark, recorded by Tony Benn in 1977, was telling: 'I forgot to tell you, twenty years ago I saw you kiss your father . . . and it brought tears to my eyes because I used to kiss my father too'.

Training in discretion equipped men to lead double lives. His Victorian contemporaries were mystified by the contrast between Frederic Leighton's high public profile in the Victorian art world and his apparently non-existent private persona. Leighton's bank statements, his own will and his sister's revealed Lily Mason, wife of a commercial traveller and her son, his godson, Fred (born 1875) as particular objects of Leighton's affection. Fred Mason was as discreet as his godfather. After his death in 1953 Fred Mason's children put two and two together and concluded that their father was Lord Leighton's son. The banana king Roger Ackerley (born 1863) only posthumously revealed the existence of a second, secret family. The story has been told from two sides. His son Joe (born 1896) worked on the manuscript eventually published as *My Father and I* (1968) from 1933 to 1967, the year of his death. Joe's half-sister Diana Petre (born 1912) told the tale of her upbringing in *The Secret Orchard of Roger Ackerley* (1975). To safeguard their reputations, families accommodated transgressors. The cover-up did not mean that shortcomings were either forgiven or forgotten. One way or another, the 'guilty' were liable to be punished. The actor David Tomlinson (born 1917) opened his autobiography (published in 1990) with this arresting vignette:

> Some years ago my brother Peter was on his way to Heathrow on an airport bus. It was, I suppose, pure chance that the traffic stopped at Chiswick. Glancing sideways Peter was astonished to see our father sitting up in a strange bed, in a strange house, drinking a cup of tea.

It transpired that, while he was serving his articles with a solicitor in Mildenhall in Suffolk, David Tomlinson's father Clarence had fallen in love with one of his landlady's daughters. By 1913 Sophie and Clarence had two children. Then, bowled over by a more suitable young woman, he married her, much to Sophie's distress. Clarence did not cut himself off from Sophie and her children – indeed the couple added to their family. Clarence's first 'marriage' lasted until Sophie died at the age of 85. Until he retired, Clarence spent the working week with his London household and went back to Folkestone for the weekend. Florence Tomlinson discovered 'the other half of the family' when she was carrying her third son. Her husband, serving as an officer in the First World War, posted a letter intended for Sophie in an envelope addressed to Florence. He and the two Mrs Tomlinsons schooled themselves to keep up appearances. David Tomlinson became aware that he had seven half-siblings only when he was 42. Never once did his father, a notoriously short-tempered man, accidentally call one of his Folkestone boys by a Chiswick boy's name. When the truth came out, the fatal letter was produced in evidence.

As far as we know, Clarence Tomlinson was the unrespectable exception in his family. Bloomsbury came to personify deviance. The group rose like a phoenix from the grave of Leslie Stephen (born 1832), founding father of the *Dictionary of National Biography*. In 1904 his orphaned children moved from stuffy Hyde Park Gate to louche Gordon Square. In this unchaperoned menage Thoby Stephen's sisters met his Cambridge friends – and in due course Vanessa married the 'very amusing' Clive Bell (born 1881) and Virginia the more austere and dependable Leonard Woolf (born 1880). The Bloomsburies were conspicuous as writers and makers, politically too. They had conscientious objections to fighting in the First World War. As the war ended, the Stephens' cousin Lytton Strachey (born 1880) published his polemic against *Eminent Victorians*. His targets were the pillars of society personifying organised religion, do-goodery, the public school, the Army and the Empire. The Bloomsburies' domestic eccentricities were not advertised. Both Bells took lovers. The conventional form of birth announcement – 'On Christmas Day [1918] at Charleston, Firle, Sussex, the wife of Clive Bell of a daughter' – was the perfect vehicle for recording the social fact of baby Angelica's parentage while masking the identity of her natural father from those outside the magic circle. 'Even in the privacy of their letters', Vanessa Bell (born 1879) and Duncan Grant (born 1885) never referred to '"our" daughter'. Nevertheless, suspicious relatives, like William Vaughan, headmaster of Wellington, cold-shouldered the 'Grants'.

Although sex between consenting adult males was illegal until 1967, public schools, the ancient universities and literary and artistic London accommodated practising and celibate homosexual men – and women too. In the Twenties and Thirties commentators commonly divided the male undergraduate population of Oxford into sporty 'hearties' and 'aesthetes' who trailed an aura of homosexual chic. Naturally the Grammar School drab swots were ignored. When Tom Driberg (born 1905) was charged with indecent assault against two unemployed Scots miners in 1935, powerful allies rallied to Driberg's aid. Lord Sysonby and Colonel Egerton, 'tall, ramrod-straight, eminently "distinguished-looking", with a carefully brushed silver-grey moustache', turned out as character witnesses. Lord

Beaverbrook, proprietor of the *Daily Express*, paid the King's Counsel for the defence and used his influence to keep the case out of the headlines. request, Gerard Irvine preached an Antipanegyric at Driberg's requiem. Irvine took up the challenge of the 'tease', the cold lechery.

As late as the 1960s homosexuality was something to be kept under wraps. In the revised edition of his biography of *The Beatles* (1985), Hunter Davies revealed that Brian Epstein (born 1934), the group's manager, had given permission to 'mention his homosexuality'. Epstein died before the book was published in 1968. To protect the feelings of Epstein's mother Queenie, Hunter Davies referred to Epstein's unhappy 'love life' in a code that younger and more worldly readers would have had little difficulty in breaking.

A retreat from discretion was a theme of the late twentieth century. Extra-marital relationship and births, in particular, were more often acknowledged. Lady Diana Cooper was born in 1892. It was generally believed that her father was not her mother's husband, the Duke of Rutland, but their neighbour Harry Cust. She had known the Cust story since her teens (a male friend of her own generation accidentally let the cat out of the bag), but her references to her father in *The Rainbow Comes and Goes* (1958) were to the duke. In old age she liked to represent herself as 'a living monument to incontinence'. It must be difficult for most readers born after 1960 to appreciate the stigma of illegitimacy. Until well into the second half of the twentieth century, bastardy was a disability, a legal, social and psychological blight. The unfolding of the family history of T. E. Lawrence, 'Lawrence of Arabia' (born 1888), is an instructive. Lawrence was the son of an Irish baronet who abandoned his family name along with his wife – 'the Vinegar Queen' – and his daughters to run off with their governess is too grand and housemaid too humble a label. There was no divorce and no remarriage. Robert Graves, who wrote *Lawrence and the Arabs* (1927) with its subject's help, acknowledged that 'Lawrence began as a name of convenience . . . his father, now dead, came from County Meath in Ireland'. In *The Long Weekend* (1940), published after Lawrence's death but during the lifetime of his mother, Graves went further, describing him as 'the son of an Irish baronet'. The article on Lawrence written for the *Dictionary of National Biography* (1949) identified his parents as Thomas Robert Chapman and Sarah Madden without commenting on their marital status. In 1955 Richard Aldington (born 1892) published a biography that spelled out the facts. Its reception was hostile. According to Basil Liddell Hart (born 1895), it read 'tediously like the report of a backstairs enquiry by a private detective who has been looking through keyholes'. 'The fact' of Lawrence's illegitimacy was well known to his circle of friends. 'But his biographers did not contemplate such indecency as that of laying bare this essentially private matter and presenting it for public discussion while his mother and elder brother, a missionary, were still living.'

Lawrence's emotional life had 'more shadow than sunlight in it'. Anthony West (born 1914), the illegitimate son of H. G. Wells and Rebecca West, had seen a boy beaten for calling a school fellow a bastard: he was appalled to learn that, in his case, this degrading term was the literal truth. Catherine Cookson (born 1906) wrote her autobiography (published in 1969) to 'openly associate herself' with words that had long been her secret shame – 'illegitimate' and 'bastard'. An incalculable number of children conceived outside marriage were, like Cookson, tucked in at the end of a grandmother's family as an 'afterthought', affiliated to an ignorant or compliant husband or passed off as a niece, nephew or cousin.

Couples who lived 'in sin' were subject to similar, though in their cases self-inflicted, strains. Roy Hattersley (born 1932) found out that his father had been ordained as a Roman Catholic priest only when he received a letter of condolence from the Bishop of Nottingham recalling the time when he and Rex Hattersley were students in Rome and young priests in England. Between 1983, when he published *A Yorkshire Boyhood*, and 1989, when the second edition came out, Roy Hattersley discovered that some of the facts about his parents' 'unusual courtship' had been 'romanticised'. In keeping with the less-inhibited spirit of the times, he offered a 'more accurate' account in *Skylark's Song*, the third novel in a trilogy about his parents and their families.

As a young man, David Leitch discovered that his foster parents had never married and, therefore, they had been unable to adopt him legally. So 'they did something which by their standards was wildly eccentric. They simply moved fifteen miles away and introduced me to the neighbours as their newborn son'. To their quasi-intimates, the Leitches were a 'fine', an 'impeccable couple even'. They 'would have been astounded to learn' of their unmarried state and of the 'screaming matches, the near homicidal attacks, the suicide attempts they both made'. His mother's boast was 'We never had a cross word'. She was 'a crab at home and an apple away', as they said in Suffolk.

These ingrained habits of secrecy paid dividends in the Second World War. The army of code breakers kept their war work secret even from those closest to them for decades until the story broke – thus there was what she calls 'a regrettable gap of six years' in Sara Turing's biography of her son Alan (born 1912) published in 1959.

Occupation and preoccupation

Occupations ran in families. Clerical and political dynasties were remarkably persistent. In the 1960s one clergy wife claimed that her children were 'directly descended from parsons back to 1515' – with the gap of one generation. The aristocratic Cecils have played a part in national politics since the sixteenth century. Brought up in a great Liberal clan, Adam Ridley (born 1942) counted the carriages in Queen Elizabeth's Coronation procession to identify the illiberal South African Dr Malan and 'started the boo' which the crowd around him took up. The Victorian-born couple William and Margaret Wedgwood Benn were both MPs' children. Their grandchildren played 'elections' and took part in demonstrations. When Melissa Benn was not quite 3 she was taken to see her father in the Commons chamber and her grandfather in the Lords. She grasped the proceedings well enough to recognise the Lord Chancellor as 'another Speaker'. When the Inner London Education Authority held its last debate in 1990, Emily Benn (born 1989) was in the Council Chamber: her grandfather's grandfather had been a founder member of the authority a hundred and one years earlier.

Medical practice were handed down from father to son. Richard Cobb (born 1917) identified the medical dynasties as 'the only hereditary element' in the middle-class population of his home town, Tunbridge Wells: Old Dr Ranking, Dr Ranking and Young Dr Ranking 'had been in practice for a total of eighty-five years'. Baring's, Rothschild's and Hambro's were family banking houses in the 1980s. From 1838 to 1964 three generations of Carrs ran the biscuit works in Carlisle. For workers as well as bosses biscuit-making ran in the blood: Athol McGregor followed in the footsteps of his father and grandfather. Colledges worked at the Denby Pottery for more than a century and a half. Glyn Colledge (born 1922) started work as a trainee designer in 1938; when he retired in 1983 he was, like his father before him, the firm's director of design. National institutions were family firms. Until the middle of the twentieth century a good proportion of the staff of the British Museum came from 'Museum families'. When Tony Benn became Postmaster-General in 1964 he encountered 'many hereditary postal workers'. New industries were not immune. In East London families operated as informal employment agencies in telecommunications in the 1960s and in computing in the 1970s.

The publisher John Grey (born 1909) adopted his mother's surname when he entered the family business in 1930 and carried on the dynasty as John Murray VI. Nevertheless, the hereditary principle is often obscured when the succession passes through the female line. John Gielgud (born 1904) came from the Terry dynasty of theatrical grandees. When she went to a play, his grandmother Kate, who had left the stage to marry, was seated in the Royal Box; the audience applauded her entry. At Westminster School Gielgud won the verse-speaking competition but he had no gift for movement – 'the most meaningless legs imaginable' was one critic's verdict. And he never mastered accents. It was the Terry connection that secured his first walk-on part at the age of 17 and kept him afloat during the first decade of his stage career. After his conviction for 'cottaging' in 1953 the family led the ovation that greeted him at the London opening of *A Day by the Sea*.

For much of the twentieth century children were a presence in the workplace. When they were little girls, Judy Boast (born 1940) and her sister, daughters of the general manager of the British Sugar Factory in Ipswich, lived more or less on site. The annual beet sugar 'campaign' started in October and lasted through to March; all that time the lime-kilns that cooked the sugar were never allowed to go out. On the night before the campaign started, the Big Boss's daughters 'would walk to the factory all dressed up in best frocks and white socks'. As Judy remembers it:

> We would stand at one end of a long pole with some easy-burning material attached to the other. A worker would light said material and my sister and I assisted by other workmen would thrust the flaming pole into the lime-kiln. There would be a roar, which I found quite alarming, and the huge oven-like things would ignite. The campaign was underway.

The men and their bosses celebrated with beer; the girls had pop and crisps.

Decades later the sweet heavy smell of cooking sugar beet still triggers memories of the ceremonial firing of the kiln. Health and Safety legislation has removed many such rituals from the annual round of family lives.

Skills learned in the family proved curiously transferable within the world of work. A poll taken in 1999 suggested that *Bagpuss* was the all-time favourite among television films made for children. Like other series made by Peter Firmin and Oliver Postgate, it drew on their families' talents. Emily, Peter Firman's daughter, posed for the pictures of the Emily in the story. Joan, his wife, made dolls and props. Professor Yaffle, the wooden woodpecker, owed a good deal to the personality of Oliver Postgate's distinguished uncle G. D. H. Cole, formerly Chichele Professor of Social and Political Theory in the University of Oxford. Valerie Thompson (born 1956) ended up in the City. Her training began in her father's greengrocery business:

> even at ten or eleven years old . . . we could add everything up in our heads. Trading apples and oranges is not too different from trading securities . . . If you're trading fruit and veg, they're perishable goods and if you don't sell them today, you've lost everything – that's how I learned to assess risk.

Broken families, mended families, families of choice

The rising number of openly broken families is a theme of our story. But families could be mended and extended too. Death or divorce cut ties and opened up opportunities for new associations; in consequence, children who lost parents often found themselves in families with 'an odd shape'. After his father died in 1940, Patrick Procktor's maternal grandparents 'in some ways [took] over as parents'. According to its editor, Rawle Knox, *The Work of E. H. Shepard* (1979) – the man who drew Pooh – was 'very much a family book'. For his material, Knox relied heavily on Shepard's daughter Mary, who was his stepmother. Chapters were contributed by Rawle Knox's sister, Penelope Fitzgerald, and by Humphrey Ellis, 'practically a relative-by-labour'.

Elective families

People without families created their own. Army officers older than their peers were traditionally known as 'Uncle' or 'Father'. Eileen Power (born 1889) and her sisters identified their intimate friends as 'Honorary Powers': they had to be 'able to recognise the Power idea of a joke at sight'. William Walton (born 1902) was absorbed into the family of his Sitwell patrons, 'so much so, indeed that he took on some of the Sitwell mannerisms and was thought by many to be a by-blow of Sir George's' – their bastard half-brother, in other words. Frank Richards (born 1875), creator of Billy Bunter and Greyfriars School, treated his housekeeper as a sister or a niece. When Edith Hood's widowed father competed for her attention, he was added to the household and when Edith herself suffered from prolonged and recurrent bouts to illness, Richards hired a nurse to take care of her. In the early

1930s E. M. Forster (born 1879) fell in love with Bob Buckingham, a London policeman. When Buckingham married, his wife May came to terms with Forster's demands on her husband's time. Forster stood godfather to their son when he was born in 1933. The relationship lasted. In the 1950s Forster helped the Buckinghams to buy a house. Never married, an only child and childless, it was to the Buckinghams that Forster turned when his health failed. They took him in to their home to die. Helen Sutherland (born 1881), a childless woman whose marriage had been annulled, the only surviving child of only children, was a collector of art and a patron of poets. The artists she helped gave her 'a kind of *family life*'; her pictures were 'a sort of family party' and 'the flowers in my garden are my friends, my guests, my relations'.

The commercial potential of elective relationships was not ignored. Until launderettes and ready-to-eat meals became commonplace, single men were 'mothered' by landladies. A firm trading under the significant title Universal Aunts set up an office in Sloane Street in the early 1920s. Househunting, escorting children, reading to invalids, cooking, cleaning, watering plants in window boxes, walking dogs were tasks for Universal Aunts. From the 1920s, the presenters of BBC broadcasts for children were advertised and embraced as honorary aunt and uncles. A viewer born in the late 1960s described his relationship with the *Blue Peter* team: 'I remember how John Noakes, Peter Purves and Lesley Judd were like my uncles and aunt, friends of the family, as my own family split up in 1978 when my father left us'. Petra, the *Blue Peter* dog, was 'a dog for everyone'.

Family animals

When Vanessa Bell's household arrive at Charleston in 1916, it consisted of herself, her sons Julian and Quentin, 'a nurse, a housemaid, a cook, Mr Grant, Mr Garnett and Henry (who was a dog).' In 1953 the readers of the *Young Elizabethan* were invited to design coats of arms for their families. Dogs, rabbits and ponies were conspicuous. In the 1960s hard-up lone mothers acknowledged their dogs' place in the family. One reported, 'When we're without, she's without'. Another confessed, 'We used to have a dog but it was too expensive. I feel so guilty. The children don't mention him, but sometimes they get his photo out and then the tears run down their faces'. In 2000 a Suffolk man still scarred by the break up of his marriage a quarter of a century earlier remarked how upsetting the episode had been for everyone involved: the adults, the children and the dogs. The Cambridge pet Crematorium opened in 1979. *Dogs Today* was only one of the magazines for pet keepers to have an obituary column.

Reading

Ackerley, J. R., *My Father and Myself* (Bodley Head, 1968).
Aldington, Richard, *Lawrence of Arabia: a biographical inquiry* (Collins, 1955).
Avebury, Diana (ed.), *Nanny Says, as recalled by Sir Hugh Casson and Joyce Grenfell* (Dennis Dobson, 1972).

Byatt, A. S., *Sugar and Other Stories* (Chatto & Windus, 1987).

Byatt, A. S., 'Memory and the making of fiction'. In Patricia Fara and Karalyn Patterson (eds) *Memory* (Cambridge University Press, 1998).

Cobb, Richard, *Still Lives: sketches from a Tunbridge Wells childhood* (Chatto & Windus/ Hogarth Press, 1983).

Copper, Bob, *A Song for Every Season: a hundred years of a Sussex farming family* (Heinemann, 1971).

Critchley, Julian, *A Bag of Boiled Sweets: an autobiography* (Faber & Faber, 1994).

Evans, George Ewart, *The Strength of the Hills: an autobiography* (Faber & Faber, 1983).

Forster, E. M., *Commonplace Book* (Scolar, 1985).

Frankenburg, Charis, *Not Old, Madam, Vintage* (Galaxy Press, 1975).

Furbank, P. N., *E. M. Forster: a life, volume 2: 1914–1970* (Secker & Warburg, 1978).

Graves, Robert, *Lars Porsena, or the future of swearing and improper language* (Kegan Paul, Trench, Trubner, 1927).

Grove, Agnes, *The Social Fetich* (Smith, Elder, 1908).

Grundy, Trevor, *Memoir of a Fascist Childhood: a boy in Mosley's Britain* (Heinemann, 1998).

Hattersley, Roy, *A Yorkshire Boyhood* (Chatto & Windus, 1989).

Hattersley, Roy, *Skylark's Song* (Macmillan, 1993).

Heald, Tim, *Denis Compton: the authorized biography* (Pavilion, 1994).

Hudson, Mark, *Coming Back Brockens: a year in a mining village* (Jonathan Cape, 1994).

Isherwood, Christopher, *Lions and Shadows: an education in the twenties* (Leonard and Virginia Woolf, 1938).

Kennedy, Margaret, *The Constant Nymph* (Heinemann, 1924).

Leitch, David, *Family Secrets* (Heinemann, 1984).

Macbeth, George, *A Child of the War* (Cape, 1987).

Meynell, Francis, *My Lives* (Bodley Head, 1971).

Mitford, Jessica, *Hons and Rebels* (Gollancz, 1960).

Murray, John G., *A Gentleman Publisher's Commonplace Book* (John Murray, 1996).

Nuttall, Jeff, *King Twist: a portrait of Frank Randle* (Routledge and Kegan Paul, 1978).

Parry, Colin and Parry, Wendy, *Tim: an ordinary boy* (Hodder & Stoughton, 1994).

Petre, Diana, *The Secret Orchard of Roger Ackerley* (Hamish Hamilton, 1975).

Postgate, Oliver, *Seeing Things: an autobiography* (Sidgwick & Jackson, 2000).

Raine, Kathleen, *Autobiographies* (Skoob, 1991).

Rebellato, Dan, *1956 and All That: the making of modern British drama* (Routledge, 1999).

Ross, A. S. C. *et al.*, *Noblesse Oblige* (Hamilton, 1956).

Souhami, Diana, *Gluck, 1895–1978: her biography* (Pandora Press, 1988).

Swift, Rebecca (ed.) *Letters from Margaret: correspondence between Bernard Shaw and Margaret Wheeler, 1944–1950* (Chatto & Windus, 1992).

Tomlinson, David, *Luckier than Most: an autobiography* (Hodder & Stoughton, 1990).

Took, Barry, *The Max Miller Blue Book* (Robson, 1975).

Turing, Sara, *Alan M. Turing* (Heffer, 1959).

Walton, Susana, *William Walton: behind the façade* (Oxford University Press, 1988).

Westminster, Loelia, Duchess of, *Grace and Favour* (Weidenfeld & Nicolson, 1961).

Willmott, Phyllis, *A Green Girl* (Peter Owen, 1983).

2   Between the wars, 1920–1939

THE TIMES

'Scourged by the bloody war'

Historians tend to play down the significance of the First World War as a chronological boundary. Those who lived through it saw it differently: 'that happened before the war, during the war or after the war', they said. No wonder. This was, after all, the 'War of a Million [Imperial] Dead'. Tens of thousands had lost limbs. Casualty lists displayed in schools gave boys the impression that England was steadily 'bleeding to death'. The sculptor Francis Derwent set up the Tin Noses Shop at Roehampton Hospital for servicemen with ruined faces. He modelled masks using the photographs taken for mothers, wives and sweethearts as his patterns. The 'Hysterical Diseases of War', as they were called, left men blind, deaf, mute, immobile. Restored to his happy childhood home in Cookham in December 1918, with his 'dear little mummy' and his music-teacher 'Par' playing Mozart on the piano, Stanley Spencer (born 1891) began to think that he had been killed and sent to heaven.

The war cast a long shadow. Advertising his pamphlet on birth control, which came out in 1926, C. P. Blacker (or his publishers) used a much larger font for his MC (Military Cross) than they did for his professional credentials: MA, MRCS, LRCP. For many too young to remember it, or born after its close, the First World War was a defining episode in their family history. Ellen Unsworth, a Liverpool doctor's wife, named her twelfth and last child Anthony Cyril after his brother Cyril (born 1897) who died on the Somme a few days before the baby was born. Violet Bonham-Carter (born 1887) named both her sons (born 1922 and 1929) after her brother Raymond, who died in the war. Irene Thomas's father chose her name to fit her birth date 'from a saints-almanac card that an old lady had given him while he was in France'. Hugh Peppiatt (born 1930) recalled an encounter with a tailor after the *Second* World War: hearing his name, the tailor asked, '"Are you any relation of Captain Will Peppiatt?" I said, "Yes, he was my uncle". "Oh," he said, "he died in my arms".' Hugh Peppiatt 'was so moved' that he 'immediately burst into tears and so did the tailor'. A generation on, Peter Parker dedicated *The Old Lie: The Great War and the Public-School Ethos* (1987) to his parents 'in memory of their fathers' – 6827 Private A. R. N. Parker of the Honourable Artillery Company and Captain F. R. Surridge MC of the Royal Army Medical Corps. Richard Cork (born 1947) commemorated his grandfather Ernest Smale 'who fought in it' in *A Bitter Truth: Avant-Garde Art and the Great War* (1994). Niall Ferguson (born 1964) dedicated *The Pity of War* (1998) to his grandfather, who joined up as a teenager. In the 1990s families campaigned for the rehabilitation of men shot for cowardice or desertion, a fate frequently kept deadly secret for decades even within the family. Eighty years after his death, the name of Lance-Sergeant Willy Stone was added to the war memorial at Crook in County Durham at a ceremony attended by relatives and representatives of his regiment, the Durham Light Infantry. At the end of the century a statue of a young blindfold soldier was commissioned to commemorate Willy Stone and other casualties of military justice.

Hard times

Times were perpetually hard for many working-class families. As a London father reminded the Salvation Army officer who rattled a tin under his nose, there were '52 self-denial weeks' in his year. The slump of 1929 hit coal, cotton, iron, steel and shipbuilding, the old props of England's industrial might. In 1932 one in three miners, half the workers in iron and steel, two in three of shipyard workers were unemployed. In 1936 Ellen Wilkinson (born 1891), Member of Parliament (MP) for Jarrow – 'The Town That Was Murdered', she called it – marched to London with 200 unemployed steel and shipyard workers from her constituency. The slump forced people to embrace change. The Stephens brothers uprooted themselves from the blighted North-East and moved to booming Bristol to work in the building trade. N. F. Fowler, a skilled engineer, moved from Manchester to Chelmsford to find work. Other men swapped trades. Kenneth Clarke (born 1910) was a watch-maker. Sacked when he asked for a rise, he found work as a pianist in a cinema: 'I'd rather sweep the streets than be unemployed' was his motto.

Mechanisation cost jobs. Office machinery displaced clerks. Machines 'fed regularly with cut tobacco, mile long reels of paper, printing ink and paste' turned out 'cigarettes by the million'. The advertising slogan 'untouched by human hands' signalled job losses in the food industry. In the 1930s many textile, tailoring, boot and shoe, cutlery and pottery hands were 'on short time' – and short wages. Older men, in their fifties and sixties, were often the first to be laid off. With illustrations by Eric Ravilious, *High Street* was an elegant memorial to men who had made goods by hand. By 1938 here were 'only three firms of taxidermists working in London'. There was 'very little work' in the plumassier's line: hats with big feathers had gone out of fashion. Repairs were the bread-and-butter of the saddler and harness maker. He kept horse brasses 'only . . . because ladies like to buy them to hang on beams'. But the knife grinder, who pushed his home-made machine 'about the streets . . . sharpening knives, scissors and tools' was still going strong. A good many housewives had no option but to make-do-and-mend.

Work was often seasonal. When the spring thaw freed Baltic timber, there was

ample work for dockers in King's Lynn. But for much of the year men who were not
the foreman's cronies fed their families on home-bred rabbit and vegetables raised
on allotments and in greenhouses contrived from discarded glass negatives and old
picture frames; they patched the cooking pots with old cocoa tins. Billy Reagan,
who grew up in Liverpool, remembered how his father used to look forward to
snow: 'He'd be looking through the window and he'd say, "Send it down, JC".' The
same prayer went up in Yorkshire.

Three-quarters of the population lived in cities, towns and suburbs but these
were hard times on the land too. When the farm that employed them was sold as
building land in 1928, Rottingdean men were thrown out of work. The crop of
bungalows that sprang up on the Sussex Downs was their lifeline: 'First one then
another took up the hammer, trowel, and paintbrush'. The mostly elderly colonists
provided other employment. Jim Copper, the farm bailiff, turned carpenter and
'muckman', cleaning out cess-pits with his son Bob (born 1915) as muckman's
mate. Sybil Marshall's father had a small farm on the Cambridgeshire Fens. In the
late 1930s, two years running, every potato he grew 'rotted down and had to be
spread back on the land . . . the whole fen stank of rotting potatoes'. Teaching
physical education at Sawston at the opposite end of Cambridgeshire, George Ewart
Evans was struck by 'the contrast' between the boys from the 'purely agricultural
villages' and 'the suburban villages' like Granchester. The farm labourers' sons
were 'often grossly underweight'; 'their skin was pale and almost diaphanous'.

Middle-class families were in trouble too. Rosemary Boxer was born in 1931. Her
childhood was shadowed by 'world recession and decline of empire . . . Father's
younger brother put his head in a gas oven, while one of Mother's sisters whose
husband had lost his job in India tried to abort by throwing herself downstairs'.

Barbara Pollard remembered her mother passing her toys over the fence to
friendly neighbours to save them from the bailiff's men. Helen Forrester, the eldest
child of a feckless, bankrupted middle-class couple, cut off from their families,
isolated from neighbourly support networks, living in squalor, and ignorant of the
public baths, remembered herself in her middle teens:

> hair draggling round my shoulders, its greasiness combed through with my
> fingers; septic acne sores all over my face; hands with dirty, broken nails,
> sticking out from an ancient cardigan with huge holes in its elbows, no blouse,
> and a gym slip shiny with accumulated grime. Red blotches of bug bites were
> clearly visible on my naked legs and thighs . . . and my toes stuck out of the
> holes in the laceless gym shoes on my feet.

Hardship is relative. In spite of his aristocratic connections, Winston Churchill
(born 1874) neither inherited nor married wealth – he supported his family and
servants with his pen. In the summer of 1926 he produced his prescription for
frugality. (There is no evidence to suggest that it was imposed.) 'Big car should be
. . . practically laid up'. There should be 'no more champagne . . . bought. Unless
special directions are given only white or red wine, or whisky and soda will be
offered . . . No more port to be opened without special instructions. No cream
unless specially sanctioned'. 'When alone we do not need fish. Two courses and a

sweet should suffice for dinner and one for luncheon'. 'Two white shirts a week should be quite enough for me for dinner in the country'.

Impoverished families missed more than money. Often, friends 'dropped off', 'shopping, once a pleasure and amusement, became a nightmare'. Health suffered. An unemployed millwright described his wife as 'often very poorly without being really ill'. She suffered from depression, asthma and bronchitis but 'her worst troubles' were her eyes and her teeth. 'She cannot see to thread a needle or read and often complains that her eyes hurt her, but we cannot afford glasses . . . her teeth cause abscesses but we cannot afford to go to the dentist'. A woman with an ulcerated leg stopped going for treatment because she could not afford the bus fares.

Unemployment was a human-interest story. In the 1930s *The Listener* carried the testimonies of people put out of work by the slump alongside advertisements for cine cameras and holiday cruises to the Norwegian fjords. In the run-up to Christmas 1936, the *Morning Post* collected presents for the children of unemployed men in Tyneside and West Cumberland. When the *Post* folded, the *Telegraph* took over. In 1938 Lancashire was added to its list. In January 1939 *Picture Post* ran the story of Albert Smith, a 35-year-old Londoner, a married man with four surviving children who had lost his job as an enameller as a result of an industrial illness (his teeth rotted and had to be removed). 'And' – the piece concluded – 'Albert Smith is only one of two million'.

Modern times

Bets bought dreams. By the end of the 1930s 10 million people did the football pools every week. A turn on a pin-table cost a penny – the prize was generally a packet of cigarettes. Cinemas – even seedy 'flea pits' – opened windows onto glamorous and thrilling worlds. By 1939 three out of four households had a wireless, often bought on the instalment plan. In Nottingham, the feckless working-class Sillitoes were 'transfixed' by broadcast serials. 'There was nevertheless a strong undercurrent of anxiety that the shopkeeper might walk in to claim his set back before the entertainment was finished'. Films, records and broadcasts – as well as live appearances – made the Rochdale-born Gracie Fields (born 1898) a national darling. When she had an operation for cancer in 1939, prayers were offered for her recovery and the wireless carried daily bulletins.

The demand for cars and electrical goods, 'artificial silk' and other synthetic fibres brought prosperity to the towns where they were made: in Oxford, 'Detroit on a smaller scale', and in Coventry few people were out of work. The Midlands were generally prosperous. An item that appeared in the *Sunday Express* in 1936 mentioned Ronald Cartland's fondness for Cadbury's chocolate: 'He munches it as he drives along in his Austin motor car, fitted with Triplex glass. Why not? Austin cars, Triplex glass and Cadbury's chocolate are all produced by factories situated in his Birmingham constituency'. The MP was a living advertisement. Cunningly constructed campaigns made people spend money on 'things they had never thought of buying' before. Copywriters played on fear ('Do you suffer from body-odour?' 'Is your lavatory clean?'); sloth ('ready cooked foods', 'gramophones that change their own records', 'the gearless car'); greed and snobbery. By the end of the 1930s, there was concern that children were going out of fashion.

> An electric washing machine, a refrigerator, football matches and pools, the little flutter on the 2.30, the greyhound track . . . the instalments on the house, the furniture, the new car, the television set, the insurance and the licence for the car, the camera and its gadgets, the dog . . . the lipstick and powder puff, the permanent waves . . . the hire-purchased dress

combined to 'cheat the cradle'. The crime writer Margery Allingham (born 1904) certainly had 'kid v. car' arguments with her husband.

Cinema advertisements contributed to the popularity of Meccano construction kits, the great middle-class boys' toy of the inter-war period. Electric trainsets date from 1920. Dinky cars, which almost every child could afford, arrived in the 1930s. The childish appetite for consumption coexisted with an old-fashioned thrift which led comfortably-off people born in Victorian England 'to fold [Christmas] wrapping paper tidily for next year but also to tie up the string . . . in neat bundles and – most important of all – to make sure that all labels were handed back to the donors ready for re-use'. Old-fashioned poverty forced Middlesbrough boys like the future star player Wilf Mannion (born 1918) to hone their footballing skills with 'cans, rag balls . . . a pig's bladder from the butcher's'.

Advertisements were not the only means by which new tastes were cultivated. *The Week-End Book*, first published in 1924, had sold over 200,000 copies by the end of the 1930s. It was conceived by Francis Meynell (born 1891), a significant and little recognised subverter of old attitudes. He was a conscientious objector in the First World War – and among the first Englishmen to have a zip in his trouser flies. The title he chose for his book was a conscious vulgarism: the upper classes went away from 'Saturday to Monday'. The section on First Aid contained an encrypted prescription for an aphrodisiac. Amusements included the Free Association Game 'based on psychoanalysis . . . which is always jolly'. Alongside folksongs, Meynell printed music and the words of the first two verses of the bawdy favourite from the First World War *Mademoiselle from Armentieres* with an invitation to transcribe the rest on to the blank pages at the back of the book. There was an anthology of verse. The sensuous, and then little known, works of John Donne (died 1631) and the bitter lines of the poets of the First World War appeared alongside squibs which would now be considered offensively racist. Between the wars cultural and class prejudices remained powerful forces.

INCOME AND ENVIRONMENT

Family economies

Although investments and dividends varied in scale and character, almost every English family was an economic partnership. As we have seen, occupations were inherited. Robert Sherriff was born in 1896. His family had connections with the Sun Insurance Office that went back a hundred years. My grandfather was principal agent from the Office in Buckinghamshire in the days of Queen Victoria and my father had served the Office for forty-five years, As I grew up there was never any discussion about what I should do when I left school, it was taken for granted that I should go into the Office.

In the prosperous classes, marriage was an occasion for endowment. James and Jean MacGibbon married in 1934. A trust set up by his mother contributed more to their income than his publishing job; she also gave them a large lump sum 'to set up house with'. When Joyce Grenfell (born 1910) married in 1939 her wedding presents included the freehold of a four-bedroom house.

In hard times affection, honour and, in the last resort, the law of the land placed an obligation on kin. Evidence from the privileged classes abounds. In 1924, Ken Milne developed tuberculosis (TB) and was forced to resign from his post in the Civil Service, his brother Alan (born 1882) assumed responsibility for the education of Ken's four children and, when Ken died in 1929, Alan settled a substantial sum on his widow. The writer Robert Graves (born 1895) and his wife Nancy Nicholson found themselves in money trouble in the 1920s – the village shop they had bought failed. As Graves remembered, 'My mother very kindly bought the cottage for five hundred pounds and let us have it for ten shillings a week.' Nancy's father, the distinguished artist William Nicholson (born 1872), sent her 'a hundred pound note in a matchbox as his contribution'. Parents' sense of responsibility overrode deep prejudice. The painter Hannah Gluckstein (born 1895), daughter of a wealthy businessman, rejected her family's bourgeois Jewish way of life. She abbreviated her name – it was as Gluck that she exhibited her work – cropped her hair and wore mannish clothes. Her father, appalled though he was, ensured her continuing solvency. The prim don J. H. Postgate (born 1853) refused to recognise his son Raymond's marriage to Daisy, daughter of George Lansbury, founding father of the Labour Party and 'uncrowned king of London's East End'. All the same he sent his son money 'to spend on making your flat more comfortable' with the injunction to 'consider this . . . strictly confidential'. When his daughter-in-law had an ectopic pregnancy in 1920, Postgate sent a cheque as a contribution towards the medical fees.

Working-class families rallied round too. When Addie Hoggart died, her dead husband's family took responsibility for their three young children. As her son Richard (born 1918) tells us:

> No part of the family could be expected to take more than one. So Tom went to Aunt Madge in Sheffield and stayed there until he was finally called up in the last war. I expect they sent him farthest because he was the oldest. Molly went to the elderly half-aunt in the next street, widowed and with one or perhaps a couple of unmarried daughters still at home.

The duty to pauper kin, embodied in the Elizabethan Poor Law and reiterated in the New Poor Law of 1834, underlay the means test. The Unemployment Insurance Scheme of 1920, which covered most manual workers and many 'black coats', was designed to cope with people who were between jobs, not with sustained joblessness. Reluctant to subject large numbers of highly skilled and, more to the point, highly organised workers to the humiliation of poor relief, the government extended the period during which insurance benefits could be claimed. By 1931 the Insurance Fund was broke. The hated household means test was introduced. In 1934 the Public Assistance Board took on responsibility for the unemployed, leaving children, the sick, the old, widows and deserted wives the responsibility of the localities, as they had been since the sixteenth century.

Help came from beyond the family too. When Charles Muir died in 1934, the firm that had employed him as an engineer found work for his sons Chas (born 1918) and Frank (born 1920). Religious and cultural communities played a part in supporting needy members. When Jim Callaghan's father, a coastguard, died in 1923, a deacon of the Baptist church in Brixham took the family in. They were kept going by charity: young Callaghan collected scrap wood from the shipyard and fish from the auctioneer. When he moved to Maidstone to work as a Civil Service clerk in his teens, it was the Baptist chapel that found him lodgings and it was at chapel that he met his future wife. Ronald Gabriel (born 1928) remembers his parents' campaign to bring refugees out of Nazi Germany. The Gabriels' mansion flat in Maida Vale served as a launch pad to a new life in England.

Paid work was not officially regarded as 'the normal condition' of married women. So ingrained was the assumption of dependency that, to avoid running up dentists' bills after their retirement into domesticity, young women had healthy teeth pulled and replaced by false ones. State-imposed marriage bars applied in publicly funded schools and in the Civil Service. In reality, wives' earnings were important to the family economy – and not only among the working classes. Charles Quennell's architectural practice ran on to the rocks in the First World War. A *History of Everyday Things in England*, on which he worked with his art-school-trained wife Marjorie, was the family's lifeboat. Their son Peter described his parents' working partnership. His father

> inked in the architectural background and left a series of neat blank spaces . . . these spaces were to hold my mother's figures . . . A large square called for a man on horseback; an oblong gap for a woman and a pretty, lively child . . . Once she had completed her task, my father brought up the background to join the outlines of the figures, and added the artists' joint initials M&CHBQ cunningly intertwined.

The house in which the distinguished accompanist Gerald Moore (born 1926) grew up had two brass plaques by the front door – one advertising his father's dental practice, the other his mother's lessons in music and elocution. Lodgers were an important source of income. Edward Heath's father was a builder in a modest way of business in the seaside town of Bexhill; his mother took in summer visitors. Ronald Searle (born 1920) was the son of a Post Office engineer working in Cambridge. The Searles put up the lady violinist from the Kinema until the talkies displaced her. For years afterwards the family lived in the basement of their house while undergraduates from the university occupied the upper floors. The absence of electricity and bathrooms added to the landladies' burdens. A Cumberland quarryman's wife crowded her own family into a single bedroom and turned the parlour into a dormitory for three or four lodgers; she made the pillowcases they used out of old flour sacks. Both these women took on other paid work: Nellie Searle filled cigarette packets for slot machines; the quarryman's wife cleaned the local church and school and fostered hounds when hunting was out of season. Living space was exploited in other ways. The wife of an unemployment coal carter in Liverpool turned their parlour into a 'general shop'; the kitchen was let as a hairdressing saloon. Farm workers' wives had to make-do-and-mend. Shoe repairing was their province. One Shropshire lad had a coat made out of an old army blanket. Coats past wearing were transformed into rag rugs. They were expected to scrub floors and clothes in the farmhouse for a pittance. One woman who had waited at a shooting party lunch and washed up afterwards was not paid at all, as the farmer's wife explained, 'I thought you'd be lonely when your chap was out' beating the game birds from the covers. Elspeth Huxley admired her Wiltshire neighbour Scilla Boulton who 'reared eight healthy children' on parish relief after ill health forced her husband to give up a steady job on the railway.

> In my mind's eye she sits surrounded by feathers in a small dark outhouse, plucking fowls for twopence a time – good pay when she had a large order and plucked forty a day . . . In their small garden she generally managed to grow extra vegetables for sale. She cleaned the village hall for a few shillings weekly. In September she picked blackberries and wheeled them in an old pram into Cirencester, seven miles, to sell to a man who used them for making dyes . . . The children helped as they grew older.

In the textile and pottery industries there was work for the wives of unemployed men. Archie and Mary Boothroyd both worked at Hirst's mill in Dewesbury; Mary was in work more often than her husband. She used to say, 'I know I am not employed for my sex appeal. I'm employed because my rate of pay is lower'. In Sheffield Nellie Ashton went back to work as a 'buffer girl' three weeks after she had her son Joe (born 1933) – her husband was out of work. It was a well-paid but unpleasant job. The 'girls' risked burns and cuts from the polishing tool and could not avoid the pumice dust that was blasted into their skin, their hair, ears, noses and throats. In Cambridge married women worked as laundresses and bedmakers, looking after students' college rooms. Do-gooding academics' wives feared that 'with no one at home in the dinner hour', the bedders' children were 'apt to be neglected'. Londoner Leonard Toomey's recollections support this view. His father was a stone mason, frequently unemployed; his mother was a cleaner working shifts at the War Office: 'We never saw her. There were no meals as such'.

Children played their part in the family economy. In better-off families this was informal and rarely made an immediate difference to the family income. Rayner Unwin's contribution was exceptional: a publisher's son (born 1925), he acted as reader of manuscripts intended for children, earning a shilling for each report – it was on his recommendation that his father Stanley (born 1884) bought J. R. R. Tolkien's *The Hobbit*, first published in 1937. In Derbyshire, Farmer Hool's children learned to use miniature hoes and sickles and drove cattle quite long distances to fresh pastures with their father following behind in his car. At harvest time farm workers and their children, armed with sticks, turned out to kill rabbits and hares flushed from the last of the standing corn. The meat made a cheap meal. After the harvesters had gone, children gleaned for chickenfeed. Laurie Arnold (born 1925) grew up on a smallholding in the Cambridgeshire Fens. 'We were kept away from school', he recalled, 'when we became capable of doing anything, in order to perform any task that was required at that time. It could have been gooseberry, apple or strawberry picking, threshing, harvesting – you mention it.' When they picked their apples, mother and father would do 'the ladder work' while the younger children dealt with the fruit on the lower branches. Children dispatched to borrow from neighbours learned a specialised vocabulary of diminutives as Winifred Foley (born 1914) remembered: 'a stump o' candle'; 'a pinch of tay'; 'a lick of marge'; 'a screw of sugar'; 'a sliver of soap'; 'snowl of bread'; 'a marsel of cheese'.

In the towns too, children's earnings made a real difference to working-class families' budgets. Ronald Searle and his younger sister helped their mother to fill cigarette packets. Later Ronald chipped in his earnings as a choirboy and, after his voice broke, as a butcher's boy. The comedian Bernard Manning was 'the singing paperboy'. Every night he delivered three hundred copies of the *Manchester Evening News* with a friendly smile that paid dividends in tips. Children in rough areas in London profited from other people's leisure: they minded cars and bikes outside football grounds; resold discarded music hall programmes, followed horses and carts and sold the dung they collected to rose growers and worked as 'Jews' pokers', doing household chores on the Sabbath. They conspired to trick other poor people who lived in bug-infested rooms plagued by bluebottles, beetles, fleas, lice and nits by packing bran and lavender essence to be marketed as 'Panzene – kills all known breeds of insects'.

The children of the business elite had the least contact with the world of work. Jean MacGibbon (born 1913) remembered how her father – a partner in the family's accountancy firm – 'left the house in his bowler hat, carrying a slim leather attaché case on his way to "business" – a confusing term since "doing big business" meant "going to the lavatory"'. Dundas Hamilton (born 1919) saw his father set off for the Stock Exchange taking with him a

> spare pair of socks and a pair of more comfortable slippers to put on in the office. As a small child I thought the Stock Exchange was a place called 'The Stockings Changed' and I imagined him sitting in this enormous building doing nothing but taking his socks off and putting them on again.

Habitats

Home comforts that today we take for granted – electric light, piped water, baths and showers, flushing lavatories – were by no means universal between the wars.

Neon advertising signs might light up Piccadilly Circus but late in the 1930s, social scientists reviewing working-class living conditions in Bristol took one 60–watt bulb burning for an average of 20 hours a week as the acceptable minimum electric lighting for a household. Many families relied on gaslight, oil lamps and candles.

In 1929 William Roberts (born 1898) made a small painting which goes by two titles: *A Family* and *Bath Night*. The family is in its living room. Father is reading his paper in the background; Mother is scrubbing the knee of a boy big enough to be well into double figures. He occupies not a bathtub but an armchair; an enamel bowl, the size you would use to wash dishes, contains the 'bath water'. In this family, the weekly 'bath' was an all-over wash. Reg Feltham, the son of an estate worker at Lyme Park, remembered his father fetching water from the well a fair distance from their cottage. 'He had a pair of yokes, and he had the blacksmith make chains so that he could carry four pails at a time. When he got home with the water on a frosty morning, his overcoat was often frozen so stiff that it stood up by itself'. In the Cambridgeshire Fens, families depended on rain water and water 'dipped from the dykes'. There were farm labourers worse housed than the stock they cared for: cottages were saturated with damp so that plaster hung in festoons from the walls and the stink of slurry permeated the rooms. And often, when a man lost his job, the family was turned out. Unless sympathisers took them in, the mother and children were taken to the workhouse while the man stayed to mind the belongings that had been dumped by the roadside. Overcrowding was common. In London, between the wars, Gran and Granddad Noble, their unmarried twins Ben and Harold, their widowed son Bert and his sons Peter and Ken lived in the downstairs half of a modest house. Upstairs lived their son Alec, his wife Harriet and their children Wally, Phyll and Joey. The upstairs family's indoor route to the outside lavatory was through Gran's kitchen.

Working-class children seldom had a bed of their own. The greater the poverty was, the less the space. In a basement in Ladbroke Grove in London, the home of an unemployed builder, his wife and five children, 'father, mother and son slept in one bed, the baby in a cot, two more children on a very small collapsible bed, another boy on a chair with his feet on this bed'. Families that lacked the money to buy bedding slept on straw mattresses covered by old overcoats and miscellaneous rags. Liverpool houses were infested with rats the size of kittens. To the Old Etonian George Orwell (born 1903), the woman 'kneeling there in the bitter cold, on the slimy stones of a slum backyard, poking a stick up a foul drain-pipe' and another, 'sick with the illness that killed her', struggling 200 yards to a lavatory 'shared with thirty-five other people, and waiting her turn' epitomised the degradation of slum life.

By contrast, blessed with technology and servants, a tiny minority of families lived luxuriously. The Debenhams' Peacock House, in Kensington, built in 1908, had seventeen bedrooms and six bathrooms. (Between the wars in even the most lavishly appointed houses the ratio of baths to bedrooms was much lower than it would be today.) The shower cages offered a rich repertory of sensations. A built-in vacuum-cleaner ran off mains electricity; an electrophone brought opera and plays from London theatres to the Debenhams' ears. Eltham Palace, built in the 1930s for Stephen Courtauld (born 1883) and his wife Virginia, had ten en suite bathrooms and a hot water system that allowed the whole house party to bathe before they dressed for dinner. Some cultivated households lived in primitive conditions. John Piper (born 1903) was a well-known painter, his wife Myfanwy (born 1911) was to write libretti for Benjamin Britten. A guest recalled that once, at the Pipers' country house, his wife found 'a mouse drowned in the glass of icy water beside her bed'. As a freshman at Balliol in 1936, Denis Healey (born 1917) found himself assigned a room 200 yards from the nearest bathroom.

Status and gender complicated domestic arrangements. Well-equipped households with resident servants had three water closets: one for the maids (downstairs, sometimes outside), one for the men – 'the downstairs "doubleyou"' – and one upstairs for women. George Melly (born 1926), the son of a Liverpool businessman, recalled that at night, 'although the bathroom was next door to them my mother and father almost always used the pot, though my mother, as a . . . proof of her modernity emptied it herself instead of leaving it to the maids as my grandparents did.'

In Grantham the Roberts family, supported by their grocer's shop, had neither an indoor lavatory nor running water. These were evidently classified as unnecessary frills. (As, incidentally, was 'happiness'.) Among the working classes, lavatory paper was a luxury. At home, one Londoner remembered, 'you simply tore off pieces' of newspaper 'and came across interesting things to read'. The 'neat squares . . . threaded on a string' encountered in a relation's house struck him as an elegant conceit.

Home-ownership was becoming commoner. In 1914 one house in ten was owner-occupied; by 1939 the proportion had risen to one in three. Clerks and artisans were becoming men of property. Copywriters rhapsodised about low-deposit ('£1 secures'), 'labour-saving' homes on private estates – a word still redolent of the stately home – in suburbs served by 'fast and frequent electric trains'. Suites for 'lounge', dining room and bedroom were the furnishings to aim for. Suburban optimism was expressed in the rising suns that decorated front gates, front doors, fireside rugs and wireless cabinets.

Most big cities had schemes to clear slums and build new dwellings to replace them: in 1933 the Medical Officer of Health for Manchester estimated that 30,000 houses in his area were 'unfit for human habitation' and another 80,000, 'by any reasonable standard', ought to be pulled down. Cambridgeshire Rural District Council built 200 houses between 1919 and 1926. The Borough of Cambridge hit the same landmark in 1934. Both councils commemorated their achievements with plaques that are still to be seen in Cambridge Road in Milton and, in Cambridge itself, in Bateson Road north of the river. The new homes made familiar things look shabby. Winifred Foley and her family moved from a tenement in Lisson Grove in London to a council flat – she 'never really felt at home but more like a daily cleaner': 'Our old furniture and second-hand rugs and mats were simply not good enough for our new grandeur and I was determined to replace them'.

It was not hard to tell private and council houses apart: municipal architects adopted the austere principles displayed in houses built for cultivated clients; speculative builders did not. As Osbert Lancaster (born 1908) noted:

> The all too few blocks of working-class flats, although similar in many respects to the Park Lane variety, are nevertheless easily distinguishable by reason of a number of interesting features. First, they are always situated in a much quieter neighbourhood; secondly, the rents are much lower though the rooms are seldom any smaller; thirdly, they are usually better architecturally.

Names were another give-away: 'in nine cases out of ten, if it has "Buildings" tacked on it is a working-class block, whereas if it has "House" it comes under the luxury heading'. Council houses were all of a kind – architects found it aesthetically pleasing, politicians argued that it was fairer. Speculative builders used the slogan: 'No two alike'. Owners looked down on tenants. At Cutteslowe in north Oxford, the hostility of the private semi-dwellers to their terraced council neighbours achieved physical form when, in 1934, the corporation yielded to pressure and built a wall to separate them.

CRADLE TO GRAVE

Birth and infancy

English families had been getting smaller since the 1870s. By the 1920s, the two-child family was becoming the nationally established ideal. For reasons discussed later in the chapter, the poorest parents tended to have the biggest families. Most women approaching childbirth between the wars had anecdotal evidence of its danger. The risk of death was greatest in Cornwall, Cumberland and Westmorland, where the population was sparse and travel difficult. From 1936 local authorities were required to support a midwifery service. But in remote rural districts, handywomen, who helped their neighbours in and out of the world, remained important. A woman born in 1908 recalled that, in rural Cumberland:

> Babies were born at home and, as most people had iron bedsteads, a rolled up towel was put through the head of the bed for the woman to hang on to . . . You made sure there was plenty of old sheets under her and lots of newspaper beneath that.

In cramped homes privacy, even in childbirth, was an unattainable goal. As a Sheffield woman explained, when her baby was delivered in 1925, 'my husband had to sit on the doorstep in the rain, worse still my little girl age 4 sat up in bed and looked at me, she said the next day, "Naughty mamma dirty the bed".' Upper- and middle-class babies were normally delivered by doctors. For first babies, nursing homes were favoured; later births were often at home. Pregnancy and birth, like other aspects of reproduction, were cloaked in secrecy. At 15, Ernest Turner (born

1909) was aware only that his mother 'had taken to her bed with some sort of women's illness'. His brother was born in a room across the landing from his bedroom – 'with no attendant sounds of drama' – and the announcement of the baby's birth came as a complete surprise. Women, whose husbands, parents or in-laws could afford to pay a monthly nurse, did not put a 'foot to the ground' for a month or six weeks after the birth. Poorer women depended on family and friends for respite from domestic chores. In some Anglican parishes new mothers were still 'churched'. Feminist writers have argued that the service cleansed the woman polluted by childbirth. The language of the *Book of Common Prayer* suggests that it was conceived as thanksgiving for a safe delivery. It is hard to tell what it meant to the women themselves. In communities where it was the done thing, it was easier to follow convention than to flout it.

Babies were at a greater risk than their mothers. In the families of professional men, most of the babies who did not survive died as a result of congenital malformations and injuries at birth. Among the children of unskilled labourers, environmental diseases – TB, bronchitis and pneumonia, diarrhoea and enteritis – were the killers. The death rate from pneumonia and bronchitis among the children of unskilled labourers in Durham and Northumberland alone was nine times greater than for the children of professional men all over England. But children from privileged families did die. Marigold (1918–21), the daughter of Winston and Clementine Churchill, was killed by a throat infection – a generation later antibiotics would have saved her.

Formal adoption became possible as a result of the Adoption Act 1926. Adoptive parents tended to prefer girls. A daughter was a child to love, a companion for her mother, a source of grandchildren – but not the vector of the family line and thus less of a cuckoo in the nest than a boy. Rosamund Essex (born 1900), a parson's daughter and a member of staff of the *Church Times*, adopted her son David when he was 2½. She was determined that there should be clean break between David and his birth mother. There were three routes to adoption. In the Magistrate's Court, where the fee was only two shillings, the natural mother was always called to give evidence; the County Court procedure cost £5 and might involve the natural mother; in the High Court, where the fee was £60, the natural mother was never called. Miss Essex, not a rich woman, chose the High Court: 'I was dead against the original mother knowing where the child was'.

> My son was told that he was adopted from the very start. He took the adoption naturally as I did – so much so that when he came into his teens and was away from home on a short holiday he said to a West Country bishop whom he met at some church function, 'I think you know my mother, Miss Essex'. The bishop was aghast. But he kept his cool and managed to stammer out, Yes, yes he did, and then disappeared into the crowd to think it over.

Such frankness was unusual.

The baby's paraphernalia and clothing reflected its family's circumstances. James and Jean MacGibbon's first child (born 1936), had a cot draped in layers of primrose muslin, a folding bath, a Moses basket for daytime use and a covered basket containing everything a baby could need down to a tin of baby powder. The chest of drawers was soon filled with baby clothes called a layette, all provided by mother: this June baby was to wear a Chilprufe vest, two sorts of nappy, flannel petticoat, lawn petticoat and long dresses of the finest drawn-thread voile with satin ribbon threaded through the waist. Endless matinee coats and bootees were soon contributed . . . There were Viyella nightdresses too.

This remained the standard rig-out for upper-class babies into the 1960s. Families with inherited wealth had 'nineteenth-century family robes for best'. Best naturally included christening, a ceremony that some radical middle-class parents omitted: Francis Meynell's son Ben was put down for the MCC (Marylebone Cricket Club) instead. These babies wore Harrington's muslin napkins 'next the skin', with towelling nappies over them and, 'when the baby is being carried', 'little woollen drawers'. All professional baby experts condemned 'Mackintosh drawers so much advertised'. Deep litter, in the form of a chaff bed, was the approved methods of dealing with the 'untrained infant'. Nevertheless, an outfit recommended by lay advisers included '3 pairs of rubber pants'. Upper-class babies were taken out for airings in what Lord Montagu of Bealieu (born 1926) called the 'limousines of the perambulator world'.

As far as the middle classes were concerned, Truby King (born 1858) was the great authority. Medical superintendent of a mental hospital, he was first moved to write on infant welfare by an epidemic of infantile diarrhoea in his native New Zealand in 1907. Breast feeding at regular intervals was his prescription – and it worked. Among his slogans was 'a woman's milk is not her own', it is 'the baby's birthright'. In England Truby King's principles were disseminated by the Mothercraft Training Society and the *Mothercraft Manual*, launched in 1924. He preached 'Regularity of all habits' and above all feeding and bowel movements. Both were to be done 'by the clock'. If bowel

> training be begun early, regularity can usually be brought about by the second month . . . At first it may be necessary to use some local stimulation such as that produced by tickling the anus . . . If the above mild external stimulation fails, the mother may try passing . . . the soft rubber nozzle of a small bulb-enema into the bowel.

The 'dummy' was outlawed. Thumb sucking was anathema:

> The child's hands should be kept away from the mouth . . . A simple method is to apply corrugated cardboard splints to the elbow . . . Splints should not be worn all the time but should be left off at intervals so that the child may exercise his arms.

The Truby King child disposed to rub his thighs together was suspected of masturbation. As a last resort it might 'be necessary to put the legs in splints' too.

Mrs Sydney Frankenburg, author of the best-seller *Common Sense in the Nursery* (1922), provides a clue to the appeal of the clock-bound regime to 'the mother of moderate means'. 'Knowing that a little crying will do good . . . by feeding him four-hourly by day and not at all by night, a woman is able to lead a human life'. Looking back, some parents regretted following Truby King's precepts. Cecil Day-Lewis (born 1904) condemned the 'system which made life about as rigorous, impersonal and nasty for babies as it could be made'. As he later acknowledged, his son and biographer Sean (born 1931) was '"disturbed": a sleep-walker, a fire-raiser, a nightmare-dreamer, a bed-wetter'. It is unclear whether his behaviour was a product of the Truby King regime or a reflection of the tension that existed between his mother and his promiscuous father.

Poorer parents improvised. One expectant mother 'trimmed' a banana crate 'with bags that had had cream of tartar in. It was very fine muslin. My brother worked for a wholesale grocer . . . and he used to bring the bags home'. In labouring families, the 'tails of dad's old shirts' might be used as nappies but 'a lot of babies went bare-arsed'. The trade unionist Frank Cousins (born 1904) had a vivid recollection of an incident he observed in his time as a lorry driver during the slump:

> I happened to be in a transport café on the Great North Road when a young couple came in with a child in a nearly broken-down pram. They were walking from Shields to London, because the man understood that he could get a job in London. And they came into the café and sat down and they fetched the baby's feeding bottle out and it had water in it. They fed the baby with water, and then sort of lifted the kiddy's dress up . . . and it had a newspaper nappy on. They took this off and sort of wiped the baby's bottom with the nappy they'd taken off and then picked up another newspaper and put that on for another nappy.

In the Forest of Dean working-class mothers relied on 'the sugar teat', 'a couple of spoonfuls of sugar tied in a bit of rag and moistened by dipping it into the kettle on the hob' to pacify their babies.

Most parents with the means had paid help with child care. American-born Lella Florence, whose husband was a Cambridge don, was an enthusiast for 'the separate nursery to which children retire, at least in middle-class English homes', with 'that wonderful person the nanny'. The classic nanny learned her craft as junior in a well-found nursery. But the nursery provided a berth for poor relations too. Moppet Whyte (born 1895) was a granddaughter of the Earl of Airlie. Unlike most women of her rank, she had to make her own living. Trained as a children's nurse, she found an employer in her first cousin Clementine Churchill (born 1885). Mary, the Churchills' youngest child (born 1922), called Moppet 'the guardian angel' of her childhood: 'Since my parents were often away, [she] provided continuity and organised my daily life, she was the greatest influence in my early years'. Julian Critchley (born 1930), son of a neurologist and a nurse with roots in rural Shropshire, was cared for by one of his mother's cousins who came up to London to take a paid post as his nanny.

In a story first published in the *Morning Post* in 1913, Saki (born 1870) observed that in an exchange between children and the grown-up responsible for them, 'Most of the aunt's remarks seemed to begin with "Don't" and nearly all the children's remarks began with "Why?"' Children throughout the century would find the script familiar. But between the wars there were well-documented exceptions to this rule, clustered among the left-inclining intelligentsia. Oliver Postgate (born 1925) and his older brother John 'would wander in and out of the bathroom while Daisy' – their mother – 'was in the bath, to talk of domestic matters or make enquiries about anatomy'. We have already identified Francis Meynell as a partisan of the modern. Unlike most children of his generation, his son Ben was 'brought up on principles which would now' – he was writing at the end of the 1960s – 'be attributed to Doctor Spock'. Ben Meynell was supposed to know what was best for him. His father recounted a telling anecdote: 'The small Ben is being pressed to say what pudding he would like for his lunch and after listening to a number of suggestions he stamps his foot and, almost in tears, cries, "Can't *cook* choose?"' Nicholas Tomalin (born 1931) recalled that 'When my progressive father was asked by the progressive headmaster of a progressive school whether the Tomalin family "kept open bathroom", I joined in his scornful laughter. Of *course* we did. What a stuffy man! I was *six*'. Broad-minded frankness was not confined to the metropolitan intelligentsia, however. According to her daughter Nancy (born 1917), Norah Spain, the Roedean-educated wife of a land agent, was prepared to explain 'bugger' to a small girl without hesitation and in graphic terms: 'It's when a man puts his thing up another man's bum and jigs up and down'.

Among the servant-keeping classes it was assumed that a woman's duty to her husband was absolute. The first woman to take her seat in Parliament, in December 1919, was not a seasoned campaigner for female suffrage but the wife of a sitting MP who had been catapulted into the Lords by his father's death. Nancy Astor (born 1879) was an improbable pioneer: American-born, mother of six and – though this was not generally known at the time of her election – a divorcee. The Empire demanded cruel sacrifices of her servants and their families. As her biography of her younger son Alan demonstrates, Sara Turing (born 1881) was a devoted mother. On leave in England with the boys, she committed their quaint sayings to paper so that her husband could share her pleasure in them: 'He announced yesterday, "The rhubarb has made my teeth feel as if the white has come off"'. In India with her husband, she treasured letters from his foster-mother 'Grannie' Ward and from Alan himself. Grandmothers and aunts, natural and mercenary, provided homes in the holidays for many boys and girls whose parents were serving King and Country abroad.

Health

The pattern of infant mortality has already been sketched. Many childish illnesses defeated the medical profession in the recent past. The cluster of symptoms that points to a diagnosis of diabetes was recognised in ancient times; in the 1670s the Oxford physician contrasted the 'honeyed' taste of diabetics' urine with the normal saltiness; a hundred years later the sweetness was identified as sugar. It was not until 1922 that the first experimental treatments with insulin were undertaken in Canada. Before that children with diabetes died. The infectious diseases of childhood: whooping cough, scarlet fever and diphtheria were life-threatening. Tuberculosis affected people of every class but it was commonest among the poor. Children in overcrowded homes, in close contact with the disease were especially vulnerable. Ellen Wilkinson's declaration that the high incidence of TB in Jarrow, her County Durham constituency, was the product of 'poverty, poverty, poverty' was endorsed by the findings of a research project carried out in the town in 1932. 'The association of tuberculosis with poverty is of greater importance than any other variable studied'.

Poor feeding meant poor health. A majority of children examined in London in 1927 and in County Durham in 1933, though 'not "ricketty" in the everyday sense of the term' showed 'signs of rickets' – calcium deficiency – 'to the clinical observer'. Among English teenagers, there was 'a marked difference in the heights of boys drawn from different classes'. Poor boys were 2.6 inches shorter than the sons of artisans and 5.8 inches shorter than the sons of professional men. (At 13, Wilf Mannion (born 1918), one of the ten children of a blast furnaceman from Middlesbrough, stood 4 feet 2 inches tall.) Condensed milk (known as 'conny onny' in Liverpool) and margarine were the food of the poor; fresh milk, butter, fish, meat, eggs, fruit and vegetables were the food of the better off.

Domestic service familiarised some working-class women with the patterns of privileged families' diet and recreation; others followed advice from books that they borrowed from the Free Libraries. A Coventry woman, six years married with a single child, read books on 'child welfare' borrowed from the public library and spent five hours in the park on fine days. The smaller a family, the easier it was to feed it well. A former cook with two children was able to provide grapefruit, bacon and egg, bread, butter and marmalade for breakfast; fish, meat and green vegetables for dinner. With examples like this before them, it is easy to see why birth control was widely perceived as 'the child's charter'. For many poor women it was an ideal out of reach.

Education

Education was another badge of rank. Up to the age of 14, when the great majority of children left, attendance was compulsory and – in the elementary schools that catered for 90 per cent of the population – free. These schools were staffed by their ex-pupils, teachers' pets, employed as pupil-teachers; they learned by observation as well as formal instruction. A minority won places at training colleges. Where numbers permitted, pupils were segregated by age and gender; in London you can still see examples of the classic three-decker with the Infants' department at ground level, with the Boys' and Girls' departments above. Elementary schoolteachers made snobbish and ambitious parents. Enoch Powell was born in 1912. Among his 'earliest recollections' was the memory of his mother putting up the alphabet round the kitchen wall so [he] could learn it'. His parents sent him to a private school.

In the nineteenth century Thomas Henry Huxley (born 1825) had designed a ladder to take able children 'from the gutter' to university. It was by any standard a long and hazardous climb. The rungs closest to the gutter were particularly slippery – Kenneth Lindsay, who reviewed the 'free place' system in the 1920s, concluded that 'greasy pole' was an apter metaphor. Only one child in ten left the elementary school for a secondary school; only one in a thousand who had started in an elementary school reached university. The regulation that allowed able children to take on part time work before the official school leaving age was revoked only in 1921. The clever children of poor parents could compete for a county scholarship to take them secondary school. Winning one was not the end of the story. Letters turning down high school and grammar school places, 'written in pencil on blue paper torn from a sugar bag', underlined the gulf between the culture of unbookish working-class families and schools where Latin was part of the 'core curriculum'. In London scholarships went overwhelmingly to the better-off boroughs, led by Lewisham, and, across the metropolis, to an elite of schools attended by the better-fed, better-clothed, better-spoken, better-behaved children of men in regular, skilled work. In rural counties like Oxfordshire, wages were low and elementary schools were small, scattered and often staffed by unqualified teachers. In industrial cities like Bradford, when times were good, high starting wages drew school leavers to the mills. Poverty frustrated ambition. While she was at the high school, Sybil Marshall's father had encouraged her to save her county council bursary to fit her out for university. 'But when harvest approached, the need for a new horse on the farm became pressing. There was simply no help for it, and my £32 went a long way to the cost of a beautiful piebald mare'. And Sybil Marshall became an uncertificated teacher in an elementary school.

In the early 1930s, George Orwell taught at The Hawthorns, which catered for boys whose parents' priority was to keep them out of the elementary schools. It occupied two rooms in the home of its proprietor, who worked at the HMV gramophone factory. Parents who aimed for more than mere segregation were prepared to invest heavily in education. The three Betts children, whose father was a tax inspector, and Kingsley Amis, an only child, whose father worked in the offices of Colman's, the mustard company, attended grammar schools as fee-paying pupils. Fees were 'a crippling burden on the [Betts] family finances'. A year's fees cost Mr Amis £90 at a time when his annual salary was £500.

Preparatory schools trained boys to enter public schools and naval academies. Their essential tasks were to eliminate regional accents and to get pupils through the Common Entrance examination. Leading prep schools fed particular public schools. A sensible mother could help a new boy fit in by making sure he had the right underclothing – vests and pants, not combinations. If cold baths were a school rule, he should get used to plunging in at home. A thoughtful mother would break the news about Father Christmas and other nursery fables before his first term as a boarder. Mrs Frankenburg's *Latin with Laughter*, published in 1931, was designed to give little boys a head start in the classroom. There was still a market for it forty years on. Thoughtful parents and grandparents recognised the importance of keeping in touch with children temporarily exiled from home. Between 1914 and 1923 Sir Henry Thornhill (born 1894) sent an extraordinary series of jokey and instructive illustrated letters and cards to his grandchildren. When the time came for Teddy, the eldest (born 1912), to sail home from India to join an English school in 1922, he found letters from his grandfather waiting for him in ports of call and the grandfather in person was waiting on the platform of Fenchurch Station. 'Every word in [Sir Henry's] letters' was a 'virtual kiss'. The strings of repeated 'Os' and 'Xs' at the end of letters to and from children at boarding school stood for hugs and kisses. Mrs Frankenburg could be relied on for common-sense advice: carbon paper enabled you to duplicate the 'family news' that you wanted to pass on to scattered children.

Prep schools were small and often family-run: 'a small school made a large family'. The quality of life in the very much depended on the temperament of the proprietor and his wife. Ashampstead at Seaford in Sussex, run by Captain and Mrs Wilson, had an average roll of 35 boys. The Captain's brother, Mr Pat, taught French verbs to the accompaniment of 'choreographic motions with his long arms and legs: extended lunges and pirouettes'. Boys learned auction bridge. Sometimes, to break the routine, the whole school spent a day in bed 'on a diet of bread, marmalade and Bovril'. At Sherborne Prep in 1920 Louis MacNeice (born 1907) won first prize at the Fancy Dress Ball. He went as 'a prehistoric man'. As the head pointed out approvingly in the end of term report he sent to MacNeice's clergyman father, he had 'rolled in the mud' to 'add verisimilitude to his get up'. Alastair Horne had bleak memories of Ludgrove where the boys' necks were cleaned with methylated spirits for Parents' Days 'so we went to greet our parents, all pink and shining above our collars, but all filth below'. The parents of Stephen Spender (born 1909) unwittingly sent him to 'a brothel for flagellants'. The ordeal had to be borne with stoicism. For a boy in a culture that valued the stiff upper lip, 'blubbing' was the ultimate disgrace.

'The main task of Public School education', Professor A. S. C. Ross declared, in the aftermath of the 1950s debate on the shibboleths that marked the language of the U [upper class], 'is to keep U-boys U and turn non-U boys into U-boys'. As the demand for public school education grew, new schools were founded. The choice available to fathers who had not themselves been to public school and those with an inclination to break the family habit increased. Gresham's, Holt, was a revitalised Elizabethan grammar school. It attracted parents who appreciated the bracing Norfolk air, the emphasis on science and music, the accommodation – every boy had his own cubicle – and the emphasis on self-discipline. Stowe, housed in an eighteenth-century mansion set in a park studded with grottoes, temples and pavilions, opened in 1923 with 99 boys and 10 masters. J. H. Roxburgh (born 1888), its founding head, 'a master of discreet publicity', outlawed boy-made rules and introduced tennis, golf and fencing as alternatives to team games. Stella Gibbons' *Cold Comfort Farm* was a set book. Roxburgh lacked the courage to abandon the public school traditions of fagging and beating but he knew boys' given names, diminutives and nicknames too. Introduced to a prep school boy, 'young Bruce', Roxburgh's response was 'Commonly known as Nigs'. Stowe had its critics. According to John Gale, who joined the school in the late 1930s, 'absurd ritual' made Stowe 'a sort of fake Eton'. Plays on the school's name abounded. The boys were Stoics; at roll call – 'stance' – they answered 'Sto'. The motto was 'Persto et Praesto' – 'Fast and First'. Bedales was the first school to offer coeducation from nursery to university entrance. Its founder John Badley (born 1865) had been at Rugby as a boy. It had 'taught him how *not* to teach history, mathematics and modern languages and how *not* to regard games as all important'. Badley's wife, 'Ma Bee', was a feminist and an active suffragette. Bedales was a pioneer in the fields of English literature and drama; 'for many years it was possible to maintain a string quartet on the Music staff'. Fees were high. Between the wars, Bedales was the choice of 'advanced' parents. Grammar and county secondary schools were 'sort of fake Public Schools' with 'beaks' in gowns – just as boys (and their parents) had been led to expect by the books and boys' papers they read. Paul Vaughan (born 1925) went to Raynes Park on the Kingston Bypass, a sort of Stowe of the suburbs: the school motto and the school song were by W. H. Auden; T. S. Eliot once gave out the prizes. Under its Old Etonian head, Richard Bailey, Quarry Bank School in Liverpool had something of a similar flavour. Predictably the boys were 'Ashlars' – their 'quarry roughness' smoothed away.

Higher education

Between the wars higher education was by no means the only route into the professions. Bourgeois schools like Dulwich College sent a majority of leavers straight into the city and the banks and merchant houses that exploited the resources of the Empire and other regions of the developing world. London and the civic universities attracted able students and academics of distinction but a place at Oxford and Cambridge remained the birthright of privilege and the goal of the ambitious child or parent. A city like Leeds which pulsed with 'the ceaseless beat of industry', with 'belching smoke by day and flames by night' could not compete with the glamour of dreaming spires and punting parties. Men like Malcolm Muggeridge's father, who had tasted higher education through the ancient universities' extension classes, took vicarious delight in expressions like 'sporting my oak' – the Cambridge equivalent of a 'do-not-disturb' sign. To send their sons to an ancient university, fathers were prepared to make financial sacrifices. Peter Quennell went up to Oxford on a scholarship and a small allowance; he later learned that this represented the proceeds of his father's life insurance. Undergraduate society was dominated by the 'poshocracy'. In the 1920s an Oxford undergraduate might still inform his tutor 'with imperious condescension' that he had 'managed to get four days hunting' a week and would, therefore, miss all the lectures and tutorials in the coming term. In 1940 Edward Heath (born 1916), who went up to Oxford from a Kent grammar school, wrote a piece for the *Spectator* that revealed the discomfiture experienced by the 'Secondary Schoolboy' 'whose home and whose parents did not come up to the standard set by other undergraduates'. Heath's account of his predicament is borne out by Hallam Tennyson (born 1920). To the Poet Laureate's great-grandson, Heath, the builder's lad, was 'a stocky, red-faced boy with black brilliantined hair and a loud "common" voice . . . In view of the contempt with which he was treated it seems remarkable that he did not become a violent revolutionary'. At Trinity College, Cambridge, a decade earlier, the lower-middle-class loner Enoch Powell stuck to his books with grim determination. His chief relaxation was a evening constitutional from his college 'to the railway station and back', among the bleakest options in a handsome town. 'On Sundays he enjoyed a more scenic route along the Backs'. Grammar school boys were expected to swot. Colleges were single-sex; at Cambridge women were confined to Girton and Newnham.

Though the route from nanny in the nursery to boarding school and 'varsity' was followed by a tiny minority of English boys and girls, story books and periodicals gave many more a second-hand, stereotyped experience of this sort of life. As George Orwell's analysis of boys' weeklies suggests, there were characters that almost every reader could identify with:

> In the *Gem* there is . . . heroic far boy, Fatty Wynn, as a set-off against Bunter. Vernon-Smith, 'the Bounder of the Remove', a Byronic character, always on the verge of the sack, is another great favourite. And even some of the cads probably have their following, Loder, for instance, 'the rotter of the Sixth', is a cad but he is also a highbrow and given to saying sarcastic things about football and the team spirit.

The wireless offered new opportunities to learn the modes and manners of the privileged. *Children's Hour*'s target audience was brought up in 'a good middle-class home' and attended 'a good school' (though the 'Uncle' who signed off with 'pleasant dreams and a hot bath' was reminded that daily hot baths were a luxury that not everyone enjoyed). Others could eavesdrop – Irene Thomas, born into what she called the upper working class just after the First World War, acknowledged the educational debt she owed the BBC. Young people who listened to *Children's Hour* at 5 p.m. were likely to catch the programme that came next – the *Six O'Clock News*.

Growing up

Menstruation was woman's periodic 'curse'. E. Arnott Robertson (born 1903), a doctor's daughter, is credited as the first writer to use this term in print. The teenage narrator of *Ordinary Families* (1933) describes 'the griping pain' that made her 'double up unobtrusively', the paralysing 'sick wrench in the stomach'. Although sanitary towels had been in the shops since the 1890s and tampons arrived in the 1930s, most women and girls wore home-made elastic belts to which they hooked rolled-up towelling squares like babies' nappies. These napkins were laundered and reused. The poorest women competed for whatever fabric could be spared – shirt-tails and worn-out sheeting. Sexual inhibition was drummed into boys and girls at home and at school. Shame and embarrassment meant that girls were often inadequately prepared for the experience of their first period. Alix Kilroy's mother, who had trained as a midwife, represented menstruation as 'a matter of pride', 'the entry into womanhood' and explained 'quite naturally and matter-of-factly how babies were born'. 'But information about the act of sex was another matter'. Directly challenged by her 17-year-old daughter, she responded, 'There is a place in your body where the man can get in'. Many women had a jaundiced view of sex – as usual the privileged are best recorded. According to twice-married, American-born Nancy Astor (born 1879), it was 'not so wonderful', 'just like going to the lavatory'. Her grown-up sons honoured her revelation by referring to sex as 'Number Three'. Lady Astor's contemporary Lady Vesci found sex – 'all the fiddlin' and heavy breathin'' – 'very tiresome'.

For many, including Nick Tomalin, sex education began in the playground. A boy sang him 'a variant of "My Bonnie Lies Over the Ocean"' in an exquisite choirboy soprano: "My Daddy Lay Over My Mummy" three times and finished the verse with "And That is How I Came to Be!" I was twelve at the time, but can still remember the incident with great clarity, because suddenly everything came clear to me'. Books were another important source of information about sex. Versions of the popular sex-education manual known as *Aristotle's Masterpiece* had been in circulation since the seventeenth century. Victor Pritchett (born 1900) found a copy 'hidden behind the chamber-pot in the cupboard' in his parents' bedroom. Gavin Maxwell was born in 1914. His widowed mother gave him 'a batty and highly misinformative' Edwardian sex manual called *What a Young Boy Ought to Know*. According to its author, Dr Sylvanus Stall,

> 'Self abuse' does 'harm to the body and harm to the mind . . . a boy will not feel so vigorous and springy; he will not have so good an eye for games . . . will look pale and pasty . . . indigestion . . . spots and pimples . . . He will probably be at the bottom of his class and get many a licking. He will surely be a duffer at games and it is a hundred to one he gets laughed at more than any boy in the school for his blundering simplicity.

In the Tomalins' house there were 'row upon row of searingly revealing books on the subject of sex' by psychiatrists and novelists.

Sex before marriage

Between the wars young men and young women from respectable families were brought up to accept a culture of premarital abstinence. Well-known lines of doggerel sum up the case for caution:

> There was a young lady so wild
> She kept herself pure undefiled
> By thinking of Jesus
> Venereal diseases
> And the danger of having a child.

The penalties for young men who set others a bad example might be severe.

William Empson was born in 1906. When a condom was discovered among his possessions at Magdalene College, Cambridge, in 1929 he was summarily dismissed from his recently conferred research fellowship.

Marriage

Until 1929, with parental consent, a legal marriage could be contracted by girls as young as 12 and boys as young as 14. Evidence submitted to the Select Committee, which considered the proposal to raise the minimum age of marriage indicated that a couple of dozen 15-year-old girls married every year; most were pregnant. The Age of Marriage Act 1929 fixed 16 as the minimum; minors, under the age of 21, required their parents' consent. In fact most couples started their married life more than a decade after they left school. Brides were generally 25 or so, their husbands, on average, three years older.

By 1920 women had the vote – though not yet on equal terms with men. Women had to wait more than half a century for the legislation intended to secure equal pay and equal opportunities. Spinsters, left on the shelf, were pitied because, without a man and his income, they had little hope of achieving a home of their own. In 1921 a quarter of women aged between 30 and 34 were single. In 1931 a fifth of women in their early forties were still unmarried. In imagination and in reality they were casualties of the First World War. Convention, a shortage of cash, the difficulty of independent housekeeping or a sense of obligation kept unmarried adults under their parents' roof. The ties binding sons and daughters to widowed mothers were particularly strong and presented an obstacle or an alternative to marriage.

Siblings and surrogate siblings set up house together. For a single woman, sharing with a friend was often preferable to the cost and challenge of independent housekeeping or the petty restrictions of a boarding house. Some of these partnerships lasted a lifetime.

In choosing a marriage partner 'till death us do part', prudence was the watchword. When June and Doris Langley Moore asked their young female readers to assess 'How well are you adapted to each other in tastes and interests, in temperament, in social position, in standards of living and in age', they echoed the counsels of the wise down the ages. Three hundred years earlier William Gouge gave much the same advice: 'That matrimonial society may prove comfortable, it is requisite that there should be some equality betwixt the parties that are married in Age, Estate, Condition, Piety'. These were not the only considerations: a suspicion of inherited disease counted against a prospective partner – 'everybody avoided TB families'. When he discovered that her father had died of general paralysis of the insane, Kathleen Hale's lover was horror struck, their relationship went through a crisis resolved only when a blood test proved that she was clear of syphilis. When, after the First World War, for the first time in his romantic career, Gervas Huxley (born 1894) 'had a secure future to offer the object of his affections', 'getting married seemed to be one of the expected and desirable features of settling back in to civilian life'. He and his bride were the same age – 25 – 'shared a similar class background' – Huxley had been at prep school with her brother – and 'had many tastes in common': 'Both families were warmly encouraging'. The prudent match failed.

The licence afforded to engaged couples varied. When Frank Pakenham (born 1905), a peer's son, visited his fiancée Elizabeth Harman (born 1906) while she was working for the Workers' Educational Association (WEA), the couple she was lodging with in Stoke-on-Trent 'vacated their double bed and put us into it. We placed the bolster . . . between us . . . to remind us that we must "wait till marriage".' There is evidence that many women who felt confident of their partner's loyalty were at least persuadable into sex before marriage. At the end of the 1930s when the date of parents' marriages began to be recorded on their children's birth certificates, it became evident that nearly a third of first babies were conceived out of wedlock. At the same time Dr Isabel Hutton, author of *The Hygiene of Marriage*, believed that marriages were often unconsummated because 'a man may be afraid of inflicting pain upon his wife'. Alec Waugh (born 1898), whose only previous experience had been with prostitutes on the continent, 'had no idea of the amount of tact and skilful patience that is required to initiate an inexperienced girl into the intimacies of sex'. The combination of the woman who 'didn't want to' and the man 'who didn't know much about it' was a poor prescription for sexual satisfaction or marital happiness. Incompatibility was not yet a justification for divorce. Herbert Morrison (born 1888) started life as an errand boy and worked his way up through the newspaper trade. He and Daisy Kent married in 1919. Morrison was active in politics; she was intensely shy. Their sexual relationship seems to have ended soon after the conception of their only child. They saw little of each other from one week's end to the next. Yet the marriage lasted 32 years – until they were parted by Daisy's death.

A flight from parenthood?

The cost of bringing children up has surfaced several times already. The campaign for family allowances or 'state wages' for mothers was a feature of the years between the wars. Enlightened employers like the London School of Economics (LSE), the chocolate makers Cadbury, Pilkington, the glassmakers and Tootal, the textile firm, introduced some form of bonus for parents. At the LSE it took the form of educational allowances. In some families a causal link between a rise in income and the assumption of new financial obligations can be inferred. Sidney and Eva Larkin were in their mid-twenties when they married in 1911 on his appointment as Chief Audit Accountant to Birmingham Corporation. Their daughter Kitty was 10 years old by the time her brother Philip was born. Again promotion – to the City Treasurer's post in Coventry – appears to have been the trigger.

Dr Marie Stopes (born 1880), an academic, not a medical doctor, pioneered an information revolution: 'the dissemination of the knowledge of Contraception by General Propaganda', was how C. P. Blacker put it. As she explained, 'the control of conception' could be achieved 'either by shutting the sperms away from the opening of the womb or by securing the death of *all* (instead of the death of all but *one*) of the two to six hundred million sperms which enter the womb'. She advocated the use of a small rubber diaphragm in conjunction with cocoa butter pessary in which quinine was the active ingredient. She called the cap she preferred the 'pro-race'. Between the wars 'eugenics' and 'race' did not carry the fascist taint they later acquired. Reactions to *Married Love* (1918) and its successors *Wise Parenthood* (1918), *Radiant Motherhood* (1920) and *Enduring Passion* (1928) were mixed. Medics disapproved of her presumption and her purple prose. Her books were widely regarded as a branch of 'improper literature' likely to corrupt the young. A working-class Catholic MP declared that *Married Love* was 'not fit for decent homes': Stopes had published 'the knowledge of the prostitute'. The Roman Catholic press was equally vituperative. 'Birth control' amounted to the 'legalised prostitution of marriage'. It was 'an abomination . . . infinitely worse than the unnatural vices that were practised in the cities of Sodom and Gomorrah'. At the same time there was an enthusiastic welcome – many of the men who printed it 'snitched a copy'. It was widely accepted that Stopes 'made an immense difference to the happiness and well-being of thousands of couples'. The letters she received demonstrated the physical and emotional pain and distress that arose from ignorance. However, as Dodie Smith (born 1896) observed, although 'thanks to the ever-blessed Dr Marie Stopes' she was fully informed about the sexual act, 'about the foothills of sex' – foreplay – she 'knew nothing'.

The poor were the eugenicists' prime target. Blacker suggested that, in an average year, 1000 teachers would generate 95 babies; 1000 general labourers, with lower earnings and less secure employment, would produce 231. A survey of mothers in the poor district of South London served by Guy's Hospital revealed that, of 78 babies born in the autumn of 1924, 47 were 'definitely unwanted'. Pro-race caps cost more than many working-class couples could afford. Lella Florence surveyed the first 300 clients of the Cambridge Women's Welfare Association who had signed up between August 1925 and 1927. More than half had found the 'methods of family limitation either so ineffective or so distressing or troublesome that they abandoned the attempt to use them'. The cost of contraception was not the only obstacle to planned parenthood:

> The vast majority of our patients have no bathroom or any suitable sanitary facilities for douching. In many cases they share a single outdoor lavatory with lodgers or another family. They live in tiny overcrowded houses, and more often than not share their bedroom with several children.

In 1930 the Church of England abandoned its opposition to birth control and local authorities began to permit instruction on family planning techniques in their clinics. Many working-class couples had neither the privacy nor the spare cash to take advantage of these shifts in policy.

Abstinence was an effective, if grim, option. Charis Frankenburg helped to run the Birth Control Clinic in Salford: 'We constantly heard that a woman dared not show affection to her husband – "It would mean another kid".' 'A sailor's wife went into hiding whenever his ship was expected' to avoid being 'caught'. A woman who attended the Family Planning Clinic in Holloway reported that she and her husband had had 'no unions for thirteen years for fear of pregnancy'. Another woman discovered that her husband had resorted to masturbation. He had been 'an ideal daddy' as his heroic abstinence indicated: 'Since little Reggie came he has had no connections with me at all' but she was 'sure he will do himself some harm' by '*abusing himself*'. Sue Dexter, whose first child was born in 1935, remembered her mother-in-law's advice 'to put two legs in one stocking'. Paper-thin walls gave the writer Henry Williamson (born 1895) a sound picture of life in the cottage next door. He observed the stress induced by poverty and the discipline of separate beds. 'Revvy' Carter, invalided out of the army after the Somme, survived by odd-jobbing – he got his nickname from working in the rectory garden. 'Mrs Revvy would yell . . . her temper caused by over-work, close-air, bad teeth, and under nourishment'. Every night

> Revvy would say 'Up over the timber hill into blanket field', to Ernie in his arms. They always slept with the windows closed; Revvy in bed with Ernie, his Missus in bed with Madge and the baby. About once a month Ernie was shifted, asleep, into the other bed.

Withdrawal was the proverbial contraceptive. Railways supplied the favourite metaphor: 'Don't go all the way to Blackpool'. 'Get off at Gateshead' – instead of the terminus at Newcastle. When an accidental pregnancy occurred, people said, 'she must have caught her foot in the sheet'. Anal intercourse was another means of avoiding pregnancy: how common it is impossible to say. A Liverpool woman confided in Maud Melly: 'My husband does it up my behind not to have more kids. He empties the chamber-pot down the sink, when me mother's in the (h)ouse and he calls me a Roman Catholic bastard – now that's not nice is it?'

The Offences Against the Person Act 1861 outlawed abortion. The Infant Life (Preservation) Act 1929 permitted the termination of a pregnancy to save the mother's life. Organised campaigns to reform the law on abortion began in the 1930s. Women who supported birth control clinics also joined the Abortion Law Reform Association. A judgment of 1939 extended the definition of preserving the mother's life: termination could be justified if the pregnancy threatened to leave her a 'physical or mental wreck'.

Termination on other grounds was illegal – but abortions were available in the back streets and in the consulting rooms of medical practitioners, for some of whom it was a money-spinner, for some a means of alleviating distress. Minnie Roberts represents the informally qualified practitioners; at her trial in 1925 she claimed that she had 'treated 800 cases in twenty-five years'. Elizabeth David (born 1913), an upper-class woman whose sexually active, fertile years spanned the 1930s, 1940s and 1950s, was childless: 'I always managed to get rid of mine', she said. A midwife described the desperate measures poor women took to get rid of an unwanted pregnancy. They dosed themselves with Beecham's Pills or gunpowder, they inserted 'a bone crochet hook up the vagina', 'keeping it there with cotton wool padding till the abortion took place'. Mrs Stephens, a building worker's wife, told her son Robert (born 1931) how she tried to end the pregnancy that led to his birth with a hot bath, gin and a crochet hook. Harriet Noble told her daughter Phyllis that she 'could have knifed' her husband Alec when she was being conceived; after producing three children in three and a half years she aborted her fourth pregnancy.

Household management

Naomi Mitchison (born 1897), daughter of an Oxford academic with a comfortable private income, observed:

> For us, in what I suppose I should call the upper middle class, having servants was part of the normal pattern of life.
> To understand what the household staff did . . . one has to go back to a period with few disposables . . . No fridge, no dishwasher, no electric liquidiser or whisk instead a hair sieve and rubbing in the fat by hand, no detergents, no drip dry for that matter no washing machines or spin dryers, instead scrubbing with bars of yellow soap and irons heating on the stove. Sheets and towels went to the laundry, but other things were washed at home.

Frances Donaldson, daughter of the popular playwright Frederick Lonsdale (born 1881), married between the wars. Looking back, she explained that

> For us it was an absolute necessity to have a cook, a housemaid and a nanny or mother's help for our children . . . At our level of affluence we could hardly afford all this and by the time war was declared we had a bank overdraft which, although not very big, was not negligible. Yet I never thought I could manage with less . . . Since I could neither cook nor iron nor sew, and had not the slightest idea of how a bath was cleaned or any other household chores, I relied . . . on others.

Affluent incompetence was a source of employment for the working classes. The young Mrs McAlpine, transplanted from Canada into a big bourgeois family of building contractors in the late 1920s, was 'shocked' to discover that the lady's maid sent over by her mother-in-law 'was in the habit of putting the toothpaste on her toothbrush' morning and evening. Elizabeth David (born 1913), whose articles and books transformed home cooking from the 1950s, was taught how to brew a pot of tea when she joined Oxford rep as a young actress in 1932. Knowing that she could not boil an egg, her mother Stella Gwynne (born 1884) recommended plain chocolate and Bovril as suitably 'nourishing food'. Her helplessness was not uncommon. At the start of the Second World War, newly married and with very little money, Jill and Laurence Whistler had breakfast 'laid . . . by a friendly person who came in to cook and clean at 7d an hour. Jill could barely cook at all and was alarmed by a frying pan'.

Resident servants were not a prerogative of the very rich. Mrs Hool was the wife of a big tenant farmer on the Duke of Devonshire's estates in Derbyshire and

mother of a large family. Farmer Hool's unmarried workers still lived under his roof
– at times between the wars the household numbered in the twenties. Mrs Hool
had the services of a housekeeper, a nurse who looked after her invalid daughter
and two young girls recruited annually from the workhouse on the overseer's
advice. Mrs Walton, the wife of the headmaster of a village school in
Northumberland and mother of three children, had a maid living in. In the days
before housekeeping was transformed by technology, the burden on houseproud
women without domestic help was formidable. On washday, in the house where
Mary Stott (born 1907) grew up,

> coal had to be brought up from the cellar to shovel under the copper. The
> copper had to be filled, bucket by bucket, from the taps over the sink. The bed
> linen, towels, tablecloths, table napkins and all the 'boiling' articles had to be
> carried down, dumped in the copper, and, when boiled, humped out, heavy
> with water and put through a mangle with wooden rollers, rinsed in the sink,
> mangled again, pegged out in the backyard, brought in folded (usually with the
> help of a child home from school for lunch) and later starched and ironed with
> a flat iron heated on the gas stove or the hob . . . There was so much more to
> wash than now – not only the bed linen and table napery but antimacassars,
> table runners, chair-arm protectors, cushion covers . . . Most of our underwear
> was woollen . . . washday included coping with bloodstained, evil smelling
> towelling diapers . . .
>
> My mother couldn't set the table for tea without spreading doyleys on every
> bread and butter and cake plate . . . they all had to be laundered . . . she made
> the doyleys too.

Lower-middle-class women living on the socially homogenous suburban estates
that radiated from the stations on the new stretches of the Northern and Piccadilly
London Underground lines and on the electric Southern Railway, found it hard to
recruit charwomen. However, they had the advantages of the gas cooker, the
vacuum cleaner, chrome fittings and the laundry man to ease the domestic load.

Elizabeth Fanshawe (born 1912) was the youngest of six children; her father was
a fireman on North Staffs Railways. They lived in a house where the only water
came from the kitchen tap and the only heat from the range. As soon as she was old
enough, she took her turn as her mother's helper on the weekly treadmill: Monday
– washday; Tuesday – bedrooms; Wednesday – grocery ordered from Co-op;
Thursday – ironing and so on. Mary Boothroyd, who worked as a weaver, had a
schedule of housework for every evening of the working week: Monday – washing;
Tuesday – ironing; Wednesday – bedrooms; Thursday – downstairs; Friday –
baking. When her daughter Betty came home from school, she laid the table and lit
the fire. There was no respite from work in the home; socks had to be refooted,
under and outer 'old clothes beyond repair' were transformed into rag rugs. The
culture of make-do-and-mend remained strong: a woman born in 1898 remembered turning sheets sides to middle 'and making pillowcases out of them'. In the
1980s she still had tea towels made out of her grandmother's linen sheets.

The assumption that work in the house was the wife's responsibility was ingrained. As a matter of principle, the journalist Mary Stott paid for the family's domestic help out of her earnings. Unemployed men sometimes did chores about the house while their wives were out earning; Archie Boothroyd 'closed the door and the curtains so the neighbours would not see him'.

Man and wife

Between the wars parenthood plunged couples into middle age. In Donald McGill's comic postcard world, bride and groom were transformed in the course of gestation from spooning honeymooners to humdrum bickering Mum and Dad. George Orwell (born 1903) explored McGill's anatomy of marriage in an essay published in 1942. In McGill's universe, 'marriage only benefits women. Every man is plotting seduction and every woman is plotting marriage. No woman ever remains unmarried voluntarily'. 'There is no such thing as a happy marriage'; 'no man ever gets the better of a woman in an argument'. The henpecked husband was a favourite theme but McGill's men often strayed. Depressingly often, real life seems to match McGill. Shortage of money and jealousy caused friction; expectations were progressively lowered until a bleak *modus vivendi* was achieved.

Amy Fletcher, wife of a Worcestershire parson, 'believed unhappy marriages to be a matter of course'. Every written communication that Peter Sanders (born 1938) received from his grandfather concluded with a prescription for getting by: 'Always remember Peter Silence is Golden'. Anne Muggeridge (born1862) 'read little, and even when she did read, it was very slowly, with her lips visibly moving as she spelt out the words.' Her husband (born 1864), by contrast, was 'the office boy who worked his way up to be boss', the local councillor who worked his way up to be MP. He 'spent hours at City libraries . . . pouring over French irregular verbs in order to be able to have a come-back if someone on the Croydon Council quoted a Latin tag at him'. As their son Malcolm recalled, an 'undercurrent of suspicion' that he might be having an affair 'frequently led to rows'. In old age their relationship mellowed. They sustained themselves with 'their interminable games of two-handed bridge'. In her widowhood she 'never accustomed herself to life without him. The bed in which they had slept side by side through so many nights had two hollows in it.' Looking back over the best part of fifty years, Mr Cosgrove described his married life: 'We used to fight. She had her sulks . . . You don't expect your whole life to be a honeymoon'.

Changing partners: 'the rules of the game'

Marriage was a life sentence. Divorces were exceptional: only two couples in every ten thousand divorced each year. The traditional view was that infidelity should be managed discreetly, 'à la Victorian without the knowledge of the other partner'.

Between the wars the old 'rules of the game' were still widely applied – an incalculable number of unhappily married men and women found 'the strength to lead a double life'. Open cohabitation was rare. In 1934 the sculptor Barbara Hepworth legally coupled her surname with Ben Nicholson's, to signal, mis-leadingly, that they had married. Their formal union took place four years later. Couples who did not engage in this sort of subterfuge were ostracised from decent society. Oswald Mosley and Mrs Bryan Guinness lived together off and on from 1933. Even after their clandestine marriage in 1936 their irregular menage was out of bounds for nicely brought up young ladies including Oswald's daughter and Diana's sister. The art dealer Lillian Browse remembered 'being enormously impressed as a visitor in 1935 by the name plate on the door which read "William Nicholson and Marguerite Steen".'

Divorce

Marriage was a legal contract hard to break. Only a wronged spouse could petition for a divorce. An 'innocent' man or woman who collaborated, connived in or condoned a marital offence (and was found out) forfeited the chance to end the marriage. The outcome of the case was by no means guaranteed: in the early 1920s about a third of divorce petitions were rejected (the success rate rose as time went on). To many, for whom marriage was a sacred bond, divorce was a catastrophe as unmentionable as cancer.

Until 1923 the traditional double standard of morality applied in divorce cases. Evidence of adultery was sufficient grounds for a man to divorce his wife; a woman had to demonstrate adultery by her husband aggravated by another offence, most commonly cruelty or desertion. In what today would be labelled 'friendly' divorces, the husband was expected to play the 'guilty party'. Ethel Wedgwood left her husband in 1912 after twenty years of marriage. To achieve an 'honourable divorce', the Labour MP Josiah Wedgwood (born 1872) had to demonstrate that he had committed two offences:

> The Law allows 'desertion' to be assumed if a Writ for the Restitution of Conjugal Rights is obtained and not complied with . . .
> To get myself proved guilty of adultery. I chose the simplest way – took a suite of rooms at the Charing Cross Hotel, and took a lady there who was not my wife. As a matter of fact, there was no adultery.

Circumstantial evidence came from a chambermaid who told the court that she had seen two pairs of shoes outside the bedroom door. In 1923 the law changed. For the next fourteen years adultery was the only ground for divorce. From 1937 cruelty and desertion became grounds in their own right. But still only the 'innocent' party could sue for divorce. Men concerned about the women from whom they were parting or the women whom they planned to marry continued to perjure themselves.

In *The Modern Rake's Progress* of 1934 – words by Rebecca West, paintings by David Low – one of the Rake's most damaging departures from 'gentlemanly convention' was to sue his wife for divorce. Only extreme provocation could justify such a slight on a woman's good name. The notorious 'bolter' Clare Tennant (born

1896) felt as though she was 'walking down Regent Street with a *fleur-de-lys* branded on one's shoulder'.

Among the rich, the social cost of divorce was a powerful deterrent. Dirty linen was almost literally dragged through the courts. The press coverage of a particularly sensational case moved George V to observe that 'The pages of the most extravagant French novel would hesitate to describe what has now been placed at the disposal of every boy and girl reader of the daily newspapers'.

A divorced person could not marry in an Anglican church. When one of the wealthiest and most flamboyant of English peers, Bendor, Duke of Westminster, married for the third time in February 1930, it was in a register office. His wealth and influence ensured that it was an unusually well-appointed office: 'its dreariness had been disguised, as far as possible, with flowers and decorations. Tapestry had been hung on the walls and there was a carpet and a velvet tablecloth and a silver inkpot'. The wedding party sat on Chippendale chairs.

The material consequences might also be grave. Charlotte Burghes's husband 'implacably refused to allow [her] to divorce him'. So she and her lover J. B. S. Haldane (born 1892) provided the necessary formal evidence of her adultery. The Divorce Court awarded Mr Burghes the huge sum of £1000 damages against Haldane and the University of Cambridge deprived him of his post on the grounds of 'gross moral turpitude'. Backed by his college – Trinity – and his close academic colleagues, Haldane appealed successfully against the verdict but the University's right to dismiss staff for adultery was upheld. In 1933 Herbert Read (born 1893), lecturer in history of art at Edinburgh University, left his wife for another woman. 'In due course' he expected 'to be divorced on an undefended charge of adultery'. 'To save the university a public scandal', he resigned from his post.

If the richest faced social, financial and professional penalties, for poorer men and women, mere survival was the issue. The long-serving magistrate Claud Mullins, confronted by a woman seeking legal separation from her unsatisfactory husband, was accustomed to point out that 'he was very likely to take up with somebody else; that his earnings were small and could not possibly support two households'. Most women found the argument persuasive.

The predicament of widows helped to concentrate the minds of wives across the social spectrum. Rena Randall was left with two small children to bring up on a tiny pension – her husband had been a major in Skinner's Horse. As her daughter Jane Ewart-Biggs explained,

> Her Indian Army pension in no way allowed her to follow the lifestyle of the families in the social class to which she aspired, and in those pre-war days, when society was even more polarized than it is today, there was no natural social niche for us. So with great good sense she made her investment in what amounted to a passport to those circles: the horse.

For working-class widows, things were much tougher. Jack Ashley (born 1922) Widnes, Lancashire, was the middle child of three whose father died. His mother,

Fearful that the family would be broken up . . . she worked morning and night shifts scrubbing floors . . . the sack she used as an apron was always soaking . . . As we children grew older, we helped as best we could but for some years, tasks like cutting the cardboard for our shoes and darning socks, besides the other chores of cleaning, washing and cooking, were all done by Mam.

Incompatible couples 'put a face on'.

Old age

Between the wars the chronological boundary between the economically and socially active elderly and the dependent old was not clear cut. The qualifying age for the old age pension dropped to 65 but half the men over 65 were still at work. Civil servants, teachers, insurance officers and other salaried workers had occupational pensions but, for fee-earning professionals and manual workers, it was infirmity and not age that signalled retirement. (Scilla Boulton's story is a reminder that ill health could push a man out of work in what should have been his prime.) Jack Spall (born 1930) remembered his father steering him towards a career in the police force; police officers had occupational pensions to look forward to, bus drivers like Mr Spall did not. When they became entitled to their old age pension, farm labourers who continued to work sometimes found their wages docked by an equivalent amount, leaving them no better off.

Single women in white-collar jobs campaigned for pensions at 55 but mothers, whose children were normally off their hands by the time they were in their mid-fifties, played an important part as voluntary workers in their sixties and even later. Upper-middle-class women were more likely to sit on committees; working-class women engaged in direct action, seeing their neighbours in and out of the world and stepping in to feed the hungry and protect the ill-treated child.

The predicament of the 'old-old' was often pitiable. Virginia Woolf (born 1882) observed her Sussex neighbour Mrs Grey, kept alive by the parish doctor, very old, ailing and isolated, her brothers and sisters, her daughters and husband were all dead: 'I crawl up to bed hoping for the day; and I crawl down hoping for the night'. A district nurse recalled that old people living with their families could 'get dreadfully dirty'. 'A son or daughter couldn't do anything for them. Intimate, I mean. Father was father and mother was mother. You couldn't touch them. They sat about and stank'.

Admission to almshouses and to asylums run by friendly societies was determined by the subscribers. Regulations often excluded those who had been on Poor Relief.

Not to go to the workhouse was the unspoken prayer and greatest wish of many aged working-class people. The family . . . did their best. Having nursed an aged person for a long time, the difficulties towards the end became more than the ordinary family could cope with, so it was that many of these old folk were brought into hospital finally dying.

The atmosphere in Poor Law institutions was demoralising and quality of patient care was often low.

Debility was shameful. As far as possible, disabilities of old age were concealed. In 1928 Margot Asquith (born 1865) feared that the effect a stroke had had on her husband, the former prime minister (born 1852), might become known outside the family circle: 'it would be a humiliation for *anyone* to know this', she wrote.

Death

Throughout the 1920s, much public energy went into the business of canvassing for funds, selecting and constructing memorials to the war dead. The First World War continued to claim victims. When Mr Doody, who had been gassed in France, died in 1925 his wife, a washerwoman, had to pawn her mangle to pay the British Legion for the hire of the gun carriage that bore the coffin.

Traditional attitudes to death persisted. For poor women, a dead baby might still count as 'churchyard luck'. One Cambridgeshire woman confessed:

> I was glad when it died it's no use saying I wasn't. I never wanted it, and I couldn't have done for it what I wanted to if it had lived. I got more now than I can feed properly. Three of the other kiddies who need boots have got to go without until I get the funeral paid for. The nurse and getting the little thing buried cost me £5. And I ain't fit yet to get back to work.

Examples of the old-style theatrical deathbed can be found. The poet Alice Meynell, who died at the age of 75 in 1922, had clearly planned her farewell to her son Francis: 'putting out her fragile arm towards me she said, "Here are my bluest veins to kiss"', drawing a text from Shakespeare. But, generally speaking, death became less 'visible' than it had been in Queen Victoria's day. Although he was a parson's son, his father's was the first corpse Cecil Day-Lewis saw. He was shocked by his shrunken appearance; his 'waxwork face', transformed by death, was 'the face almost of a stranger'. In private life, the upper classes' retreat from elaborate funerals and formal mourning, apparent well before the First World War, continued. The preference for privacy and simplicity was not always honoured. Jacky Fisher, Admiral of the Fleet Lord Fisher of Kilverstone GCB, GCVO, died in July 1920. He left terse instructions for his funeral

> The nearest cemetery
> No flowers
> No one invited except relatives
> No mourning.

> Words under tablet at Kilverstone Church as arranged in memorandum in my writing case.

The words were 'Fear God and Dread Nought'.

Public priorities prevailed. Fisher's funeral took place in Westminster Abbey. Sailors drew the gun carriage bearing his coffin through the streets. In the Abbey there was a 'vast congregation'.

> The procession moved up the length of the nave . . . the choristers, white surplices over scarlet, in front, then the canons and other dignitaries of the Abbey and the Dean. Behind the Dean was the crimson cushion on which the dead man's Orders and Decorations were displayed, a glittering mass of stars and ribbons

and last the coffin 'borne by eight bluejackets' and 'crowned with the Admiral's hat and sword'. Fisher's body was cremated at Golders Green. His ashes were buried beside his wife's grave at Kilverstone, the Norfolk estate left to Fisher's son by a childless friend of the family.

Burial remained the norm. Only one person in a hundred was cremated in 1930. H. G. Wells described the cremation of his wife Jane, who died in 1927. He and his sons

> went together to the furnace room. The little coffin lay on a carriage outside the furnace doors. These opened. Inside one saw an oblong chamber whose fire-brick walls glowed with a dull red heat. The coffin was pushed slowly unto the chamber and then in a moment or so a fringe of tongues of flames began to dance along its further edges and spread very rapidly. Then in another second the whole coffin was pouring out white fire. The doors of the furnace closed slowly upon that incandescence. It was indeed very beautiful . . . I have always found the return from a burial a disagreeable experience, because of the pursuing thought of the poor body left being boxed up in the cold wet ground . . . But Jane, I thought, had gone clean out of life and left nothing behind to defile the world.

By the late 1930s extravagant working-class funerals were a peculiarity of the East End of London. In the countryside traditional practices died out. In August 1920 Mrs Deman, their cook, 'cajoled' Leonard and Virginia Woolf into watching a farmer's burial, 'by calling it a Sussex funeral, & promising that the bearers would wear smock frocks. But only 6 were to be found in the village; so that plan was given up'. The old boxy casket was superseded by the coffin sloping at the shoulders and tapering towards the corpse's feet. But village undertakers might still invite their clients to go upstairs to the stockrooms in their big houses to choose 'the satins, silks and lace edging' that they wanted.

The corpses of paupers and others too poor to pay for their own burial were handed over for dissection in medical schools. In 1921 the news that John Crosby, a veteran of the Indian Mutiny, was to be dissected caused a furore in Romford; his body was retrieved and buried with full military honours. In spite of such demonstrations of hostility, anatomy continued to be taught using the corpses of the destitute – over the winter of 1934–35 of the 261 bodies dissected only 9 were donated.

Domestic shrines commemorated those who died before their time. Tommy Agar-Robartes was killed at Loos in 1915. He was 35. The possessions he had with him at the Front were returned to his mother Lady Clifden in Cornwall. She kept the alligator-skin case that contained, among other things, his 'sword, field periscope, hip flask, leather writing set, walnut talc holder, field stove, brushes and moustache comb' in the attic of Lanhydrock House. In 1970 the house passed into the care of the National Trust. The items finally went on show in 2000 after the death of Agar-Robartes's last surviving relative. Violet Annie Dix (1909–19) was the sixth – and by ten years the youngest – child of a Saffron Walden businessman and his wife. A trunk full of her belongings deposited in the town's museum by her niece Mrs Helen Rose in 1973 testifies to her life and the impact of her death. Nothing was thrown away, from the Cradle Roll Certificate issued by the Baptist church to the note that accompanied the flowers on her coffin: 'A last posy from the garden our darling loved. Now she blooms in paradise'. There is a letter to Santa Claus, the running order of games for a birthday party, darned socks. Such shrines and reliquaries have much to tell us.

Christian beliefs and explanations had traditionally coexisted with other attempts to make sense of the world. The terrible death toll of the First World War stimulated a revival of interest in spiritualism. The physicist Sir Oliver Lodge (born 1851), Sir Arthur Conan Doyle (born 1859), who created Sherlock Holmes, and Pamela Glenconner were among those who described communications from sons who had died. Lodge's book *Raymond* went through twelve editions in three years. From beyond the grave Raymond (1889–1915) chaffed his mother about 'a mistake of a day in his memorial tablet . . . The day of the month does not correspond with the day of the week. "You can't eradicate it. The mistake has been made and will stand forever. It's the record of a mistake"'. Lady Glenconner's son 'Bim' Tennant (died 1916) passed dozens of what were known as 'Book Tests': 'directions for finding the book were given': 'first as to the room, then the book-shelf, then the number of the book on the shelf, and lastly the page, followed by the words which tell the gist of the message or its application'. One of the tests led Lady Glenconner to the copy of *Walton's Lives* in the drawing room at Glen, the Tennant family's home in Peebleshire. On page 74 in the life of Dr Donne, she heard an echo of Bim's voice. John Donne called the people of his native village 'the living furniture of the place'. 'This', his mother pointed out, 'was one of Bim's terms, "furniture" and he would use it for people; it was one of his words'.

Reading

Barnett, Charis (Mrs Sydney Frankenburg), *Common Sense in the Nursery* (Christophers, 1923).

Blacker, C. P., *Birth Control and the State: a plea and a forecast* (Kegan Paul, Trench, Trubner, 1926).

Campbell, John, *Edward Heath: a biography* (Jonathan Cape, 1993).

Campbell, John, *Margaret Thatcher: volume 1, The grocer's daughter* (Cape, 2000).

Courtney, Cathy and Thompson, Paul, *City Lives: the changing voice of British finance* (Methuen, 1996).

Davies, Russell, *Ronald Searle: a biography* (Sinclair-Stevenson, 1990).

Essex, Rosamund, *A Woman in a Man's World* (Sheldon Press, 1977).

Ewart-Biggs, Jane, *Pay, Pack and Follow: memoirs* (Weidenfeld & Nicolson, 1984).

Florence, Lella Secor, *Birth Control on Trial* (George Allen & Unwin, 1930).

Foley, Winifred, *A Child in the Forest* (BBC, 1974).

Forrester, Helen, *Twopence to Cross the Mersey* (Cape, 1974).

Frankenburg, Mrs Sydney (Charis Barnett), *Latin with Laughter* (Heinemann, 1931).

Goodman, Geoffrey, *The Awkward Warrior: Frank Cousins, his life and times* (Davis-Poynter, 1979).

Graves, Robert, *The Long Weekend* (Faber & Faber, 1940).

Graves, Robert, *Goodbye to All That* (Cassell, 1957; Penguin 1998).

Greenwood, Walter, *Love on the Dole: A tale of two cities* (1933).

Hoggart, Richard, *A Local Habitation: life and times, volume I, 1918–40* (Chatto & Windus, 1988).

Holroyd, Michael, *Basil Street Blues: a family story* (Little, Brown, 1999).

Huxley, Elspeth, *Gallipot Eyes: a Wiltshire diary* (Weidenfeld & Nicolson, 1976).

Huxley, Gervas, *Both Hands: an autobiography* (Chatto & Windus, 1970).

Jackson, Alan J., *Semi-detached London: suburban development, life and transport, 1900–1939* (Allen & Unwin, 1973).

Kee, Robert (ed.) *The Picture Post Album* (Barrie & Jenkins, 1989).

Kennedy, Margaret, *The Constant Nymph* (Heinemann, 1924; Virago, 1983).

Liddiard, Mabel, *The Mothercraft Manual* (J. & A. Churchill, 1923).

Lodge, Oliver, *Raymond: or life after death, with examples of the evidence for survival of memory and affection after death* (Methuen, 1916).

MacGibbon, Jean, *I Meant to Marry Him: a personal memoir* (Gollancz, 1984).

Marshall, Sybil, *A Pride of Tigers: a Fen family and its fortunes* (Boydell, 1992).

Melly, George, *Scouse Mouse, or, I never got over it: an autobiography* (Weidenfeld and Nicolson, 1984).

Mendel, Vera and Meynell, Francis (eds), *The Week-End Book* (Nonesuch, 1924).

Meynell, Alix, *Public Servant, Private Woman: an autobiography* (Gollancz, 1988).

Moore, Doris Langley and Moore, June Langley, *The Bride's Book, or the young housewife's companion; compiled and written by two ladies of England* (Gerald Howe, 1932).

Neill, A. S., *That Dreadful School* (Herbert Jenkins, 1937).

Orwell, George, *The Road to Wigan Pier* (Gollancz, 1937).

Postgate, J. R., *A Stomach for Dissent: the life of Raymond Postgate* (Keele University Press, 1994).

Priestley, J. B., *English Journey* (Heinemann, 1934).

Quennell, Peter, *The Marble Foot: an autobiography, 1905–38* (Collins, 1976).

Richards, J. M., *High Street* (Country Life, 1938).

Richardson, Ruth, *Death, Dissection and the Destitute* (Routledge & Kegan Paul, 1987).

Robertson, E. Arnot, *Ordinary Families* (Jonathan Cape, 1933).

Routledge, Paul, *Madam Speaker: the life of Betty Boothroyd* (HarperCollins, 1995).

Sillitoe, Alan, *Life without Armour* (HarperCollins, 1995).

Soames, Mary (ed.), *Speaking for Themselves: the personal letters of Winston and Clementine Churchill* (Doubleday, 1998).

Vaughan, Paul, *Something in Linoleum: a thirties education* (Sinclair-Stevenson, 1995).

West, Anthony, *Heritage* (Random House, 1955).

West, Anthony, *H. G. Wells: aspects of a life* (Hutchinson, 1984).

White, Jerry, *The Worst Street in North London: Campbell Bunk, Islington between the wars* (Routledge & Kegan Paul, 1986).

3 'Not brave, just British', 1939–1945

WAR TIME

On 25 April 1939, for the first time, the *Daily Telegraph* carried news on its front page. The headline of the lead story was

> BRITISH AMBASSADOR TO WARN HITLER . . .
> CONSCRIPTION IN ENGLAND IF PEACE PLAN IS REJECTED.

In the summer of 1939 the personal columns on the front page of *The Times* played on readers' fears of aerial bombardment. The potent initials ARP (Air Raid Precaution) introduced many of the advertisements:

> ARP – YOUNG CHILDREN 5–8 years; lady and daughter would receive a few young children in delightful COUNTRY RESIDENCE (7 acres) in the Chilterns; home life with every care and modern convenience; farm produce; references exchanged; terms including elementary tuition 3–3½ guineas a week.

Boarding schools in the country reopened early for the autumn term:

> DURNFORD, LANGTON MALTRAVERS, DORSET. MR AND MRS CHRISTOPHER LEE-ELLIOT are in residence, and completely ready to receive their boys in an emergency.

Schools in the suburbs of London moved to safer areas:

> TUDOR HALL SCHOOL, CHISLEHURST, KENT has MOVED to BURNT NORTON, CHIPPING CAMPDEN, GLOUCESTERSHIRE and is now open to receive children. No warning of arrival necessary.

'Girls NOT GOING ABROAD' to be 'finished OWING TO THE EUROPEAN SITUATION', were offered 'a Domestic Science and Languages Course' at the Norfolk home of Lord and Lady Walsingham. The King Edward VII Hospital for

Officers in London removed to Luton Hoo in Bedfordshire. There was an appeal for money to send 'cripples and aged folk' from 'Hoxton slums to places of safety'. Professional copywriters evidently relished the challenge. Bourn-vita, enriched with 'nerve-restoratives', offered 'Peace-time Sleep'. Advertisements for London bed-sits – 'divan rooms' – stressed the 'thoroughly reinforced air raid refuge' in the basement. The food shortages of the First World War had not been forgotten. One small ad read: 'Breed rabbits: safeguard Larder. Three breeding Does produce nearly 2 cwt carcasses p.a'.

On 1 September 1939, two days before the declaration of war, the government's ARP schemes swung into action. The Women's Voluntary Service (WVS) – the 'Housewives' Service' – had been launched on 18 June 1938, the one-hundred-and-twenty-third anniversary of Wellington's victory at Waterloo. Thousands of women had been trained to scale their domestic skills up to feed, house and nurse the casualties of war; to drive in the blackout; to teach their neighbours how to cope with poison gas. Fashion-conscious ladies who shopped in Bond Street carried their gasmasks in leather or velvet-covered cases. Children had Mickey Mouse boxes – a sign of the transatlantic reach of Disney's world. From now on the 'fluctuating high-pitched moan' of the sirens, first tested in December 1938, would signal that bombers were on the way. Buildings and vehicles were blacked out at night. Schoolchildren, their teachers, pregnant women, mothers with toddling children and young babies were evacuated from the danger zones. Non-combatants in London; in the north-east; in the woollen towns in Yorkshire; in the cotton towns of Lancashire; in Greater Manchester; in Sheffield and Rotherham; in Grimsby and Hull; in the industrial areas of the West Midlands; in Southampton and Portsmouth had the option of evacuation to 'safe' areas. The greatest number went from London. Some parents, anticipating evacuation, set out to provide their children with reminders of home. The Bennett boys, Gordon and Alan, had a toy shop which their father, a Leeds butcher, made for them on his fretwork machine: 'It had little wooden joints that hung on bent-pin meat hooks, a counter and a block'.

The upheavals of war strained family ties. The domestic telephone was still uncommon and, since it was 'often situated in a passage hall, or some other public place', it 'was not yet an established channel for chat or confidences'. Practised letter writers were best equipped to keep in touch with a dispersed family. Laura Coates (born 1930) spent the war with her Aunt Lila in Canada. Her father, the architect Wells Coates (born 1895), undertook to 'send things', 'nice things', 'once or twice a month: things you can use and keep, and not just *use up*'. Appropriately, he 'started with a small zipp-fastened case (with your name on the outside) which has a pad, a flap for envelopes, a calendar, and a pocket for stamps and a little notebook for addresses'. Prompted by his daughter's news, Wells Coates sent her long illustrated stories about his boyhood in Japan, where his Canadian-born parents had been missionaries – accounts of tennis matches, volcanoes, sailing trips. From the family estate in Norfolk Lady Mayhew circulated 'every letter of general interest' to her six stepchildren who were variously married and settled away, in the Forces, at college and school. Letters began 'Felthorpe calling the

Family'. Lady Mayhew's descriptions of the park were designed to conjure home thoughts. The woodpecker, for instance, 'really' was 'the most marvellous bit of camouflage; with his head down and his back towards me, he is exactly the colour of our mossy lawn'. Charis Frankenburg, whose tips for parents with children at boarding school were cited in Chapter 2, adopted a similar plan when her family was separated during the war. All through the war, Andrew Gow (born 1886), a classics don at Trinity College, Cambridge, sent a monthly duplicated circular to between eighty and a hundred of his old students, the 'sons' of his college. His 'parish magazine' makes refreshingly astringent reading. College news, accounts of arcane practices in what he dubbed the 'Mysterious University', antique scandals, 'Nature Notes' and Gow's thumbnail reviews of books he had read, operas and art shows he had been to (he left his collection of Degas to the Fitzwilliam Museum) helped his scattered correspondents to hold on to their identity as Trinity men. Inevitably, some letters were returned marked 'missing'. Gow dedicated his collected letters to the fourteen who died.

The wireless helped to keep the national family in touch; it provided virtual neighbours. Vere Hodgson (born 1901), a social worker, regarded her hired wireless as a luxury. 'If I live on bread and cheese I must keep it'. Sunday 28 March 1943 was 'an indoor wireless day for me. Workers' Playtime was good . . . Also listened to Mr Middleton [an expert gardener]. Not that I have any intention of growing the things he talks about; but I like his personality and the way he says pertaters'. She found 'Mrs Buggins'' broadcasts on the Kitchen Front 'first-class fun'. Lord Haw Haw, whose talks beamed from Germany were designed to undermine civilian morale, was paradoxically regarded with some affection as a kind of family black sheep by many listeners. Even the intellectual aristocrats, reluctant converts to the wireless (and new technology in general) were prepared – if only at moments of crisis – to concede that the immediacy of broadcasting gave it advantages over the printed word: in June 1942 Frances Partridge asked her servants if she might 'listen to the nine o'clock news in the kitchen'. Outside these rarefied circles broadcast news was a constant background to daily life – on summer days passers-by could hear it through the open windows as they walked through the streets.

People displaced by the war forged new bonds. Denise Hatchard's daughters were billeted with a Derbyshire mining family. For the duration of their stay, 'this black man walking home from the pit' was, as she observed, the one they greeted as 'our dad'.

Other families were preoccupied with their own domestic hostilities. For Roy Strong (born 1935) wartime life at home in Winchmore Hill 'was largely hell', not because of the international situation but because of domestic 'dictatorship'. His father, a commercial traveller, brought home 'black market' – illicitly obtained – boxes of chocolates and guzzled them himself.

The war did not, at first, 'come up to expectations'. Wags christened this period the 'Great Bore' or Phoney War. No bombs fell on the danger zones. Within weeks almost all the women who had fled the cities with their babies brought them home again. Mothers and children proved the hardest group to billet. As reluctant hostesses had anticipated, sharing a home and kitchen was not easy. Money was a problem – working men could not afford to support two homes. Wives feared that their men might be subject to the predatory attentions of 'the woman round the corner'. Husbands made out that they could not fend for themselves (a group of London social workers organised 'a rota of solitary fathers to cook each other's suppers in turns'). Parents who had stayed in the danger zones recalled many of the 'artificial orphans', children sent to away to unnecessary safety. Scarcities were the main feature of the early months of the war. The *Happy Mag*, which had presented William Brown – 'Just William' – to his public since December 1922, came out for the last time in May 1940.

When the first bombs dropped on the London suburb of St John's Wood, the editor of *Punch* was opening a bottle of claret. 'The blast was close enough to make the cork jump straight out of the bottle'. He 'stood among the debris, corkscrew in hand, quietly interested: "If one could rely on it happening regularly"'. In the spring of 1940, as state after state on the continent capitulated to the advancing German forces, the war was boring no longer – nor was it a subject for whimsy. Unknown to the people, the War Cabinet discussed the possibility of a negotiated peace. The Local Defence Volunteers (better known as the Home Guard or 'Dad's Army') were marshalled in May. A third of them were veterans of the First World War.

In June 1940 France fell. The psychological impact was devastating. In Salisbury Cathedral Close Mrs Dimont, the wife of a cathedral dignitary, fainted 'flat-out in her drawing room' at the news. Recording the catastrophe, Violet Bonham-Carter broke off her diary in mid-sentence. Mrs Furse, whose husband had been a senior civil servant, 'buried the household silver' and prepared to retreat to a 'hide' he had built to shelter his family while their house 'was being visited, plundered or burnt' by invaders. A land girl conscripted for farm work remembered the only time that her boss stood 'still for any length of time while the hay was in the field'. It was 'the time he brought the wireless out into the yard at seven o'clock in the morning. We all stood round with our rakes and pikels [pitchforks]; the horsemen stopped their horses . . . and we heard the news of the fall of France'. A fleet of naval vessels, channel steamers, tugs, fishing boats and the once-round-the-bay 'shilling sicks' rescued the fleeing British troops marooned on the French beaches. Britain was 'alone and at bay'. The Channel – worth a guinea a pint – was all that separated the south coast from Hitler's conquering armies. Actors at the Theatre Royal, Brighton, were issued with an 'invasion £' so that, if need be, they could finance their escape inland. There were few tanks and little heavy artillery between London and the coast. Rumour had had it that Churchill's broadcast command to fight on the beaches and in the streets ended, off-air: 'And we will bash the buggers about their heads with bottles which is about all we've got'. A senior officer of the Special Operations Executive, a corps set up in July 1940 and dedicated to sabotage and subversion, remembered gloomily that 'it took the Greeks only six hundred years to get free of the Turks'.

Bottles were transformed into grenades. Vita Sackville-West

> spent an afternoon filling old wine bottles with petrol, paraffin and tar, and
> finishing them off with two of Messrs. Brock's gay blue Guy Fawkes squibs

bound tightly to the sides. These absurd but lethal missiles are known facetiously as Molotov cocktails.

War could be entertaining. One Sunday, not long after she attended 'this novel form of bottle party', Miss Sackville-West was counting waves of bombers and fighters 'roaring' overhead. '"Please madam", said a quiet voice, "would you like luncheon out of doors? Then you could watch the fights better".'

In private, the tone was often grimmer. From Norfolk, Sir Basil Mayhew wrote to his scattered children to explain his plans for 'keeping together':

Dear Family

We live in difficult and dangerous times . . .

In these circumstances I think it is desirable, bearing in mind our large and widespread family, that we should have some organised method of keeping together. I therefore command you, as head of the tribe, to continue to regard Felthorpe [his home in Norfolk] as Headquarters for all communications until such time as the chain is broken; then Headquarters will be transferred to Marlborough [the home of his eldest child Dorothy Heywood, who was the Master's wife]. . . If Marlborough gets into difficulties then Helen [her younger sister, stranded on the other side of the Atlantic at the outbreak of war], in America, will become our Headquarters for communication. It is quite probable that she will have to take up this important position, and please God bring us all together again.

Parents who could afford it sent their children away into the country or overseas. Between June and September 1940, when *The City of Benares* was sunk by enemy action, the Children's Overseas Reception Board shipped children across the Atlantic. The cartoonist David Low (born 1891) had fought appeasement with a vitriolic pen. 'Reliably informed' that his name 'stood high on the Gestapo list of those who would not enjoy a happy old age' if Britain fell, Low found 'bolt-holes' where his old mother and aunt could live under new identities. In case he was 'forced apart' from his wife and daughters, they planned 'an annual rendezvous, password and all at the White Stone Pond, Hampstead, at 2 p.m. on Christmas Day'. Some people decided that, if the worst came to the worst, an honourable death by their own hands would be better than living 'under the Nazi heel': 'If the Germans over-run England, we should put the children out and then ourselves'.

The aerial Battle of Britain – 'a ballet in three dimensions' in the eyes of the young Al Alvarez – was won in September 1940. Fighter pilots like 'Cats-Eyes' Cunningham and 'Sailor' Malan became popular heroes. Fred and Julia Lennon called their son, born on 9 October 1940, John Winston in honour of the man who had led the country in its 'finest hour'. But the tide of war did not definitively turn against Hitler for another two years. Nor did Victory in the Air mark the end of heavy casualties on the Home Front. In June 1944 Hitler launched a new weapon, the V-1, a pilotless plane which gave audible warning of its approach – it sounded like a clapped-out motorbike. Its nickname, the 'doodlebug', played down the fear inspired by its 'sheer damnable devilry'. The V-1 was aimed at London but scarred the suburbs – Buzz Bomb Alley – on the run in. The damage inflicted provided a metaphor for domestic disorder: 'His bedroom looked as though a flying bomb had hit it'. An estimated one and a half million people left London. In September the V-1s were succeeded by the V-2s, rockets that made craters that could 'easily hold two double-decker buses'. Exploding without warning, 'out of nowhere', the V-2s dealt 'horrible and sudden death'. The sound of their impact reminded people of a gas explosion, a car backfiring, even a door slamming. Missiles, which came down well short of their London target, fell on Kent and Essex – Ilford was Rocket Alley. By the end of 1944 the end was in sight on the European front – that year's edition of The Saturday Book included a photograph of one of the rare English memorials to the German dead of the First World War in an 'Album of National Characteristics' with the optimistic caption: 'Tendency to forgive and forget'.

Income and environment

In the months leading up to the declaration of war, men who had been on the dole for years were put to work to build air-raid shelters and manufacture munitions – as Picture Post reported, Albert Smith's new job enabled him to buy a set of false teeth. Even the feckless found work. But war did not bring universal prosperity. As the metropolitan population shrank, London milk rounds lost customers. And, as war distracted the attention of householders from the hire purchase of three-piece suites, the income of the people who collected the instalments dropped. The antique trade 'flopped': one Norfolk dealer got work 'in a pantomime as the front legs of a horse' while his wife found a job in a petrol rationing office. Aware that commissions for his fine bespoke furniture had dried up, Bedales allowed Edward Barnsley, head boy in 1917, to pay reduced fees for his children and made no difficulties as arrears mounted. Civilian wages went up but, until 1944, the wives and children of private soldiers and their equivalents in the other services received meagre allowances. Recognising that a good many couples 'passed for married', the authorities recognised as 'unmarried wives' women who had been dependent on their partners for six months before they joined up.

War played a part in destroying traditional farming practices. As

> food shortages grew worse, machinery came in with a rush . . . The binder, the wagons, all the horse-drawn implements went off to fetch a song at agricultural sales. Then the clanking, itinerant threshing drums disappeared . . . No more piles of chaff in the rickyards, or rat-hunts with terriers when the last of the straw was moved.

Wives stepped into their husbands' shoes as they always had in emergencies. When William Benn MP, a flying officer in the First World War, joined up, his wife took on his constituency business. This was familiar territory – to the whole Benn family, politics were meat and drink. But the war opened eyes – perhaps especially women's eyes – to other ways of living and working. For a pre-war deb: 'It was a liberation, it set me free'. Pauline Henriques, daughter of a Jamaican businessman who had transplanted his family to middle-class London just after the First World War, lodged in Carlisle with a railway clerk and his wife. She was appalled to discover that her landlady was 'totally and absolutely subservient' to her husband. 'She never ate with him'. War provided Yolande Holroyd (born 1902), the unmarried daughter of a company director, with her first job – driving 'a library van round prisoner-of-war camps in the Home Counties'. Katharine Briggs (born 1898), another single woman brought up in middle-class comfort, found the manners of her fellows in the Air Force hard to take. She remembered 'sitting in a canteen with a tablecloth in front of me spotted with other people's spillings, and watching them stir their teas and put the spoons back in the sugar bowl'.

A woman, working in the steel industry, remembered the isolation of many pre-war housewives: 'Housework gets monotonous day in day out, so it was a change, and we really enjoyed it and enjoyed the company'. Hers was a common reaction: 'After all, for a housewife who's been a cabbage for fifteen years – you feel you've got out of the cage . . . It's all so different, such a change from dusting'. The 'good money' paid for war work tempted mothers to take jobs. For some of them, unrelated childminders were such a novelty that they lacked a label for the role: a Manchester riveter working on Lancaster bombers took her baby son to his 'day-time mother'. Firms rarely tailored hours to fit in with school hours. Children, a house and a paid job added up to hard labour. Some women needed 'an alarm clock on a tin tray under the bed' to get them up in the morning.

For Mary Custance (born 1915) the evacuation meant the end of her settled life as a schoolteacher. Since she was single, 'she was considered to be mobile'. After three months in Kent she was sent back to London. When France fell she escorted children from London to Devon. Escort duty became a feature of her life. When there was a shortage of teachers in Halifax she was drafted there. By December 1943 there were getting on for 74,000 women serving in the fields as members of the Land Army. Rachel Knappett worked on a 130-acre farm in south-west Lancashire. She joined two horsemen and a tractor driver, the pig-and-hen man and the Irishman – 'in that part of the world nearly all the farms [had] an Irishman'. She had known the labourers she worked alongside by sight since she was a little girl – but they had lived worlds apart. The men 'decided that it would be improper to swear' when a young lady was 'within earshot'. Since, in their circle, in that part of the world, 'bugger' was 'used to express any possible emotion – affection, rage, happiness, derision, surprise and despair', this self-denying ordinance imposed an intolerable strain. When the first inevitable 'bugger' slipped out and she didn't fall 'flat on the floor in a swoon', the ice was broken. But a young lady she remained. The fruit and veg merchants who called at Bath Farm acknowledged the class difference between this land girl and the labourers she worked alongside. They tipped the men who loaded their 'motor wagons' with cash but they brought Rachel Knappett 'little goodies such as a bar of chocolate, an orange, a bunch of cherries or a lettuce'.

Evacuation thrust the poor under the noses of the privileged and highlighted the differences between town and country, between the quality and their inferiors, between the houseproud and 'the great unwashed'. Class antagonism was sometimes expressed in powerful terms. The literary landowner Osbert Sitwell described the evacuees at Renishaw as 'fried-fish-shop types' who 'might have been designed by Cruikshank' – grotesque caricatures of what Sitwell regarded as the human norm, in other words. The writer F. Tennyson Jesse told friends in the United States that it was 'as though a flat stone in the garden had been raised and pale wriggling things that had never seen the light of day were exposed'.

Habitat

Fear of air raids drove some families into 'funk holes' in the country well before the official evacuation. The writer Guy Chapman, his wife, her sister and her sister's children 'rented a large strong ugly house, with a superb garden, a good orchard, and a splendid vegetable garden, over half an acre of easily worked soil, the finest [he] ever laid spade to'. Percy and Barbara Muir moved out to Takeley Street in the spring of 1938. Like other couples who scuttled out of London, they traded twentieth-century comforts for safety – their Essex retreat was primitive by comparison with their London home. The cost of running the generator made electric light 'a luxury to be used only if we had guests'. To avoid frozen and burst pipes, when the weather was cold, they drained the water system before going to bed. A mouse found its way into the drawer where Barbara Muir kept Rendell's Wife's Friend, her coconut-oil-based contraceptive pessaries, and ate them. The authors of a guide to Living in the Country (published in 1940) acknowledged that withdrawing to the country was 'a partial answer to reduced incomes as well as to war-weary minds'. The national supply of 'food is going short and will go more short', in the country you could grow your own eggs, meat, fruit and vegetables. They did not conceal the less palatable aspects of rural life: the rats, the fleas, black beetles, flies, mosquitoes, wasps, ants; septic tanks, cess pools and earth closets. Many country dwellers depended on the village pump. A wartime visitor to Morecambe Bay observed an old lady 'placidly filling a pan with snow to boil for the washing up' – the river which supplied her with water was frozen.

The secret army of code breakers at Bletchley found themselves variously accommodated – in a ducal palace, in a ruinous manor house infested with mice and swallows, putting up in The Hunt Hotel at Leighton Buzzard, The Shoulder of Mutton at Old Bletchley or boarding with landladies in Wolverton (grim – one hot bath a week) and Newport Pagnell ('much nicer'). Land girls were billeted in 'castles, Manor Houses, Old Rectories, Hotels, Roadhouses, Cottages, Sports Pavilions, Converted Stables, Ministry of Works Hutments, and Converted Chicken Houses'. These miscellaneous premises were supplied with a piano, a wireless and a sewing machine, the essential accoutrements of a well-appointed middle-class home. Like girls at boarding schools, the land girls slept in dormitories. The warden (like a house mistress) had a bedroom and a sitting room; cooks and assistant wardens had bedsitters, 'the domestics' shared rooms.

Evacuees' hostesses were shocked by habits that spoke of poverty and dire overcrowding: 'Some of them will not sit at the table, but want to sit on the floor and have the food handed to them . . . Some do not know how to use a knife and fork, they only use a knife'. One child 'said he never went to sleep lying down, he perched himself by the bedpost . . . clinging to it with his head resting on it. There had never been room in the bed at home for him to lie down'. A small boy 'observed that: "The country is a funny place. They never tell you you can't have no more to eat, and under the bed is wasted".' He was not the only child to see the space beneath a bed as the natural place to sleep – though to be fair he would have had as much headroom as he would have in a bottom bunk today.

Where potatoes were an important crop, schoolchildren had a fortnight's tattie-picking holiday. Rachel Knappett observed that it was

> in the matters of dinners and boots that one sees the most obvious differences between country children and those who belong to families evacuated from the cities. One has the impression that the country mothers are very much in the habit of sending out dinners for farm labourers – home-made meat and potato pies, large and satisfying, jam or treacle 'butties' (sandwiches) and thick chunks of cake. This goodly fare is all packed up in well-worn leather bags which have seen plenty of service and look fit for plenty more. Many of the country children wear clogs and those that don't have an impressive array of nails in the soles of their boots.
>
> Those who equip the town children do not understand the needs of potato pickers so well. Their dinners are more slender and carried about in their pockets or in little cardboard attache cases which seem quite incapable of surviving the rigours of their existence. Often these children wear strap shoes which suffer sadly. Another difference is that country girls, almost without exception, are provided with stout sack aprons which they gird about their small bodies with a practised air.

Host communities mounted 'hair raids' against the lice and nits evacuees brought with them. But the traffic in vermin was not all one way. When Nicola Harrison, a 6-year-old from a south London council estate, was evacuated to Lancashire, she found herself infested with nits and lice for the first time in her life. Surprisingly, they were 'an enormous comfort. I can remember lying in bed pulling them out and cracking them; they make the most wonderful noise. I thought, not quite that they were my pets, but they were very much a part of me'.

Homes were put into wartime livery. Windows were blacked out and, especially in danger zones, protected against blast damage. (After air raids Londoners had to negotiate 'green glaciers of broken glass' settled 'ankle deep on the pavement'.) As a precaution, some householders covered their windows 'with net curtains dipped in a sort of glue', others preferred strips of criss-crossed gummed paper which gave the impression of leaded panes and thus 'a horrible air of Ye Olde Oake Tea-Roome'. One London household used gummed paper to spell out the message 'NO BOMBS ADOLPH PLEASE' and topped the display with sticky-paper Union Jacks.

Anderson shelters were one of the key pre-war Air Raid Precautions. Households with suitable gardens – and incomes under £250 a year – were offered the components – corrugated steel panels and nuts and bolts to hold them together – free. Better-off households were charged £7. The shelters, 6 feet long and 4½ feet wide, were sunk into the soil (and therefore prone to damp and liable to flood) and covered with a thick layer of earth or sandbags. Alice Bridges, a working-class housewife from Birmingham, took great pride in her family's arrangements.

> After looking inside heaps of shelters I have decided that mine is as much like home as anyone's. I bought a 'Spiraldivan' just before the war for taking up and down when we had visitors . . . Fortunately it fits just into the length of the shelter, it is 2 feet wide which just leaves room for J's little bed at the side which consists of my padded deck chair put very low and levelled up with cushions and a footboard. We have 18 inches square to stand in, fortunately we are both very slight.
>
> My husband has fixed 4 hooks for us and a bullet-proof steel door which we can lock. He has also made us a candleholder . . . and arranged it so that it can slip into a holder on the wall . . . the condensation is the biggest problem.

She stored a tin of emergency rations under the bed and 'my leather case with all important papers in it and first aid'. Gardening catalogues advertised shrubs to camouflage 'the mounds of air-raid shelters: berberis, cotoneaster, cydonia etc.' The Morrison shelter was designed for indoor use: the steel table roughly the Anderson shelter's width and length, with wire netting between the legs made the occupants look 'just like rabbits in a hutch'.

Families improvised their own bolt-holes. Cellars were colour-washed and made homely with wicker chairs, cushions, rugs and pictures. A Norfolk family chose the bathroom as the 'refuge room because it is downstairs and has only one small eighteen-inch square window and has outside walls eighteen inches thick . . . We take in a tin of Smiths' crisps, three bottles of lemonade, several packets of chocolate from business stock, and some old magazines to read'. On the Isle of Wight, three generations of a family used the broom cupboard under the stairs as their shelter. It was furnished with a table and chairs for the grown-ups, a cot for the baby and a selection of implements – spades, hatchets and pickaxes – to dig a way out if the need arose.

In London, Underground stations were the scene of a 'kind of lie-down strike'. People 'paid their three-ha'pence and then proceeded to encamp quietly on the platforms'. By the end of a month the Tube was 'so much home' to the families who sheltered there 'that they take off their shoes and stockings, loosen their collars, feed their babies and carry on their personal quarrels' oblivious of their neighbours. The Tube was not bomb-proof. At Balham station 600 were killed, at Bank 111 died. The basements of Oxford Street stores were turned into dormitories. There was a glamorous 'sleeping colony' in the strongly built Dorchester Hotel. Until it was hit in November 1940, the Granada cinema in Wandsworth Road in Lambeth became 'a shelter and sleeping quarters for staff, regular patrons, and anyone who was bombed out': 'many old people took up regular quarters there'. In suburban Kent, the owners of the Chislehurst Caves recognised their potential as communal shelters. Nottingham people used the caves under the castle. Retrospect has rosied the accounts of shelter life. The 'stench' features in many contemporary descriptions. Peggy Graves, working as a nurse in London, commented on the foul smell of 'urine-soaked siren suits' continuously 'worn by small children'. Mothers, who wore the same clothes night and day, also 'smelt of shelters'. In London and other badly affected areas, bombed-out families were put up in rest centres which the Women's Voluntary Service set up in school and parish halls.

Household goods were in short supply. Newly married couples and victims of bombing could buy Utility furniture. As the designer Gordon Russell gleefully recalled, 'There wasn't enough timber for bulbous legs . . . or enough labour for even the cheapest carving . . . It must have been a bit of a shock that a type of design which had been pioneered for years by a small minority [like Russell himself] whilst the trade looked on and laughed – should prove its mettle in a national emergency'.

When she decided to rent a flatlet at the end of 1941, 'people' thought Vere Hodgson 'mad'. She had no furniture of her own except a mirror, an armchair and 'an air-raid mattress'. The outgoing tenant sold her 'a bundle of curtains and a divan cover'. She 'did not like the look of second-hand beds' but – 'Glory, Glory, Hallelujah!' – had the good fortune to get hold of a new mattress through an acquaintance who worked in a department store. A former colleague provided 'a bookcase, a bedside table and a stool, also a corner cupboard'. 'A desirable second-hand shop' yielded a camp bed and a cottage chair. She 'managed to buy a bucket in Portobello Rd for 4/3d. Ridiculous price – but I was thankful to get it. Mr Hillyard managed to buy me a dustpan in the City'. The asking price for a 'complete and pleasing set' of cups and saucers was £7. Prices rose as the war wore on. At a house sale in the Cotswolds in July 1944 'two fleecy blankets . . . fetched £14 10s' and 'three patched unbleached [linen] sheets . . . £7 10s'. Frances Donaldson described the challenge of wartime home decorating from the point of view of a well-connected member of the upper-middle class. A friend introduced her to the decorator John Fowler, who

> made curtains for my sitting room out of dark green blackout material (no coupons) relieved with a fringe of alternating dark and light green silk. He also managed to sell me three extremely pretty oil lamps (there was no electricity at Gipsy Hall at that time). Then Hannah took me to see a Mr Cole who made wallpapers.

Shortages hurt the well-off least. When soap rationing came in, Charles Graves and his wife had nothing to worry about: 'there was a false alarm about it some months ago and Peggy laid in a stock of all sorts of soap'. At the first air-raid warning, Helen Brook 'rushed off to D. H. Evans and bought so many toilet rolls, they lasted us well into peace time'. The poorer or less provident did not fare so well. By December 1940 lavatory paper doubled in price. Just before Christmas 1942, as Violet Bonham-Carter observed, 'Fortnum's luxury altars were covered in w.c. paper'. A school for the daughters of officers was reduced to providing 'squares of old newspaper in the lavatory paper holder'.

Items suitable for Christmas presents became almost unobtainable. Briefing an adult guest expected at Badminton in 1944, the Duchess of Beaufort proposed that if he would 'kindly bring something of your own for me to give to you, I will supply two things for you to give us'. Many presents were home-made. The assiduous diarist Richard Brown (born 1902) was inclined to skimp his entries in the run-up to Christmas. In December 1944 he wrote, 'presents are so scarce that once again I'm making things and this year it's a helluva programme'. His tally included a workbox for his young daughter Margaret (in 1941 he made her a dolls' house), aeroplanes for her brother Godfrey, six bookends and a spill holder.

Household management

When Barbara Muir moved to rural Essex in 1938, farm labourers' daughters still left school to go into 'service'. By 1943 they found jobs in factories, hospitals and shops that left a girl 'with her evenings free and more money in her pocket'. Established servants switched career. After twelve years their much-loved nanny 'Buddy' Winch left the Benn household for war work; out of their employment, she remained an important member of the family.

Older servants tended to stay put but, as the war went on, the owners of great households found themselves with much diminished staffs: at Knole there was one housemaid for 250 rooms. Dailies disappeared. To Andrew Gow, it was 'something of a mystery'

> where the [college] Bedmakers and Helps have gone to, for I cannot readily picture the absentees disguised as Wrens, Waafs or even Land-girls. I suppose, however that with husbands and daughters earning more, family budgets have been swollen, and that some have downed mops for that reason.

In London it was impossible 'by hook or crook to get a char or a man of any kind to clean'.

Evacuated to the country and deprived of the amenities they had become accustomed to, young working-class women were 'as helpless as French aristocrats during the revolution'. They were

> used to buying everything at Woolworth's, wearing it or using it until it got dirty or torn and them throwing it away and buying fresh. Without Woolworth's, not only their milliner, hosier, grocer, ironmonger and furnisher were gone but their laundry and seamstress too.

Older women, by contrast, had retained the skills of make-do-and-mend. Nella Last, in her fifties, set about making cot blankets for needy babies out of 'books of tailor's patterns' and 'old socks cut open and trimmed'; she contrived the mattresses out of sugar sacks. This voluntary work distracted her from her routine housework – 'pictures and furniture that were once polished every week, now got done when I had the time'.

On the Kitchen Front

Food – what could be got hold of, the soaring prices – is a running theme of diaries, letters and reminiscences about the war. Even in London, air raids were the exception rather than the rule but the dietary emergency affected almost everybody everywhere, almost all the time. Osbert Lancaster (born 1908) produced a pocket cartoon for the *Daily Express* – gallery-goer contemplates a composition including wine, fish and lemons: 'Extraordinary the way these painter fellows seem to be able to work entirely from memory.' Gourmands consoled themselves with pornographic fantasies. Evelyn Waugh (born 1903), who wrote *Brideshead Revisited* in the early months of 1944, confessed that he had 'infused' the novel 'with a kind of gluttony, for food and wine' which, later, 'with a full stomach' he found 'distasteful'. He revised 'the grosser passages' for the second edition, which came out in 1959.

Food rationing was introduced in January 1940. Sugar, butter, bacon and ham were the first items affected, then, in March, meat. Offal was not rationed and 'liver, chitterlings, sheep's heads and suet, tripe and bones, all made welcome supplements to the wartime rations'. Phyllis Noble's mother found an idiosyncratic way of stretching the family butter ration: 'she popped a lump into her mouth, chewed it a bit and then spat it on to the bread'. Bread, the staple of working-class diets, was never rationed during the war. All the same, the off-white National Loaf brought in in 1942 was unpopular – 'nasty, dirty, dark, coarse, indigestible' was one verdict. Tea, then England's staple drink, was rationed but, in the 1940s, coffee was too much of a minority taste to make rationing necessary. Points, a scheme for sharing out goodies that appeared erratically, was intended to make shopping less of a chore. Housewives became conditioned to queueing.

Lord Woolton, a businessman with a social conscience, was appointed Minister of Food in April 1940. He set out to mobilise the nation's housewives for the vital campaign on the Kitchen Front. To rally his troops, Woolton conscripted talent from advertising agencies and the BBC. Patriotism and humour were his weapons of choice. Waste was outlawed: it was illegal to feed wild birds. What was not eaten by human beings was destined for the omnivorous pig. Backyard stock-keepers made hard choices: Nella Last, who kept poultry for eggs and meat, killed a cockerel in August 1942 'eating too much valuable mash'.

Fuel was short. Tucking boiling soup or stew up in a haybox saved fuel and the cook's time, since there was no possibility of the food burning. A nest of scrunched-up newspaper was the townee's substitute.

War affected the supply of fruit. Eating out in December 1940, Charles Graves was faced with 'banana fritters and also a fruit salad largely composed of bananas'. This was a late sighting of the item that came to symbolise the exotic. In May 1941, the Midland Hotel in Birmingham

produced a tray of sweets . . . There was stewed rhubarb, an open flan and a
tart. 'What is in the flan?' 'Rhubarb.' 'What is in the tart?' 'Rhubarb.' 'What is
in the mixed fruit salad?' 'Rhubarb and tinned plums.'

In the winter of 1940–41 oranges were the only fruit Vere Hodgson could afford; by
March 1944 the sight of orange peel on the street was rare enough to be worth
recording in her diary and, when a GI gave a 'few fresh oranges and lemons' to
friends in Totnes, 'the people in the entire block came to look at them including a
couple of youngsters who had never seen the fruit before'. Lemons were scarce
enough to star as prizes in raffles. In February 1941 Vere Hodgson 'managed to get a
few eating apples'. They were expensive: 'I treated myself' and 'carried them home
as if they were the crown jewels'. In July, when cherries and gooseberries came into
season, they cost even more than the traditional Fortnum and Mason luxuries –
lobster, salmon, caviar. Grapes (£4 a pound in 1944) were far beyond her pocket.
But the Lord Woolton Restaurant in Notting Hill Gate was offering 'Steamed Fish
or Rabbit with Parsley Sauce', cheap and 'really good'. In December she 'tried the
powdered milk' for the first time. 'Not bad. You take some warm water, sprinkle the
powder on and whisk it in. Then it begins to look something like milk and is all
right for cocoa, puddings or in an emergency'.

Where you lived and the length of your purse were inevitably key factors in
determining the food you could get hold of. Early in 1940 Marlborough College ran
very short of potatoes. The Master's wife sent an SOS to her stepmother, Lady
Mayhew, in Norfolk. In motherly fashion, Lady Mayhew resolved the immediate
crisis. Potatoes were dispatched, 'some by post . . . a cwt by train'. A brisk covering
note pointed out that potatoes were readily available in the London wholesale
markets, 'if you pay carriage'. In the war and during the period of rationing that
followed, money talked on the black market.

Leading London restaurants like the Ivy still offered menus in pre-war style.
In September 1942 Frances Partridge lunched there on 'smoked salmon, cold
grouse, chocolate mousse'. All through the war London clubs enjoyed supplies of
unrationed game dispatched by their shooting and fishing members – 'rush baskets
of salmon', venison, hares, rabbits, grouse, snipe woodcock. Lady Montagu sent her
son Edward, at Eton, pheasants still in their feathers with a label tied round their
necks. Thanks to a father, the girls of St James's, West Malvern, ate venison.
Londoners resettled in Essex tried less glamorous game, squirrels caught in Hatfield
Forest. 'The taste was agreeable and slightly nutty, but there wasn't much meat on
the little carcasses and when skinned they looked horribly like rats'. Theodora
Fitzgibbon, a skilled and inventive cook, made the most of unrationed rabbit:

> I made big jellied pies with a scrap of bacon and onion; braised rabbit in dark
> beer with prunes, which made it taste vaguely like pheasant; or with cider and
> tomatoes; or with curry spices or paprika; or stuffed and baked rabbit, – when
> we would pretend it was chicken; and if it was very young, Peter would joint it,
> and we would fry it in a crisp batter. Frying was quite difficult, as lard was
> rationed and olive oil only obtainable at a chemist on a doctor's prescription,
> so sometimes we were reduced to liquid paraffin.

Occasional unexpected delicacies made their appearances in the Cambridge grocers' shops – salami, for instance, which Andrew Gow felt the need to define for his old students as 'that admirable Italian sausage made of raw ham and garlic which in England one mostly meets as an hors d'oeuvre'. Salami, 'being apparently caviar to the general', was 'sold without restriction'.

Alien tastes were promoted. Muesli, 'a most wholesome breakfast dish . . . invented by the Swiss dietician Dr Biurcher-Benner', was 'a new way' of serving blackberries from the still capacious 'wild larder'. Wild greens could be made into salads and soups dressed with 'sour cream, according to the Russian tradition'. Leaf and fruit teas were another novelty worth knowing about 'in these times of tea shortage'.

Parcels from friends and family overseas took the edge off austerity. The publisher Philip Unwin remembered that, 'throughout the war, thanks entirely to a regular Christmas gift' from the firm's representative in South Africa, 'my wife was able to offer some form of . . . crystallised fruit at the festive dinner table, when it had become totally unobtainable in England.' The firm's 'Australian man' sent 'a regular monthly parcel which contained the supreme luxury – O it sounds extraordinary – a pound of good beef dripping. It meant much to be able to give a growing family a piece of fried bread again for breakfast'. Vere Hodgson's cousin Lucy sent her tinned food from Africa. She put the tongue by 'for our Victory supper'. On 8 May 1945, to celebrate Victory in Europe, 'We had ersatz champagne. Tinned grapefruit. Salad. Tongue. Tin of cray fish – and a Plum pudding. All of us had been saving these viands up for a long time'.

For the adult population, cigarettes were almost as high a priority as food – the landing rations issued to the troops involved in the D-Day landings included an allowance of twenty cigarettes for use in the first twenty-four hours.

Clothes

Rich men were well placed to survive clothes rationing. Chips Channon, a metropolitan dandy had 'forty or more' suits in his wardrobe at the outbreak of war: 'Socks will be the shortage. Apart from these, if I am not bombed, I have enough clothes to last me for years', he noted in his diary entry for 1 June 1941. Sir Basil Mayhew surrendered his coupons to clothe his growing grandchildren. Well-off women, whose stockings and underclothes were flimsier than their menfolk's, did experience privations. By 1944, Peggy Graves, a former fashion journalist, noted there were no brassieres or roll-on suspender belts to be had and the stockings in the shops were much inferior to those she had worn before the war (silk fully-fashioned hose were unobtainable in Britain). Prices had rocketed too so that a nightdress cost very nearly fifty times what it would have before the war. At Cambridge traditional undergraduate dress was under threat: the supply of mortarboards had dried up by 1942–43; by the following year 'the shortage of the stuff for gowns [was] beginning to make itself visible', undergraduates began to appear 'academically naked' at lectures.

The poor had fewer clothes to start with and, because they were generally shoddier and often subjected to harder wear, those they had wore out more quickly. Evacuation brought home to the middle classes just how ill clad the poor were. Liverpool was nicknamed 'plimsoll city'. Evacuated from Nottingham, Alan Sillitoe (born 1928) had neither the underwear nor pyjamas that the authorities instructed his mother to pack for him. Bombed-out families turned to the WVS depots. The Housewives' Army appealed to its many supporters in North America, Australia, New Zealand, South Africa and India, set up clothing exchanges to recycle garments outgrown before they were outworn and used linen stripped from charts to make children's clothes.

CRADLE TO GRAVE

Birth and infancy

During the war expectant mothers were entitled to special allowances of milk, eggs and meat, orange juice and vitamin tablets. Bottle-fed babies fared badly in shelters with no means of warming their milk supply. Doctors could do little for premature infants. In February 1940 Nella Last's general practitioner (GP) brought a premature baby to her house – its mother was sick and its grandmother was dying. Mrs Last was its only hope of survival: she installed it in a drawer, wrapped it in cotton wool with 'hot bottles top and bottom' and fed it on an eggcupful of Nestle's milk and water every hour. The baby survived.

Old traditions persisted. As Laurie Lee and Lorna Wishart discovered when they were holidaying in Hampshire in the early 1940s, it was taken for granted that a woman who 'went to church . . . in a little white scarf' was a new mother there to be 'churched'. Clothes rationing made it impossible to buy a traditional layette. Otherwise the patterns of childcare practised in upper- and middle-class families in the 1920s and 1930s survived – with a wartime twist. Helen Brook shared a house and a nanny with another young mother. The nanny was 'all starch'; children were the sole responsibility she acknowledged and, in the war-induced absence of other staff, her employers found themselves 'waiting on her hand and foot'. In working-class families, older siblings shouldered their accustomed responsibility for baby care. A WVS worker billeting a family who had been bombed out tried to simplify her task by separating the eldest boy, who was 7, from his mother and baby brother. He refused: 'Mum can't manage the baby without me. Look, he needs changing now'. And he was right.

Like Truby King, Anna Freud (born 1895), a psychologist who ran a nursery for babies and young children separated from their parents as a result of death or illness, favoured three- or four-hourly feeds even though she recognised that rigid feeding times turned some children into 'bad eaters'. But, unlike the traditional nanny, she held that children were ready for toilet training only when they were 'physically able to sit' alone, 'intellectually able' to understand what was going on and to communicate their needs to adults – and emotionally secure.

Families were growing up without fathers. In 1944 Margaret Wheeler's younger children were 6 and 4. Their father had been away for four years. 'To hear them talking about him you'd think he was some sort of mythical or fabulous person – they don't really believe in him', she confided in a letter.

Toys were improvised – one baby had a rattle made from a matchbox filled with buttons and covered with crocheted fabric. Rag dolls and other soft toys were homemade. Between calls, fire-fighters made wooden dolls' houses, forts, boats, cars, scooters and bricks.

Education

Evacuation upset the rhythm and routine of children's school lives. Crispin Tickell (born 1930) and his younger brother, whose home was in London, spent the early months of the war with their grandmother in the Cotswolds. In a sense their stay was like an extended summer holiday but, looking back, Tickell concluded that the brothers had much in common with 'other evacuees': 'We were broke. Our education was disrupted'. The Tickell brothers had cultural and material advantages that most other evacuees lacked: a great-aunt stepped in and stumped up 'the bulk of what was needed' to pay the boys' school fees at Westminster. In the summer of 1939 Al Alvarez and his mother moved to Hove. When he returned to his prep school in Hampstead for the spring term, he found himself the only pupil – all the other boys had been evacuated to the country. Eva Figes (born 1932), a Jewish refugee from Nazi Germany, came from an impoverished but culturally privileged family. Her first experience of English education was a big elementary school in a growing London suburb. Evacuated to Cirencester, she went to a small private school 'for the daughters of officers'. The regimentation of the elementary school contrasted with the informality of the school in Cirencester. At the elementary school,

> A teacher blew a whistle and the children rushed from all corners of the asphalt playground to form up in lines. Talking was not allowed, and if the teacher was feeling particularly severe he or she could make us wait indefinitely until the rows were not only silent but straight. Then we were marched inside with military precision.

Lessons were mechanical. Multiplication tables and poems were learned by rote. BBC schools broadcasts yoked the London classroom to others all over the country. 'Even games were carried out with military precision'. Leigh Heath School reflected the mores of earlier and more refined days. Eva Figes remembered it as 'peaceful and relaxed. No marching in single file; no physical training in vest and knickers'. The joint principals, sisters, 'spoke to each child as an individual. Neither of them was ever heard to blow a whistle, or discipline a child with a ruler, let alone a cane', instruments she had encountered in the elementary school. They 'did not go in for new-fangled teaching methods like the wireless'.

> In the London primary school, making music meant banging away in a percussion group, but the sisters' notion of music making, so central to their

lives derived from the Edwardian drawing room of their childhood. Millie played the flute, Zoe the piano.

As a very small boy Patrick Procktor (born 1935) was sent to a boarding school of a very different stripe – his father had died and his mother was working as a housekeeper in the Dorchester Hotel. One of the more imaginative punishments meted out by the headmaster coincided with the regular Saturday night film shows: victims were 'made to lie directly under the screen so that [they] could not see the film'.

Whole schools were evacuated with their schoolmates. The archives of the Bethnal Green Museum of Childhood in London include the notice circulated 'To the Parents of the Children of St Patrick's School' in 1939, evidently handwritten in advance on lined paper with the date and time of evacuation added at the last minute. The document opens with the statement in red copperplate script:

The children are being evacuated to-morrow Friday.

Instructions follow:

If you do not want your children to go DO NOT SEND them to School.
If you want them to go with the School send them at 8.15 to the School.
(1) Don't forget to pack all their clothes.
(2) Don't forget food for one day. (No bottles.)
(3) Don't forget gas masks.
(signed) W. J. Ridge, Headmaster

With evacuation, 'the whole educational system . . . suddenly disintegrated'. Buildings were requisitioned and teachers dispersed. Children returning to Manchester during the Phoney War 'were without schools, medical attention, supervision for cleanliness, free meals, free and cheap milk, and safety from premature employment'. In London secondary schools reopened after Christmas 1939, attendance was made compulsory for those over 11 from 1 March and for those over 8 after the Easter holidays. The air raids, when they came, destroyed schools along with homes; at Plymouth in the spring of 1941 half the school places were lost.

Independent schools evacuated their pupils from the danger zones. Westminster School's first berth was Lancing School in Sussex, where an Old Westminster was head; in 1940 it moved again to safer billet – the University of Exeter. Nan Wise (born 1924) was evacuated to Cheltenham where her Birmingham high school (King Edward's) shared the premises of Pate's Grammar School. The evacuees found greetings from the Pate's girls on their desks when they arrived. A 'double-shift' system was adopted: Pate's girls went in the mornings; King Edward's in the afternoon and on Saturday mornings. Friendships blossomed between evacuees and the local girls. By contrast, when the City of London School was evacuated to Marlborough, there were, according to Kingsley Amis (born 1922), 'no host-like gestures . . . in five terms'.

In spite of wartime shortages, schools demonstrated their loyalty to tradition by sticking to pre-war rules about uniform – the boys of Christ's Hospital, dressed in their Tudor gowns, looked as if they 'were expecting the Spanish Armada' rather than the Wehrmacht. Though the losses were not on the same scale, schoolteachers suffered painful bereavements, just as their predecessors had in the First World War. Stowe was a new school founded between the wars. As its founding head recalled, 'A little short of two thousand Old Stoics served in the forces: one in every seven lost his life'.

War shaped children's leisure pastimes, *Oddentifications* helped boys to become confident plane spotters: drawings exaggerated the crafts' distinctive features. 'There were short rhymes, too, which put these originalities into words'. The war effort set back the production of new consumer goods for the more privileged end of the young civilian market. Alastair Horne's homebuilt wireless suddenly 'seem[ed] like a dinosaur' beside the 'tiny truly portable radio' he was given by his hosts in the United States.

Higher education

The number of male undergraduates dropped – though at Cambridge the decline was notably less dramatic than in the First World War. Men awaiting call-up, medics and others whose studies were regarded as vital either to the war effort or to post-war reconstruction, men unfit for military service, kept the population up. The number of women remained steady, hovering about the 500 mark, the quota fixed by the university. What Andrew Gow called 'alien institutions' evacuated from London found temporary berths in Cambridge. Gow, a classicist, saw 'nothing of the visitors' – the Cambridge habit of lecturing only in the mornings left space for them in the afternoons. Economics and architecture were 'more matey, and the lectures [were] pooled and attended by both groups'. The Froebel Institute trained teachers at Knebworth House in Hertfordshire. Other London students were evacuated to Scotland or Wales. Some institutions stayed put in spite of the bombing. George Hayes remembered travelling in to Liverpool from West Kirby on the Wirral: 'We would arrive at Central Station to find trams upside down, Lewis's on fire, the sewers burst, total chaos. And we would go into the School of Architecture and they would carry on as if absolutely nothing had happened'. Much of the 'fun' had gone out of university life, as an old Oxford hand observed. 'They feed poorly . . . and have any amount of fire-spotting and military duties to do'. Service life provided a sort of extramural higher education – and not only for the tiny minority who would have gone university in the ordinary course of events. Penguin Books played their part by a message encouraging readers to: 'Leave this book at a Post Office when you have read it so that men and women in the services may enjoy it too'. Thanks to material sent by the Red Cross and other agencies, more than 5000 British prisoners of war passed vocational exams while in captivity.

In the world of apprentices, customs persisted in spite of the emergency. Roy McGill started work as a telegraph boy in 1944, at the age of 14. His service opened with a rite of passage, an initiation into the culture of the Post Office: 'The senior telegraph boys grabbed me, turned me upside-down, held me over the toilet, lowered my head and pulled the chain . . . That was called bogging'. In other trades the ritual often involved taking the novice's trousers down and blacking his genitals.

Growing up

Segregated at school, boys and girls often grew up knowing very few members of 'the opposite sex'. Tony Benn, a boy without sisters, considered subscribing to the *Girls' Own Paper* to bridge the gap. Campaigners for chastity before and within marriage and prophets of free love continued to preach their conflicting gospels. At 17 John Gale 'had never slept with a girl. Somehow the thought of syphilis, nerves, the fear of bungling, and even the presence of a real live girl rather than a pin-up all combined to put off what should have been not too difficult'. His mother 'felt one should wait for the "real thing" when one was married'. His father advocated 'as many affairs as possible and a late marriage'.

At Morley College in London, students were confronted with the shocking Amber Blanco White. An ornament of Newnham College, Cambridge, daughter of the director of the London School of Economics, she had, as Amber Reeves, taken H. G. Wells, a married man, as her lover and father of her first child. Her family had been rescued from public embarrassment by the gallant intervention of Blanco White who married her and assumed paternity of her daughter. Thirty years on

> Tall and skinny, with gappy slightly protruding teeth, Mrs Blanco White was plain and middle-aged, but charmed us with her humour and vivacity. At one session, which was on the importance of the sexual side of life to mental health, she ended up miming in front of the class the various positions which she said could be used to make sexual intercourse more fun . . . She was a proponent of free love who advised us never to tell a spouse about a lover and pointed out that living together as lovers did not have to mean being married.

In her middle age, Amber Blanco White was still ahead of the times. For Mirren Barford, an Oxford graduate, sex before marriage would have been 'like opening your presents before Christmas morning'.

In the Forces the conventional double standard of morality applied. The Services saw it as their duty to protect young women from sexual experience and young men from its consequences. Wrens going to dances 'were obliged to wear . . . and to have verified by inspection "blackouts", rugged black knickers with stout elastic at waist and knees'. Troops were issued with condoms. This was 'an unreal event' to men serving in isolation in North Africa, 'who had for months been restricted to following the prick-teasing antics of Jane in the Forces' newspaper'. One wag said that they were 'for tossing yourself off on Sundays'. Condoms were primarily intended as protection against venereal diseases, well known as a 'camp-follower of war'. As the Penguin Special published three years into the war explained, 'the disruption of the family unit, movements of large sections of the community, increased promiscuity arising from unsettled conditions, and the return of troops infected in foreign theatres of war . . . all contributed to the spread of sexually-transmitted disease'. The message, sandwiched between other health promotion slogans such as

Coughs and sneezes spread diseases
Catch the germs in your handkerchiefs

was that the stigma attached to venereal infection was the sole obstacle to its 'reduction to insignificant proportions'.

In 'Civvie Street', North American servicemen, 'over here' from the spring of 1940, when the first Canadians arrived, were seen as a threat to the virtue of the married and unmarried women. Their ability to conjure up nylons, make-up, cigarettes, sweets, sugar, butter and even coal added to their appeal. The Canadian and US authorities strongly discouraged marriages between their enlisted men and British women. Particular pressure was put on couples whose relationships crossed religious or ethnic boundaries: French Canadian officers did not want their men to marry 'out'; US officers were conscious that in some states marriages between blacks and whites were illegal. In spite of these obstacles 100,000 women married American servicemen and sailed across the Atlantic as GI Brides. Working on similar principles, the British government banned marriages between British subjects and prisoners of war. June Tull and Heinz Fellbrich were the first couple to marry after the ban was lifted in July 1947. She was disowned by many members of her family and received two sacks of hostile letters from strangers. As ever, frustrated marriages led to illegitimate births. GIs stationed in England fathered thousands of children – estimates range from 7000 to 100,000. The English families responded in predictable ways. They put pressure on the mother to give her baby up or pass it off as the child of a grandmother, an aunt or a cousin. The motives of parents who deliberately sabotaged their daughters' chance to marry the men whose child they carried are harder to understand. Many of the children acquired stepfathers. When tempers were frayed, names were called: 'Yank', 'bastard'. Skeletons slipped out. One mother kept her secret until she was in her late fifties and then 'blurted out at a dinner party' that her son's father was the pilot with a foreign name whose grave they had visited in the American cemetery at Madingley just outside Cambridge. In their middle age, in the 1980s and 1990s, hundreds of the GIs' sons and daughters tracked their fathers down. One set of reunited lovers married.

Marriage

The impression of a rush to matrimony, given by the announcements which the 'officer class' placed in *The Times* in the late summer of 1939, is confirmed by the Registrar General's all-embracing data. In 1939 and 1940 marriage was in fashion.

In the following four years, the number of marriages fell. All the same 'romantic excitement' led to some hurried weddings. 'The normal period of courtship', which gave couples a chance to test their temperamental compatibility, was often skipped. Rationing affected brides. The Utility range of government-approved goods included 9ct wedding rings. Some brides' dresses made as many as seven trips to the altar. Service couples sometimes opted for 'khaki weddings' – one member of the Auxiliary Territorial Service (ATS) married her Canadian sweetheart in uniform 'with carrot tops and pinks from the garden as buttonholes'. Vita Sackville-West described the 'snowy loveliness' of a country church 'filled with sheaves of white flowering currant'. The cake might be a cardboard replica. The availability of unrationed parachute silk enabled good needlewomen to equip themselves and their sisters with luxurious trousseaux of knickers and nighties.

Many wartime weddings were followed by protracted separations. Richard and Mary Hoggart married in 1942 and did not meet for another three years. Their marriage lasted – they celebrated their forty-sixth anniversary by buying the engagement ring they had been unable to afford in their younger days. Under the strain of separation, other relationships came to grief. Letters from servicemen and women were subject to a censor's inhibiting scrutiny; the news they carried was often months out-of-date, even airmail took at least ten days. It was easy for a sweetheart or even a spouse to dwindle into 'an episode in the past'. War changed people: women whose partners were away from home found new identities for themselves as volunteers or earning good wages and not having to account for the way they spent their time or their money. For some men, the Services were 'a godsend of freedom and relative irresponsibility'. As one confessed, 'There are no women to bother about, and we yarn and smoke and have a drink just when we like'.

The legend that 'when the blackout came, London became a vast double bed' is clearly exaggerated but 'the emergency' provided excellent cover stories for men and women with an inclination to stray. Separated from his family by war work in London, Cecil Day-Lewis (born 1904) enjoyed a 'double marriage', his unofficial town wife being kept a secret from his country wife. Fire-watching and other nocturnal duties provided excellent alibis. The sense of danger and excitement 'churned up emotions' with the result that 'many men and women, under the strain of war conditions and in spite of their ordinary and absolute rule of rectitude' found themselves 'entangled'. 'Some friends grow to be lovers. Some take a stern hold upon themselves and repress their needs and desires'. In the last two years of the war a third of illegitimate babies were born to married women. The family legacies of war are considered in Chapter 4.

Old age

Older people were determined to prove that they too were 'not brave just British'. The Home Guard recruited many veterans of the First World War and some who had served in Boer War – the Director General encountered at least three men wearing medals from the Egyptian Campaign of the 1880s. The imposition of an upper age limit of 66 was not well received: after all these men came from a culture in which infirmity rather than age triggered retirement. As one member of Dad's Army put it, 'Some men have never been young whilst others never grow old. Age is no criterion for efficiency'. Defying the blitz, Frank Gielgud (born 1860) went to his office in the City five days a week. Gameness and gallantry were not male prerogatives. In Sheffield a veteran conductress who had served on the city's trams in the First World War came out of retirement at the age of 74. An old bombed-out woman arrived at the WVS Centre Bethnal Green

> with nothing more than her canary. As she walked along she hummed the music hall song about a woman flitting from one home to another, walking through the streets behind the movers' van carrying with her cock linnet in a cage, 'My old man said follow the van and don't dilly-dally on the way'.

Death

Barbara Cartland (born 1900) published a memorial life of her brother Ronald (born 1907) who had been killed 'fighting with the rearguard of the BEF [British Expeditionary Force] during the retreat from Dunkirk'. The opening pages have a strong tang of the memoirs of the fallen written during the First World War: a preface by the prime minister, tributes from Cartland's fellow MPs, fellow Tories, fellow officers, and other friends. They celebrated him as 'a marvellous boy', 'one of the coming men', 'a Happy Warrior', 'a natural leader'. 'He went, he fought, he died' as his father had a generation before. Flying Officer Vivian Rosewarne, co-pilot of a Wellington bomber, the only child of a widowed mother, was one of the flyers who lost his life during the Battle of Britain. He left a letter to be sent to her in the event of his death. Here are some of his words of consolation: 'It will comfort you to know that my role in this war has been of the utmost importance. History resounds with illustrious names who have given all'.

These sentiments too echo those of the men who laid down their lives between 1914 and 1919. On 18 June 1940 Vivian Rosewarne's letter was published in *The Times*. By popular request, it was reprinted in pamphlet form. Half a million copies were sold in England and abroad. The message was so much what Ministry of Information might have ordered that some sceptics guessed, wrongly as it appears, that it was the work of a professional morale raiser.

The evidence of war memorials in villages and towns suggests that the Second World War claimed fewer soldiers' lives than the first. This is not a misleading impression. Civilian deaths were much more common than in First World War – 60,000 died in air raids. The authorities had prepared for casualties on the home front. Supplies of dark brown cardboard coffins awaited assembly; unwanted bales of fabric, sometimes incongruously bright, were acquired to provide shrouds. The toll was uneven. In London alone 13,596 had been killed by the end of 1940. In Cambridge, where Andrew Gow spent the war, 30 people died, 10 of them in a single raid; in Rachel Knappett's corner of south-west Lancashire there were no deaths at all.

Statistics do not tell the human stories. Bombing brought the horrors of war to the Home Front. A London woman, who lost her mother and child in the same raid, discovered her daughter in the mortuary (her mother was never found).

> All her little hair was burned, and her face, where she'd put her fingers right across, all the fire was there and I thought: 'Oh dear now, can it be true?' Then I thought to myself: 'Well, I suppose the Lord's taken her, you know, to be right out of pain altogether', and I thought to myself, 'Well, I sooner her go that way than be maimed for life, you know a little cripple'.

A Hull air raid warden came off duty to find his wife's body in the passage between the kitchen and the washhouse, 'Her legs were just two cinders. And 'er face – the only thing I could recognise 'er by was one of 'er boots'. Mangled, headless, limbless corpses were identified by tiny distinguishing marks, a malformed fingernail, for instance, or shreds of clothing.

War victims could be buried without charge in communal graves. Many people preferred to pay for a private plot because that meant that the living could look forward to lying beside their loved ones in due course. In the mean time, those left behind found their own ways of staying close to those they had lost. Tony Benn removed the 'wings' he had won as a pilot from his uniform and wore his dead brother's instead. Dick Ketton-Cremer was killed in Crete in 1941. 'Jester his large horse and Mimi his little cat' helped to console his brother.

The war did not suspend natural death. Behind the Home Front men and women continued to die in the spirit in which they had lived their lives. In 1942 Dillwyn Knox (born 1883), religious sceptic, Greek scholar and code breaker in two wars, was dying of cancer. He refused a second operation: 'his considered opinion was that a human being ought not to be turned into a bit of plumbing'.

Reading

Allingham, Margery, *The Oaken Heart* (Michael Joseph, 1941).

Benn, Tony, *Years of Hope: diaries, papers and letters, 1940–1962* (Hutchinson, 1994).

Calder, Angus, *The People's War, 1939–1945* (Jonathan Cape, 1969).

Cartland, Barbara, *Ronald Cartland* (Collins, 1942).

Chapman, Guy, *A Kind of Survivor* (Gollancz, 1975).

Day-Lewis, Sean, *C. Day-Lewis: an English literary life* (Weidenfeld & Nicolson, 1980).

Donaldson, Frances, *A Twentieth-century Life* (Weidenfeld & Nicolson, 1992).

Donnelly, Peter (ed.), *Mrs Milburn's Diaries: an Englishwoman's day-to-day reflections* (Harrap, 1977).

Figes, Eva, *Little Eden: a child at war* (Faber & Faber, 1978).

Gale, John, *Clean Young Englishman* (Hogarth Press, 1965).

Gow, A. S. F., *Letters from Cambridge* (Jonathan Cape, 1945).

Graves, Charles, *Women in Green: the story of the WVS* (1948).

Hodgson, Vere, *Few Eggs and No Oranges: a diary showing how unimportant people in London and Birmingham lived throughout the war year* (Dobson, 1971).

Hoggart, Richard, A Sort of Clowning: life and times, Volume II, 1940–59 (Chatto & Windus, 1990).

Kaye, Barbara (Mrs Percy Muir), The Company We Kept (Werner Shaw, 1986).

Kenward, Betty, Jennifer's Memoirs: eighty-five years of fun and functions (HarperCollins, 1992).

Knappett, Rachel, A Pullet on the Midden (Michael Joseph, 1946).

Last, Nella, Nella Last's War: a mother's diary 1939–45, Richard Broad and Suzie Fleming (eds) (Sphere, 1983).

Lees-Milne, James, Ancestral Voices (Chatto & Windus, 1975).

Lees-Milne, James, Prophesying Peace (Chatto & Windus, 1977).

Mayhew, Patrick (ed.), One Family's War (Hutchinson, 1985).

Millgate, Helen, Mr Brown's War: a diary of the Second World War (Sutton, 1998).

Partridge, Frances, A Pacifist's War (Hogarth Press, 1978).

Patten, Marguerite, We'll Eat Again (Hamlyn, in association with the Imperial War Museum, 1985).

Pottle, Mark (ed.), Champion Redoubtable: the diaries and letters of Violet Bonham Carter (Weidenfeld & Nicolson, 1998).

Rhodes James, Robert (ed.), Chips: the diaries of Sir Henry Channon (Weidenfeld & Nicolson, 1967).

Sackville-West, Vita, Country Notes in Wartime (Hogarth Press, 1940).

Schweitzer, Alex et al. (eds), Goodnight Children Everywhere: memories of evacuation in World War II (Age Exchange, 1990).

Swift, Rebecca (ed.), Letters from Margaret: correspondence between Bernard Shaw and Margaret Wheeler, 1944–1950 (Chatto & Windus, 1992).

Tyrer, Nicola, They Fought in the Fields: The Women's Land Army, the story of a forgotten victory (Sinclair-Stevenson, 1998).

Willmott, Phyllis, Coming of Age in Wartime (Peter Owen, 1988).

4   A better world, 1945–1960

Reconstructing families

Families, long-separated by war service, imprisonment or internment, were gadually reunited. Wives faced 'the struggle to deal with . . . postwar problems' in partnership with 'a worn-out . . . stranger'. A fortunate minority had sustained companionship by correspondence. It would be wrong to assume that letter writing was a skill confined to the upper and middle classes – many children who attended elementary schools were fluent writers by the time they left.

Some mothers had worked hard to ensure that absent fathers had remained a steady 'presence' in their children's lives. Photographs helped. As one woman recalled, 'I wanted them to know and love their Daddy when he came back home to them. So I used to talk to them about "Daddy" and show them his picture constantly . . . I was to be amply rewarded.' A few lucky children had records of their fathers' voices made by the NAAFI (Navy, Army and Air Force Institutes). Frequently, however, returning fathers were alien invaders. Boys and girls resented 'that man who keeps coming into our house', the man who usurped the child's place in the mother's bed. Children sent abroad in the dark days when the future of Britain hung in the balance came back. Elizabeth Rothenstein, evacuated to the United States, greeted her father on Oxford station with the observation: 'You don't recognise me, Daddy, but I recognise you.' Some evacuees never returned. Don McCullin's sister stayed in the Big House in Somerset and grew up with a 'posh' accent.

Women who had had a good war on the Home Front resented the return to the old regime. During the war, while her husband was away, Margaret Wheeler became her 'own boss'; she 'ordered things' to suit herself. 'Now Charles is back . . . I am expected to drop back into my old place and be everybody's little dog. I am not in the least inclined to be'. 'The children are another cause of dissension . . . Anything wrong in their behaviour is put down by Charles to my incapable handling of them during the five years he was away'. Returning men found it equally hard to adjust. Paul Hodder-Williams 'had been a lieutenant-colonel since 1943, commanding a force five times the human complexity and wartime strength of Hodder & Stoughton'. But, as far as the chairman of the family publishing firm was concerned, he was still 'a boy'.

Remaking their world

In the late 1930s, the looming war 'seemed to offer an opportunity for a new beginning'. In August 1939 Allen Lane, the driving force behind Penguin Books, the 'poor man's university', announced a change of tack: 'we are switching very considerably' to books 'discussing the possibility of a new world when all this mess is over'. Magazines and feature films campaigned for a new society. *Picture Post* argued that needs tests should replace means tests. The closing caption of the film version of *Love on the Dole* (released in 1940) declared that 'Never again must the unemployed become the forgotten men of the Peace'. The stoicism of ordinary men and women added to the enthusiasm for a new deal. As Queen Elizabeth said of East Enders: 'The destruction is so awful and the people so *wonderful* – they *deserve* a better world.'

The welfare state

The Beveridge report, the blueprint for this better world, was published in 1944. Employing the familiar language of John Bunyan's *Pilgrim's Progress*, a work that had been in print – and popular – for the better part of three centuries, William Beveridge declared war on five metaphorical Giants: Want, Ignorance, Disease, Squalor and Idleness. At home, in the Forces and in prisoner of war camps tens of thousands of ordinary unbookish people read the report – Alan Milburn, a sporty young man, who spent much of the war in captivity, astonished his mother: 'studied the Beveridge Report. Alan! Gosh!' At the general election of 1945 the electorate voted into power not a Conservative government led by Mr Churchill, Britain's champion in the war against Hitler, but Mr Attlee and his team of Labour veterans, who had commanded the Home Front.

In the welfare state envisaged by Beveridge, men were to be the breadwinners, bringing home a family wage. (In real life there were significant numbers of men – casual workers and those on low wages – who did not earn enough to keep a family.) 'Be like dad, keep mum', one of the puns designed to remind the wartime population that 'careless talk costs lives', summed up what Beveridge saw as a fact of family life. But a wife was not 'a mere adult dependant': she was a partner whose work was 'vital but unpaid'. Beveridge had intended to add the new family allowance, a modest contribution to the cost of rearing two or more children, to the father's wage packet. Pressure from women MPs diverted it to the mother's purse, a last-minute triumph for the doughty campaigner Eleanor Rathbone (born 1872). She had helped to administer service separation allowances during the First World War. Her case for family allowances, *The Disinherited Family*, was published in 1924. A National Assistance Board was set up to provide for those who fell through the net provided by the welfare state. Its officers were instructed to carry out their investigative duties 'with courtesy and tact'.

This new dispensation was not universally welcome. Claud Mullins (born 1887) came from a family that exemplified the virtues of middle-class mutuality and self-help. His Uncle Willie was his hero. Willie was the eldest of seven. When his father died in 1853, Willie was 19. 'Without moaning he left the University' to earn his living (he later returned to Cambridge and graduated with distinction). He helped to educate his younger brothers and made a home for his two spinster sisters. Willie never married. 'Without help from public authority, my Father's family triumphed over disaster'. When his own father's health failed, Claud Mullins 'became, as the eldest son, more and more his deputy in the home'. 'In 1948', Mullins observed, 'a serious blow was struck to family loyalty'. The National Assistance Act 1948 ended 'the historic duty of relations' to support elderly members of their families who would otherwise become 'a charge on public funds'. The Mullins family's history was not unique. Alix Kilroy's university fees and her father's were paid by uncles. Her never-married aunt Maud was 'the relied-upon daughter-at-home and the second mother to her sister's children'. Grateful though she was to Maud, Alix Kilroy was conscious of the cost.

The National Health Service (NHS), launched in 1948, offered, free at point of need, medical care from cradle to grave: care during pregnancy and labour for mothers; fruit juice and cod liver oil for babies and children; lotions, pills and potions; dentistry; eye tests and lenses for spectacles (though not frames unless the old ones were 'worn out or otherwise needed'); hearing aids; artificial limbs; home helps; grants towards the cost of funerals (a benefit from which the current generation of old people was excluded). Almost everyone in the UK registered as an NHS patient. A family doctor from the Home Counties reported that the 'local aristocrat' used the NHS; only 'one or two business people, and especially their wives, and one or two old widows' had insisted on remaining private patients. The demand for treatment was huge and unpredicted – and naturally greatest where unemployment had bitten deepest in the 1930s, in the areas of heavy industry and atmospheric pollution. Decades of self-sacrifice were revealed: GPs saw women with 'prolapsed uteruses literally wobbling down between their legs'. The state of the artificial arms and legs discarded when new limbs were fitted 'was a grim reminder of the extent to which the crippled poor had been neglected'. By the autumn of 1951, 152,000 free hearing aids had been supplied. The bills frightened the Treasury: the first means-tested charges were not long in coming. Even in the 1940s there were hints of the unmanageable cost of funding advances in medical technology. To treat the writer George Orwell (born 1903) in the last stages of tuberculosis, streptomycin, a new and very expensive drug, was privately purchased in the United States by his friend and patron David Astor and imported by special licence. Orwell proved allergic to the drug (he died in 1950) but the remaining doses saved the lives of two other patients. Antibiotics revolutionised the treatment of TB. Immunisation helped to prevent it. During the First World War a pair of French researchers, Leon Calmette and Jules Guerin had developed a vaccine against the disease – Bacille Calmette-Guerin or BCG. Its use was not finally sanctioned by the British medical authorities until 1953. From then on schoolchildren were immunised against TB early in their secondary school careers.

Austerity

The end of the war in August 1945 did not bring 'paradise on a plate'. Privations persisted on the Home Front. The first emblematic bananas were unzipped in 1946 but, that July, bread rationing was introduced. Friends living abroad ordered biscuits and other export-only luxuries and had them sent to treat-starved English households. Violet Bonham Carter hoarded unopened 'a tin labelled "Biscuits"' that she had been sent from New Zealand with Christmas or 'some great "grand-children" occasion' in mind. The Congregational church in Highgate, Australia, sent food parcels to its sister church in Highgate, a relatively well-heeled part of London. In 1947 the boar's head paraded at New College, Oxford, on Christmas Day was the *papier mâché* substitute used during the war. But, earlier that same year, Oxford and Cambridge colleges held the first May Balls of peacetime. The 'New Look' came in. Nipped-in waists and long, extravagantly full skirts, the antithesis of the square-shouldered mannish wartime fashions, were mouth-watering but unattainable. 'The first really lovely wedding dress' seen in London after the war was made in Paris by Pierre Balmain and worn by the daughter of the Argentine Ambassador. The bonfire of the ration books was a long time coming. The black market thrived. Scarcity bred 'spivs', shady traders who lived up to the motto 'only fools and horses work'. 'Export or Die' was the official slogan. The clothes, furnishings and toys displayed with wit and flair in the still-empty galleries at the Victoria and Albert Museum in the autumn of 1946, to the admiration of more than a million visitors, were not intended for home consumption. 'Britain Can Make It' was the message. 'Britain Can't Have It' came the weary response.

The weather was unkind. To the Chancellor of the Exchequer, Hugh Dalton, 1947 was 'annus horrendus'. The worst winter weather since 1881 coincided with a coal shortage. With ice flows off the coast of Norfolk, there was a ban on the use of electric fires at home between 9 a.m. and 12 noon and from 2 p.m. to 4 p.m. – the midday reprieve is a reminder that a large number of husbands and schoolchildren came home to dinner. To keep their morale up, miners, the front-line troops in the war against the cold, were rewarded with extra rations and nylon stockings for their wives. With the thaw came the floods. In Oxford swans glided in through bedroom windows. The water receded leaving sodden furnishings, prone to mould and hard to replace. Plans for a Festival of Britain, conceived in 1945, were endorsed by the government in the 'bad bleak year' of 1947. It was to be 'a rainbow – a brilliant sign . . . promising better [metaphorical] weather'. Paradoxically, as it turned out, the early 1950s saw devastating coastal flooding. In 1952 Devon suffered. In 1953 it was the east coast's turn. On 31 January a train travelling from Hunstanton to King's Lynn ran into a 'wall of water' carrying with it a bungalow washed inland from Heacham. At Canvey Island in Essex the bodies of flood victims lay on the pavement until they were identified. A fireman remembered that the 'worst thing was finding the bodies of people you had known all your life'. Since the nineteenth century the 'London peculiar', 'pea-soup' fog, had been a feature of the city winter. The smog of December 1953 brought everyday life in London to a halt for four days. The death rate shot up by 250 per cent as dozens of people with weak hearts and lungs succumbed. The following year smog masks were supplied on the National Health. The Clean Air Act 1956, which required people to burn 'smokeless fuels', reduced atmospheric pollution. By the end of the 1950s soot was no longer 'part of our lives'.

'Britain bounces back'

In the 1950s, things began to look up. The Festival of Britain, which opened in May 1951, was part commemoration of the centenary of the Great Exhibition in the Crystal Palace, part showcase for British design – a follow-up to Britain Can Make It. It was also 'A Tonic for the Nation', a 'cheer up effort', 'planned fun' for a planned society, a 'real family party'. After years of blackout and fuel shortage London was floodlit for the Festival. 'Miniature versions of the South Bank Exhibition' visited four inland cities and ten cities on the coast (carried there by the Festival ship, *Campania*). Bedfordshire County Council badged its village signs, back in place now that the war was over, with the symbol of the Festival – Britannia re-created for the second half of the twentieth century – young, gallant, crisply liveried in red, white and blue, set off with a gay little frill of bunting. Talking on the Home Service, the precursor of BBC Radio 4, J. B. Priestley drew attention to the proliferation of locally organised celebrations:

> If I had to award a prize for terrific goings-on in a smallish place, my choice, I think would be Dunster parish, which from June 13 to 17 will have medieval booths, hucksters, jugglers, beggars, men in stocks, monks chanting round the church and priory gardens, minstrels, a band of recorders, three teams of archers, five morality plays, spinning and weaving, wool brought in on pack horses and spun on the site, the hobbyhorse, Morris and country dancing, exhibitions of local antiques and handicrafts, sports and tea for the children and a firework display. I call this prodigal.

The people of Dunster chose to hark back to the town's days of prosperity as a centre of the trade in woollen cloth – evidence of the persistent English preoccupation with a largely imaginary past – a preoccupation that coexisted, illogically, with the generally enthusiastic take-up of novelties in real life.

Synthetic fibres became familiar. In October 1951 *Varsity*, the Cambridge University student newspaper, carried a report that 'the first nylon shirt' had made its appearance in the city:

> Its owner has announced that he intends to wear it without a change during the coming academic year. Apparently one throws these shirts in water in the evening, crumples them in a ball, and then puts them on the next day, clean and needing no iron.

Nylon bedding and garments made the bachelor's life simpler – and undermined the value of the housewife's traditional skills.

The accession of the young Queen Elizabeth in 1952 conjured up glorious visions of a Second Elizabethan Age. *Collins' Magazine*, aimed at grammar school girls and boys, changed its name to the *Young Elizabethan*. News of the 'conquest' of Everest by members of a British-led team broke, aptly, on the morning of the Coronation. The day was wet. A National Serviceman recalled 'marching in the pouring rain through the streets of London . . . a few paces behind the Mounties, and caked half-way up the chest in their horses' droppings'. But spirits were not dampened. Some workers were enjoying their first paid day off. Many people watched television for the first time – more than half the viewers enjoyed the spectacle in someone else's home. TV's career as a 'friend collector' had begun. The impact of television on family life is a subject to which we shall shortly return.

Ray Gosling, a mechanic's son brought up in Northampton, remembered his father soldering saucepans, mending watches, cannibalising bicycles for his own household and his neighbours' too. The Goslings' bandages and dishcloths were made at home. This old make-do-and-mend philosophy was on the way out. Thinking back, an East Ender remembered, 'things changed. I don't know how; my father didn't change his job or anything like that. Things just seemed to get much better. We started to buy new things.' Working men began to feel 'middle class'. Pawnshops shut. Full employment, the security blanket of the welfare state and the new goods on the market fostered a culture of materialism. *Which?*, the Consumers' Association Magazine guide to good value launched in 1957, provides evidence of a new and bewildering range of choice of goods and services. Premium Bonds, which offered investors cash prizes instead of interest, were introduced in 1956. Car owning became commoner – the first stretch of motorway, now the Preston bypass, was opened in 1958. The M1 from Watford to Rugby opened the year after; the first motorway service station, on the M1 at Newport Pagnell, dates from 1960.

Television had been a casualty of the war. Its spread in the 1950s was both emblem and engine of a changing style of life. TV and steady wages gave families the confidence to become consumers. About 25 million people watched the Coronation in 1953, the biggest viewing figure to date. In 1955 ITV, 'commercial' television funded by advertisements, went on air. The facts of commercial life meant that the family audience got what it wanted: 'girls, wrestling, bright musicals, quiz shows and real-life drama'. The prescription changed little over the decades that followed. Snobs complained that give-away shows fed an appetite for something-for-nothing and feared that advertising jingles would oust nursery rhymes. Indeed in primary school playgrounds, girls used them to provide novel rhythms for their skipping and ball-bouncing routines. A few years on *Coronation Street* was the inspiration for new rhymes:

> Ena Sharples, how about a date?
> Meet me at the Rovers at half-past eight.
> You buy the milk stout, I'll buy the crisps,
> You'll do the rumba and I'll do the twist.

The social and intellectual elites were late and reluctant converts to the new medium. In 1958 none of the political party leaders owned a set. For many ordinary people, on the other hand, particularly those who had been transplanted to new estates and new towns, the television was 'a bit of a friend'; some women saw it even more positively, as an ally: 'television holds you together', 'television keeps husbands at home'.

Harold Macmillan (born 1894), the cartoonists' 'Supermac', was right when he claimed in 1959 that 'most of our people have never had it so good'. Take note of 'most'. Families with irregular incomes, big working-class families (and by the 1950s four children constituted a large family), families without fathers, all found the going very hard. The state pension was too low to provide adequately for those without other means. And, although the Poor Law had been replaced by the welfare state, the old and homeless mothers and their children were still billeted in the great union workhouses erected to accommodate Victorian paupers. All the same, Britain appeared to be turning into a more equal society. Egalitarian gestures abounded. Property owners and university graduates lost their rights to additional votes. The Coronation honours list included the jockey Gordon Richards. In 1953, Len Hutton, the first professional cricketer to captain England, led his team to victory. In 1958 lay life peers joined the law lords and the bishops in the Upper House of Parliament; from now on men – and women – could enter the Lords without dragging their heirs behind them. The rare hereditary peeress could take her seat. In the same year debutantes were presented to the Queen for the last time.

Black faces

Between the wars many English working-class families were cared for by Indian doctors or bought goods from Sikhs selling door-to-door. In ports like Liverpool there were communities of black seamen. During the war black servicemen from the West Indies and the United States were posted to England in significant numbers – 8000 West Indians served in the Royal Air Force (RAF). Nevertheless, the arrival of the *Empire Windrush* in labour-hungry England in June 1948 symbolised the start of the first major wave of organised immigration. During the 1950s, the number of West Indians and Asians in England doubled. Skilled men from the Caribbean, mostly in their twenties, came to England to take mostly semi-skilled and manual jobs in the Post Office, on the railway, tubes and buses and in the NHS. Women and children followed. In London these immigrants clustered in Brixton, Notting Hill and Ladbroke Grove, living in furnished rooms in large houses built for the Victorian bourgeoisie. Local shops and markets began to sell salt fish, goat meat and spices and (in the 1950s, before air freight became cheap) exotic tinned vegetables.

Language that would be deeply offensive today was used unhesitatingly forty or fifty years ago. In 1951 the socialist Kingsley Martin (born 1897) used the phrase 'nigger in the woodpile' as naturally as he might have 'spanner in the works'. Ruth Glass (born 1912), a social scientist, investigated West Indian settlers in London for a study, *Newcomers*, published in 1960. 'Coloured' is her preferred expression:

among West Indians in Britain there are . . . people of every shade of colour; those who look like Negroes, Mulattoes, Indians, Chinese or like Europeans . . . There is a good deal of class consciousness tied up with 'colour snobbery' . . . Light pigmentation conveys social prestige, thus the desire to marry 'fair'.

Among children 'the greatest insult is to say, "You are blacker than me".' When she reprinted a chapter from *Newcomers* in the late 1980s, Glass left the period terms intact but, for editorial purposes, she naturally used the by then current vocabulary: 'Afro-Caribbean' and 'black people'. Sheila Patterson (born 1918) was the author of a classic study of the Cape Coloured Community in South Africa, published in 1953. The opening paragraph of *Dark Strangers* (1963), her study of West Indian community in Brixton, is headed 'Colour Shock and Strangeness'. It describes her first reconnaissance trip to Brixton.

I was immediately overcome with a sense of strangeness, almost of shock . . . At least half of the exuberant infants playing outside the pre-fab day nursery were *café noir* or *café au lait* in colouring. And there were coloured men and women wherever I looked, shopping, strolling or gossiping on sunny street-corners with an animation that most Londoners lost long ago.

Patterson commented on her use of language in a footnote to the page: '"Coloured" is used throughout in its colloquial sense, although I realize that the term is open to criticism'. The close reading of texts of even the near past provides an excellent training in cultural awareness.

West Indian settlers faced a hostile reception. The prejudice that black servicemen had encountered during the war had not evaporated. An analysis of advertisements placed in the *Kensington Post* between November 1958 and January 1959 revealed that about one in eight private landlords were overtly discriminatory. Ruth Glass discovered that 'most of the estate agents and landlords whose advertisements are "neutral" . . . also refuse to take coloured tenants'. Landlords' prejudices were comprehensive. Tom Driberg recorded an advertisement placed in the *Middlesex Independent and West London Star* in 1951 that read:

Only professional black-coated workers in secure financial positions need apply. No Poles, no Czechs, no socialists, no children, no young married couples.

Race riots occurred – most seriously in 1958. The Keep Britain White Campaign 'hunted' 'niggers' in Notting Hill in London armed with 'flick knives, stilettos, razors, bicycle chains, carving knives'.

Homosexuality

As a National Serviceman, Bernard Palmer observed

a long-established male marriage, apparently connived at and condoned by all, from the colonel down . . . They had taken up together in the war, and never since separated; the regiment, in its quiet monotonous way, saw to it that their relationship survived. Nobody seemed to see anything in the least incongruous about this.

Tolerance of particular couples coexisted with hostility to anonymous, stereotyped 'queers'. In the early 1950s a number of men in the public eye were prosecuted for homosexual offences. A moral panic was fanned by an exaggerated report of the number of cases of importuning that came before the courts. Viscount Samuel evoked the Old Testament: 'the vices of Sodom and Gomorrah . . . appear to be rife among us'. Lord Montagu of Beaulieu, his cousin Michael Pitt-Rivers and Peter Wildeblood were tried at the Winchester Assizes. Peter Wildeblood (born 1923), a journalist, published a well-received account of his experience of jail. His reception, when he was released, demonstrated a sympathy well beyond the boundaries of bohemia. His parents' friends, 'the middle-aged inhabitants of a small country town', mostly 'avoided discussion of the case' but welcomed him back 'as though nothing had happened'. His neighbours in Islington were more open: 'We read all about it in the papers, and we thought it was a rotten shame!' Lord Montagu enjoyed a similarly heartening welcome back: friends threw parties; Hugh Gaitskell (born 1906), Leader of the Opposition, greeted him warmly in a Mayfair restaurant. In October 1953 John Gielgud (born 1904), knighted earlier in the year, pleaded guilty to importuning. Shortly afterwards the West End audience at the London premiere of *A Day by the Sea* gave Sir John a standing ovation.

In 1954, provoked by these and other high-profile cases and the recognised nuisance of 'public and flagrant' soliciting by women 'streetwalkers', who faced small fines if they were arrested for soliciting, the Home Secretary set up a departmental committee on Homosexual Offences and Prostitution. The bracketing of these 'deviant' groups is telling. (Civil servants coyly referred to 'Huntley and Palmers'.) The committee, chaired by John Wolfenden (born 1906), Vice-Chancellor of the University of Reading and, unbeknown to the public, the father of a flamboyantly homosexual son, reported in 1957. Its proposals for 'cleaning up the streets' led to the Street Offences Act 1958. The suggestion that private homosexual acts between consenting adults should no longer be a criminal offence (the 'Pansies' Charter', as it was called by a hostile journalist) was in Wolfenden's words too much of a 'political hot potato'. Legalisation was postponed until the 'liberal hour' in the 1960s.

Family economies

When it came to choosing a job, young people were expected to follow in their parents' footsteps. Mining communities were self-perpetuating. Sons followed their fathers down the pit and married miners' daughters. The architectural historian John Harris (born 1931) came from a family of upholsterers. When he left school in 1945, an apprenticeship in Heal's upholstery workshop awaited him. He had not been consulted: it was assumed that he would join the family trade. In some parts of Britain working patterns were changing. In the West Country 'prosperous and well-established' lines of yeomen farmers died out. 'The conjugal family with one or two children' – the twentieth-century ideal – had proved 'a very imperfect instrument for farming a holding over a long period'. In London, the dynastic principles that had governed recruitment to the print industry and the docks were eroded. As home ownership became commoner and consumer goods more plentiful, the desire to achieve a high disposable income increased. In Oxford, in the 1950s, 'skilled craftsmen and college servants' found that they could 'earn more as semi-skilled production-line workers making Morris cars' at Cowley. The Vauxhall car factory drew families to Luton. As one car worker explained: 'When I came out of the RAF my wife wanted income rather than an interesting job for me'.

As servicemen returned to civilian life, married women conscripted to the waged workforce for the duration of the war went home. Many of them had earned good wages and had enjoyed the freedom to spend them (in the denuded wartime shops). After the war was over most women seen to have accepted that managing a home and family was a full-time job. In 1959 'Podge' gave 'Mummy' *The Penguin Book of Comic and Curious Verse* for Christmas. Among the verses was the well-known anonymous obituary 'On a Tired Housewife' embarking on an eternity of blessed idleness. Either donor or recipient underlined the title and added three exclamation marks. Professional opinion was critical of mothers who took paid work. War nurseries, women doctors collectively declared as they closed, were characterised by 'a high incidence of infection and a low incidence of happiness'. Decent working-class men in regular employment, still paid in cash, handed over their wives' 'wages' on pay day. Miners, whose wages fluctuated, were expected to make steady contributions to the household exchequer.

Like many middle-class women whose brothers would have trained for a profession, Elspeth Shand (born 1932) went from boarding school into secretarial work. She married in 1953 and by 1960 she had three children. In the 1940s and 1950s young graduate wives also expected that motherhood, not career-building, would be the dominant theme of their lives. Valerie Hess, married soon after she came down from Cambridge in 1958, 'never seriously considered looking for a job'. Hess came from a line of educated women but, writing in 1996, she recalled that her maternal grandmother

> encouraged by her mother had left Wiltshire and gone to London at the end of the nineteenth century to train as a nurse. She made sure that her daughter, my mother, attended as good a school as did her sons. My mother was also determined that both my brother and I should be equally well educated. However, none of these generations of women would have expected to have a career.

Like the wives of professional men of earlier generations, when her domestic responsibilities eased, Valerie Hess became actively involved outside her home in voluntary work, as a magistrate and marriage guidance counsellor. In 1975 Elspeth

Howe (née Shand) was appointed deputy chair of the Equal Opportunity Commission. When her husband became Chancellor of the Exchequer in 1979, she resigned, changed tack and enrolled as a student at the London School of Economics.

There were signs that the days of the volunteer were numbered. Paid work, in the 'post-family phase', was recognised as something that could confer identity, a sense of purpose and a measure of financial independence. It also spared the children 'guilt feelings'. Highly educated mothers owned up to feeling oppressed by the 'endless littleness' of their domestic lives. When, in the mid-1950s, the Ministry of Education appealed for married women to return to teaching, the fit of their hours in the classroom with their children's made this an attractive option. An increasing proportion of working-class mothers went out to work. Shops, hospitals and schools offered 'little jobs', part-time, poorly paid, with few prospects. By tradition, a wife's earnings were her own and frequently it was the desire to buy some specific extra for the house or for the children that prompted a mother to take a paid job. Married women who were obliged to earn to make ends meet had a much less positive view of going out to work.

A very few couples swapped roles. George Ewart Evans (born 1909) and his wife Florence were both teachers. When George came back from the war, Florence took up a post at the village school at Blaxhall in Suffolk and her husband settled down to a routine of childcare and writing. With two children under school age to look after, George Ewart Evans, a newcomer to the village, felt isolated:

> For weeks on end I would see no one outside the family except for tradesmen. Fortunately at that time there was a full complement of these: grocer, baker, butcher, and the oil man who weekly filled up our tank of paraffin.

In Blaxhall the schoolmistress's house had neither gas nor electricity.

Habitats

A desperate housing shortage was a lasting legacy of bombing. Squatters invaded unoccupied buildings. The need to replace the 458,000 houses written off during the war and complete the task of slum clearance – cynical Londoners looked on Hitler as 'civilisation's bug destroyer No. 1' – prompted a huge and sustained building programme.

Appalling living conditions persisted. In damp one-roomed homes in Paddington just after the war,

> the most noticeable characteristic is the strong and unpleasant smell. Indeed on a first visit the middle-class stomach may find it impossible to stay longer than five minutes. These strong odours are partly due to the fact that the windows are not opened and so no current of air can carry away the smells of cooking, lavatory buckets, wet mattresses and the baby's vomit hurriedly wiped up.

The Rent Act of 1957, which abolished wartime controls for new tenancies, encouraged unscrupulous landlords to harass existing occupiers in the hope of persuading them to leave – the tactic known as Rachmannism, after an alleged practitioner.

Outside recognised slum areas many households lacked bathrooms and kitchens. In 1950 one in five or six London households inhabited properties converted for multiple occupation simply by fitting 'front-door' locks to the rooms. These flats had no kitchen; two out of five shared a bathroom. In London south of the river, the families living in flats built by Victorian philanthropists enjoyed the amenities that represented best practice in the 1870s – a communal tap, sink and lavatory shared with the four others on their landing. Every flat had its allotted weekday washday. Sybil Marshall lived in the teacher's house at Kingston just a few miles from Cambridge. A farmer's daughter from the fens, she was accustomed to life without gas, electricity or piped water, but, as a full-time teacher with a small daughter, she found coaxing her household's water supply from the village pump a burdensome addition to her daily routine. Phyllis Willmott, born into a working-class London family, was entranced by the primitive sanitary arrangements in her father-in-law's house at Great Chesterford in Essex where she was a cherished guest with no responsibility for household drudgery (this was her father-in-law's responsibility). 'There was electric light but no bathroom or piped water'. The Doulton bowl on the washstand was filled with 'heated-up rain water'. She delighted in the walk down through the flowery garden to the privy. 'And it was no hardship to sit in the whitewashed privy in which the wooden bench seat had been scrubbed to a bonelike yellow by Ben's daily ministrations'. As late as 1956 Burghley, a prodigious Elizabethan house, had neither gas nor electricity: the first electrical installations were leads for a razor and a television set.

'Prefabs' were conceived as an emergency solution to the housing crisis. By the standards of the time, the box-like factory-made prefabricated bungalows were very well equipped with gas or electric cookers, clothes boilers, fridges sometimes, and ample cupboard space. Though intended as a stop-gap, prefabs were, and continued to be, popular with the families that occupied them. Prefabs went up in 1945, next came more conventional looking factory-made houses intended for permanent occupation, and finally, traditional, brick-built housing. After the prefab phase (something like 157,000 were built), most council-built dwelling were two-storey 'cottages'. However, big-city planners favoured high-rise flats. By 1957 the London County Council (LCC) was scraping the sky with its first fifteen-storey block. Today, phrases like the 'vertical Garden City' and 'sculpture in space' have a naively optimistic ring to them but as Oliver Cox explained in 1951,

> these large blocks were not the result of an architect's whim, or a speculator's desire for profit; they are a direct result of the planned attempt to provide every Londoner with a house of his own, without ejecting a large proportion of London's population.

To families affected by bomb damage and poor housing, this was a welcome proposition, as one East London mother confirmed: 'My girls wouldn't go out of Bethnal Green. After the war a couple of them got those Nissen huts – they kept them like dolls' houses and when the time came they were able to get places in these new blocks'. These tight-knit family-based communities were not peculiar to working-class London; a Lancashire woman, married in 1940, had her mother, her mother-in-law, two sisters and four aunts within easy walking distance.

Bolder East Enders spilled out into new towns and new estates in Essex, Hertfordshire and Bedfordshire. In new towns like Harlow there were no grand-parents, few teenagers and plenty of babies. Separation from kin encouraged the colonists to acquire cars and telephones. Peter Willmott and Michael Young, who tracked migrating families from Bethnal Green to Wanstead and Woodford, were struck by 'the variety of people's lives'. They encountered old-fashioned 'Mums' in thick, sagging cotton stockings and 'enormous flowered overalls' who sat their visitors on 'hard upright chairs next to drying nappies' and offered 'sweet tea and sterilised milk' and 'modern' women who 'colour-rinsed' their hair, wore make-up and skin-tight nylons, 'engulfed' their guests in 'deep velvet-covered settees' and gave them sherry. For the 'modern' couple, keeping ahead of the Joneses was a novel – and favourite – sport. 'DIY' – 'Do-it-yourself' – entered the English vocabulary in 1958. The notion that a home expressed the taste and personality of its occupants, had been the preserve of the comfortably-off upper and middle classes. Now it infected yet another section of the population. 'Home improve-ments', Formica surfaces ('one wipe and it's clean'), suites of new furniture, household equipment, a telephone or a car were relished as a 'knock in the eye' for the neighbours.

In spite of the spanking new housing, these estates lacked the amenities of the communities they replaced. In the St Ebbe's district of Oxford 915 inhabited houses, no more than ten minutes' walk from the city centre, had been served by sixteen family-run pubs; seven fish and chip shops and cafés; two butchers; one dairy; nine pawnbrokers, second-hand clothes and junk shops; three boot-menders; three hairdressers and three undertakers. 'There was a general store with 100 yards of any front door.' In Nottingham the clearance of St Ann's displaced 30,000 people and closed 50 pubs and 500 small shops. Ray Gosling, a leader of the campaign to preserve the old community, lamented the loss of its distinctive character: 'We fought against having high-rise flats, budgie boxes in the sky, and we won. We've got plasterboard rabbit hutches on the ground instead'. The old web of kinship and neighbourhood connections was destroyed, 'a history was wiped out'. The friendly TV in the corner offered displaced families an alternative community. In their new dwellings, families flouted the architects' intentions. They ate in the corridor kitchens designed only for the preparation of food, lived in the dining room and used the lounge for special occasions or as a convenient place to store bikes and sewing machines. We must not exaggerate the amenities of the new homes. The notion that there should be electrical sockets in every room was still a novelty. Even in newly built housing central heating was a rarity. In the winter, families still huddled together round a single fire. Jack Frost etched 'ice trees' on bedroom windows.

War damage was not confined to the inner cities. Requisitioned country houses were reduced to ruins by friendly forces. Men from eighteen different regiments had been billeted at Rolls Park in Essex. The house's 'delectable back Tudor staircase' was 'hacked up' and burned; an eighteenth-century portrait was used as a dartboard. The post-war years saw the destruction of many of these vandalised and, seemingly, redundant houses. On average, in 1955, two country houses were demolished every five days. Yet there was a brighter side to the post-war history of the country house. To exploit the public appetite for voyeurism, noble showmen invited the public into their ancestral homes: Longleat in 1949, Beaulieu in 1952, Woburn in 1955. Alternative uses were devised: Mutual Households began to convert large houses to accommodate comfortably-off retired people.

Housework

In Oxford the academic Jenifer Hart continued to 'hand over some money every week for the housekeeping' to Edith Thompson, who had joined the family in 1942, 'and so avoided having to think about domestic matters'. This fortunate state of affairs lasted until 1978. Brought up in the Fens, Peggy Brittain (born 1933) went into service at a local farmhouse straight from school. In the mornings, to do the rough work, she wore a 'great big heavy duty green overall'. The 'posh white apron' and cap she wore in the afternoons had been her mother's. But the war had dramatically reduced the supply of such old-fashioned servants. Gilbert Murray (born 1866), Regius Professor of Greek at Oxford from 1908 to 1936, found it 'painful to be living in the middle of a social revolution'. In his experience, servants, when available, now demanded unprecedented luxuries: wireless, television and outings to the cinema. Fortunately, the television was not the family's only new electrical friend. By the end of the 1950s one household in four had a washing machine. These were literally machines that washed. They left the housewife to cope with heavy wet sheets, towels and clothing. As Muriel Beadle, an American who spent a year in Oxford with her academic husband, observed, even the launderette had no hot-air drier. 'We came to accept as normal the sight of wet underpants drying on a clothes horse'. In the late 1950s Yorkshire women still hung their washing out on lines stretched across the street – in working-class districts motor traffic was still light enough for this to be feasible.

Food

Peace did not bring full larders. The newly imposed bread rationing lasted from July 1946 to July 1948. Tea and sugar were rationed until 1952; butter and other fats, meat and bacon until 1953. Sweet rationing, briefly suspended in 1949, also ended in 1953. Presented with a pound of fresh tomatoes in 1946 – the first she had seen since war broke out – Diana Grey (born 1915) burst into tears. The following year Mrs Grey's elder sister, Elizabeth David, who is often credited with educating post-war English palates, 'assuaged' her hunger for unobtainable Mediterranean foodstuffs by savouring their names 'apricots, olives and butter, rice and lemons, oil and almonds' – 'in the England of 1947 those were dirty words'. Rationing encouraged cooks to experiment with more exotic cuisines. In Theodora Fitzgibbon's view, 'nothing' was 'more pathetic, or indeed wasteful, than to treat a piece of meat the size of a spectacle case as though it were a sirloin'. Taking cues from Indian and Chinese traditions, she argued, 'a dinner party for eight people can be given on one meat ration'. Soy sauce and spices could be bought over the counter in Soho or ordered by post. Raymond Postgate (born 1896) launched the Good Food Club; members' reports on restaurants, distilled by Postgate, 'Public Stomach Number One', were published in the *Good Food Guide*.

Foreign foods were slow to catch on. Les Wiles (born 1936 in Woolwich) first came across a bay leaf during his National Service.

> Now my mother is a good down-to-earth English cook, roast beef and Yorkshire pudding and none of your foreign rubbish. Digging into my stew one day, to my astonishment I found this piece of herbage the like of which I had never seen before.

Most housewives were like Mrs Wiles. They made the sort of meals their mothers had dished up. On April Fool's Day 1957 the respected current affairs television programme *Panorama* successfully teased viewers with an item on the pasta harvest: ripe strings were shown hanging from the branches of the spaghetti tree. In 1960 only in London and the south-east did homes contain a significant number of cookery books. West Yorkshire miners were among the staunchest culinary conservatives. They had physically demanding jobs; their wives earned their 'wages' by feeding them well. If their dinner did not come up to expectations, the aggrieved husband might hurl it 't' back o' fire'. Shop-cooked fish and chips – 'a kid's supper on the street' – was unacceptable. With rationing over and money plentiful, miners' wives indulged their families in 'slight luxuries – tinned fruit, sweet cakes'. The cake mix – 'just add an egg' – made this easier. Instant coffee, which had vanished from the grocers' shelves almost as soon as it had appeared before the war, began to make inroads on the nation's tea-drinking habit. Convenience was the selling point – 'There's always time for Nescafe'. Wimpy Bars opened in 1954. Fish fingers came in in 1955. Tinned dog and cat food, convenience food for pets, became a normal item in the housewife's shopping basket.

CRADLE TO GRAVE

In a material sense most children were better off than their parents or grand-parents, brought up before the war in bigger families on much less money. Sam Friend, a Suffolk man, put the emphasis on food: 'Young 'uns today have breakfast afore they set off – a lot of 'em didn't use to have that years ago, and they hev a hot dinner at school and when they come home most of 'em have a fair tea'. A female contemporary observed, 'They don't value no toy'. The small broods of two or three that were now conventional were often competitive in childhood and continued to be emotionally distant as they grew up.

Bringing up baby

Cultures of childcare varied. In rough working-class families babies were breastfed on demand. Weaned from the breast, they were pacified with dummies and bottles, ingeniously propped so that they could feed at will. Pot-training was neglected. The shape of the local economy helped to determine parents' roles. Yorkshire miners saw the routine management of babies and small children as their wives' province. Recreation was another matter. But fun was for sons. 'It is a common sight to see the small daughter . . . standing mournfully aside while the father and son play together and then be chastised for "moaning" when she tries to attract attention'. In industrial Lancashire, where married women worked evening shifts in textile factories, they left their husbands to bath the children and put them to bed. One man, expressing his pleasure in 'a row of children glowing from the bath', described the experience as 'the nearest I've been to God'. When his wife was 'not very well', Kingsley Amis, a university lecturer, cooked the dinner, got the children's tea, put them to bed and washed up. He also stood in for her when she went riding or to the cinema.

Between the wars Mabel Liddiard, had promoted the regimented, clock-bound method of child-rearing. In her post-war writing, she recognised that middle-class attitudes to mothercraft had changed. Waterproof 'Mackintosh drawers' were still officially outlawed but a Mackintosh undersheet covered 'with a pretty piece of coloured or patterned flannelette' was now permissible. The generation of 'mother-craft' babies born in the late 1940s and 1950s were introduced to the pot from the time they were 3 days old but scolding the 'wet' or 'dirty' infant was no longer recommended: 'psychological difficulty' could ensue. The use of an enema to ensure that bowels were regularly evacuated was no longer advised. Sucking thumbs and even touching genitals, 'when not pernicious', could be ignored in a very young child. When we put ourselves into their mothers' shoes, we can understand why babies were 'potted' in their first month. Disposable nappies remained a North American luxury. A tiny minority of affluent London mothers benefited from a nappy laundering service. But Phyllis Willmott's experience was commoner. Without a washing machine, she found nappies 'a horrendous chore' – she rinsed them and then boiled them 'in a bucket of water on the gas stove'. Then, of course, they had to be wrung out and hung up to dry alongside the rest of the family wash.

Mabel Liddiard did not have the field to herself. There was a plethora of advice for parents in the press and between hard covers. John Bowlby (born 1907) was a psychiatrist with a special interest in children. His hugely influential *Maternal Care and Mental Health* was published in 1951. As a 'Report prepared on behalf of the World Health Organisation', it carried great weight. Bowlby argued that it was 'essential for mental health . . . that the infant and young child should experience a warm, intimate, and continuous relationship with his mother (or permanent mother-substitute) in which both find satisfaction and enjoyment'.

Even 'partial deprivation brings in its train acute anxiety, excessive need for love, powerful feelings of revenge, and, arising from these, guilt and repression' – and retarded development. The report was a best-seller. In 1953, in a paperback summary 'freed from many of the technicalities and prepared for the general reader', it reached a still wider market under the title *Childcare and the Growth of Love*. It was generally accepted that all under-threes and most under-fives needed their mother's pretty-well-undivided attention. Even a 'bad mother' was better than no mother at all. The father was the 'economic and emotional support of the mother'.

Between the wars the upbringing of the children of progressive parents like the Meynells and the Tomalins had been influenced by psychiatric theory. In the 1940s and 1950s a far greater number of children came under the psychiatrists' scrutiny. Autism, an abnormality of the brain that makes it difficult for sufferers to relate to other people, was first described by Austrian-trained psychiatrists working independently, one in the United States, the other in Vienna, in 1943. Diagnoses of autism in disturbed children followed.

The assumption that children needed to be drilled in regular habits was challenged, most conspicuously by A. S. Neill (born 1883), headmaster of Summerhill. Neill and his wife believed that 'childhood is playhood' and that 'a self-regulated child will not lie because there is no need to'. In June 1949 Zoe, their self-regulated daughter, 'The Child Who Never Gets Slapped', featured on the cover of *Picture Post*. The captions to the picture story summarise the Neills' methods.

> Zoe Neill Never Gets Dumped Into Her Bath
> A stool is put beside her bath so that she can climb in and out. She gets in when she wants, turns taps on and off and splashes if she chooses.
>
> The Floor Serves as Her Pavement Artist's Pitch
>
> She Cuts Up Her Own Food
>
> She Chooses Her Own Stories
>
> She Takes Scratches As They Come
>
> She Copes With All Her Own Hazards
> Her movements are sure and steady. She has never been made apprehensive by grown-up anxiety for her safety. She has been allowed to explore and climb ladders.
>
> Portrait of the Girl Who is Never Commanded to Get Down from There at Once
> At two-and-a-half self-regulating Zoe Neill chooses her own trees to climb, and climbs them and comes to no harm. But her parents do not carry the principle of self-regulation to the point of risking her life. Open fires are guarded, and upper storey windows are shut at the bottom.

The Most Surprising Thing About Zoe: She Takes a Bottle to Bed
Comparatively grown-up in many ways, Zoe won't go to bed without her baby's milk bottle and a nappy. She sometimes even asks for a bottle in the daytime.

Freedom to Ask Questions

Freedom of the Coal-Hole
She scrabbles in the coal and can get filthy without being made to feel guilty.

This unconventional upbringing did not produce a child well adapted for life in polite society. As her father recorded, when she was a little older, Zoe Neill 'had a fancy for telling staid women in shops that Daddy fertilised Mummy and she came out of Mummy's fanny'.

Elizabeth Longford (born 1906), daughter of a Harley Street doctor, wife of an aristocratic Oxford don, Frank Pakenham, and mother of eight children, published her *Points for Parents*, based on a series of articles that had appeared in the middle-market *Daily Express*, in 1952. She flattered her readers by pretending that their background was as privileged as her own. A good 'acting-box' was essential to a well-regulated household.

> Everything is grist to the mill. Great-Aunt's wasp-waisted riding-habit [riding in wasp-waisted habits was an upper-class pastime] and exquisite fichus and capes. Great-Uncle's walking-sticks. Grandfather's plume and breastplate [dress uniform in the Guards], someone's BA gown trimmed with rabbit fur [a souvenir of student days at Oxford or Cambridge].

Longford endorsed Neill's anti-smacking line: parents should take 'a vow of perpetual abstinence from corporal punishment' – but not his commitment to self-regulation – 'even a smack is better than no discipline at all'.

Dr Benjamin Spock's *Baby and Child Care* crossed the Atlantic in 1955. Spock's message was 'TRUST YOURSELF'. Common sense would provide even an inexperienced mother with many of the answers she needed. Trust and involve the baby's father. Trust the baby too: 'When he cries it's for a good reason – maybe it's hunger, or wetness, or indigestion, or just because he's on edge and needs soothing'. Spock (born 1903) urged mothers to reject the tyranny of the clock. When it came to bowel and bladder training, 'the baby will mostly "train" himself'. As far as waterproof pants were concerned Spock was permissive. But he explained the reason for earlier writers' veto: 'with waterproof pants the nappies stay much wetter and warmer and bacteria accumulate in them. This favours the formation of ammonia and nappie rash'. Like Bowlby, Spock assumed that mothers would stay at home. If a mother had to work for financial reasons or for professional satisfaction, she should find a surrogate to care for her child. He agreed with Bowlby on the chronology too – under-threes certainly and under-fives in many cases were better off with a single caretaker.

In view of this professional consensus, it is strange that visits to children in hospital were so strictly limited. George MacBeth's mother was allowed to see him twice a week: 'I felt so deprived of affection, that I would look forward to the chance of being given one particular white mug, which was shorter and more chunky and more huggable, to my eye, than the others'. An epidemic of infantile paralysis, as poliomyelitis was then graphically known, hit Britain in the bleak year of 1947, when 7776 cases were notified. Tony Gould (born 1938), struck down by polio in 1959 during his National Service, published the harrowing testimony of child victims of the disease. They remembered hospital as 'almost like a concentration camp'. Nurses showed little tenderness. Children were routinely encased in plaster. As a 5-year-old, Simon Parritt (born 1950) was a prisoner in an iron lung: 'a body-enclosing apparatus to produce ventilation' was the technical description. His parents were not allowed to visit him, they were permitted only to look at him through a window. David Widgery remembered crying himself to sleep: 'And you'd wake up and then you'd see another little boy crying himself to sleep in the next cubicle'. Ian Drury was a patient at Black Notley Hospital in Essex in 1949. The physiotherapy department, where wasted limbs were exercised, was called the 'screaming ward'. Polio was a crippling disease. Survivors who learned to walk again depended on callipers and sticks. A campaign to immunise children against polio was launched in 1958.

Schooldays

Books and broadcasts for children presented attractive pictures of boarding-school life. 'As any fule kno' the black comedy of the unreformed preparatory world was immortalised by Geoffrey Willans and Ronald Searle (no prep school boy he) in four books 'written' by 'nigel molesworth', the Curse of St Custard's. The first, *Down with Skool*, was published in 1953.

In real life the bonds uniting old boys of public schools remained powerful. In 1953, during the ascent of Everest, three Old Marlburians (OM), including the expedition's leader, Colonel John Hunt (born 1910), held an OM dinner. A blizzard forced the OMs and their guests to eat in their separate tents: 'no speeches were made owing to the circumstances'. Families that had traditionally sent their children to fee-paying boarding schools continued to; socially ambitious parents copied them. Enoch Powell, a product of a distinguished Birmingham grammar school, planned to put his son down for Eton. The extent of the 'public school' world and the touchiness of alumni of obscurer institutions are graphically demonstrated by Humphrey Berkeley's success in promoting the myth of Selhurst and its grotesque headmaster Rochester Sneath, both figments of his imagination. Berkeley's fellow undergraduates at Cambridge and the heads of many more eminent schools were taken for a ride.

Looking back, Frances Partridge concluded that the upper-class 'English system of packing children off to boarding school at the age of eight or even six is brutally cruel' but 'the trouble was that there was no day school within reach and we obviously couldn't leave Ham Spray'. The possibility of sending her son to the village school did not enter her head at the time, or later.

The Butler Education Act 1944 was the 'educational Beveridge'. Its implementation marked the end of the all-age elementary school that had catered for the great majority of English children since the introduction of compulsory education in the 1870s. Elementary education had been free for more than half a century, now secondary education would be free too. There were plans to raise the school-leaving age from 14 and provide training for young workers. To encourage the cleverest 18-year-old school leavers to go on to university, state scholarships were introduced. The 1944 Act designated three types of secondary school: grammar, technical and secondary modern. The 11+ examination, which determined a child's destination, was represented as an objective test of intelligence, language and number skills. This meritocratic ideal was rarely realised. Primary school Heads often 'considered streaming as a form of natural selection'. By the time they were 7, most children in sizeable schools had been allocated to a stream – A, B or C – a 'rough and ready' demarcation by social class and circumstances. A stream families took the *Children's Newspaper* and the *Young Elizabethan*; C stream families bought the *TV Times,* then the guide to programmes broadcast by the 'commercial' television channels. C stream children were less likely to have resident fathers or bathrooms: C stream children 'smelled'. The Beatle George Harrison (born 1943) remembered, 'Smelly kids . . . were the sort teachers made you sit next to as a punishment'. Streaming anticipated and determined the secondary-school hierarchy. The 'gut' feelings of the teachers who separated the socially privileged A stream 'sheep' from the more deprived C stream 'goats' determined the population of state secondary schools. A stream children were destined for the grammar school, C stream children for the secondary modern.

In Hertfordshire in 1954 two-thirds of the children of managers and professional men 'passed' the 11+; only one in eight of manual workers children did. None of the children from the village school at Blaxhall in Suffolk ever went on to the grammar school. The prospect of a gruelling daily eight-mile journey (five by bike, the rest by bus) persuaded the school's headmistress and her husband to swallow their political convictions and send their four children to boarding school.

However unfair the 11+ might have been, the majority of grammar school boys and girls had parents with an elementary school education. Clever men and women born into working-class families and kept out of the grammar school by an urgent need to bring home a wage or by the cost of uniform and other extras made ambitious parents. People who had won their way out of poverty to 'security . . . through hard work . . . and more hard work' saw 'studying books, passing exams and getting . . . letters after your name' as the key to their children's success. It is hardly surprising that passing the 11+ ran in families. Even so, during the four or five months that separated the day of the scholarship exam from the publication of results, parents 'worried solidly'. The broadcaster Peter Sissons (born 1942) remembered 'the ritual' announcement of the results at Dovedale Road School in Liverpool: 'The school was gathered together and those who had passed were called up to the podium one at a time with their own round of applause. The poor sods who failed were left sitting in the hall – they only realised they had failed because they weren't called up'.

Roger Scruton (born 1944) characterised his old school, High Wycombe Royal

Grammar School, as a 'fantasy . . . suburban Eton' – like Raynes Park or Quarry Bank between the wars. Middle-class parents whose children failed the 11+ sent them to private schools to avoid the stigma of the secondary modern. In the long run, first-generation parents who put their sons and daughters through grammar school and university were to pay a price they had not foreseen: their children moved away, first to study, then to work. 'People whose children don't go to university and who work locally have a better life really. Their families don't get broken up', one mother observed sadly. Grammar and high schools, wholly supported by local authorities, competed with direct grant schools (which took in both scholarship and fee-paying pupils) for high-achieving 11 year olds. George MacBeth won a free place at the King Edward VII Grammar School in Sheffield: it was a 'surname school' (he was MacBeth to masters and boys too); he remembered the headmaster 'invariably . . . wearing a gown, and frequently a mortar board as well'. The future Labour MP Ann Taylor (born 1947), the first child brought up in a council house to go to her direct grant school, remembered it as a 'snob factory'.

Grammar schools, like the public schools on which they were modelled, were normally single-sex. In towns like Malton in Yorkshire, that were too small to support separate grammar schools for boys and girls, the pupils were segregated in the classroom, boys on one side, girls on the other. In girls' schools Latin, the passport to university, was set against cookery, a branch of *domestic* science. Girls were less likely to learn physics and chemistry or metal or wood work. According to a poll carried out by the *Young Elizabethan*, a periodical aimed at academic girls and boys, its readers' literary tastes were strongly gendered. C. S. Forester (born 1899) was the boys' favourite author; Noel Streatfeild (born 1895) the girls'. Forester's world was romantic and almost exclusively masculine: Horatio Hornblower, his most famous character, was a naval hero 'cast in the Nelsonian mould'. Streatfeild's world was self-sufficiently female. *Ballet Shoes*, her most successful book, originally published in 1936, tells the story of three variously talented orphan girls, including one with a mechanical bent and a passion for cars and planes. The subjects these children studied at school and the books they read for pleasure reflected a world in which male and female roles and expectations differed. A girl, contemplating the possibility of her mother's going into politics, was adamant that she did not want 'two fathers' in her family.

Working-class children often failed to thrive in grammar schools. As a 'dee-daa', who 'thee-d and thoued', Joe Ashton (born 1933) was treated with contempt at his Sheffield grammar school. Paul McCartney (born 1942) and brought up in council houses, remembered that 'there weren't many other kids from the [elite Liverpool] Institute round our way. I was called a college pudding, fucking college puddin' was what they said'.

Despite their optimistic label, secondary modern schools were often old elementary schools trading under a new banner. In Cambridgeshire, village colleges, the product of a pre-war plan to revitalise rural society by putting a secondary school on the same purpose-designed site and under the same management as classes for adults, seem to have enjoyed greater communal esteem. The support of local businesses helped. Spicers, who made paper, and Chivers, who made jam, donated land in the villages where their factories were. Henry Morris, the chief education officer, raised private funds to commission Walter Gropius to design Impington Village College; there was a plan to acquire a Henry Moore group for the grounds. The village colleges' role as purveyors of culture – pottery classes and music appreciation societies – won them friends among the middle classes who were inclined, nevertheless, to prefer grammar or private education for their own children.

Technical schools were the neglected centre ground of the Butler Act's vision.

The direct grant and grammar schools were the academic escalator that gave access to white-collar, managerial and professional careers. There were several entry points – at 16+, at 18+, and after training college or university. Oxbridge was still seen by pupils, parents and teachers as the glittering prize: *Brideshead Revisited*, which came out in 1945, heightened Oxford's glamour. There were vestiges of the 1920s style. Ian Maxwell-Scott once paid the bill for a luncheon party with a cheque written on a tablecloth: the sum total was made up of the price of the food and drink, the cost of the tablecloth and the tip. The new town of Dagenham had not prepared Dudley Moore (born 1935) 'for the Oxford social life at all . . . It was like being plunged into an exotic battlefield'. But, according to the psychologist Liam Hudson (born 1933), a postgraduate student at King's College, Cambridge, in the early 1950s, King's could take 'clever boys from ordinary homes' and equip them so that, within a few years, they were 'virtually undistinguishable from the College's Old Etonians'.

'Kicking Daddy'

Well before the First World War the 'teens' were a recognised stage on the road from childhood to full adult status but it was only in the prosperous 1950s that teenagers became an important commercial target. Young people emerged as ever more enthusiastic consumers: *What do you want if you don't want money?* was a hit song of 1959. Early leavers had much greater spending power than those who stayed on at school. Clothes and entertainment were at the top of their shopping lists. 'Teddy Boys' wore long 'Edwardian' jackets with velvet collars (a cheap parody of coats worn by upper-class males), bootlace ties, drainpipe trousers, 'very baggy round the crutch' but so tight in the leg that they sometimes had to be eased off over vaselined ankles, and distinctive shoes – thick-soled brothel creepers were succeeded by pointed-toed winkle pickers. The Ted's hair was heavily greased and elaborately dressed with a DA – duck's arse – at the nape of his neck. Teds took to Rock and Roll like ducks to water, dancing in the aisles and slashing seats when Bill Haley's *Rock Around the Clock* was screened in 1956 – the film was banned in several towns. The rackety, drunken way of life adopted by some young middle-class men behaving badly at schools of art and architecture was another metaphorical means of 'kicking Daddy'.

National Service

In the world we lost with industrialisation young men left home to live under a master's roof as a farm servant or an apprentice. By 1939 the custom had declined almost to vanishing point. Peacetime conscription, designed to build up trained military reserves, was a new phenomenon. For a decade it disrupted the rhythms and routines of family life, courtship and work. And for men born in the 1930s and early 1940s it proved an eye-opener. From 1949 to 1960 18-year-old men, except miners, merchant seamen, fishermen and police cadets, were called up for eighteen months or two years of National Service (the length varied across the decade). Indentured apprentices, articled pupils (training as accountants, architects and solicitors), students at university or teachers' training colleges could defer their call-up. Conscientious objectors were allowed to trade work in hospitals or farms for military service. The certifiably unfit were exempt. Legend has it that drama students coached young men who hoped to fail the medical. The effects of going without food and sleep and relying instead on 'those two good amigos Nick O'Teen and Al K Hall' were generally understood.

The Army, by far the commonest destination for National Servicemen, recruited over a million of them. As the cartoonist Mel Calman (born 1931) explained, in the Army, 'half adult boarding school, half lunatic asylum', 'you had to unlearn being an individual and become a number', an anonymous component in the military machine. Recruits were allowed to bring their own 'pyjamas, handkerchiefs, leather walking shoes and nail scissors', if they chose. The 'civvie' clothes they arrived in were parcelled up and posted home. Uniforms came in two sizes, 'too bloody big and too bloody small'. And only, in David Baxter's words, 'when a man has burnt his boots, battered his brasses, cooked his hat, scorched his battledress and reinforced his trousers with soap and his packs with cardboard is he properly dressed'. Five weeks of basic training – drill and bull – presided over by hectoring 'Lance-Jacks' – 'If you don't swing that arm, laddie, I'll tear it off, stick it up your arse and have you for a lollipop' – were designed to transform 'scruffy civilians' into smart soldiers, instinctively obedient and conditioned to polish the studs on the soles of their shoes and the backs of brass buckles, buttons and badges.

The authorities were on the look out for Potential Officer Material. A good record from the Combined Cadet Force, compulsory in most public and many grammar schools, weighed in a candidate's favour. Forty years on, men who were commissioned attributed their selection to the ingenuity they demonstrated in getting a team across a river or over an electric fence. The military authorities were astute enough to realise that a clever and self-confident young man 'would do less harm as an officer'. David Baxter set out to disqualify himself from a commission. He adopted a bogus Irish brogue and asserted hostility to the Union: 'For the rest of my army career, I was free from a false position of authority, and able to skirmish for a tolerable way of life'. Like other spoiled officers, he was drafted on to clerical duties. In the clerks' domain: 'uplift was in the air and satirical graffiti on the lavatory walls'.

Conscripts served in Aden, Brunei, the Cameroons, Cyprus, Gibraltar, Kenya,

Korea, Libya, Malaya, Malta, Palestine, on the Rhine – as part of the army of occupation in Germany – and in Singapore; 395 of them were killed. For survivors, National Service was a formative experience. They were 'confronted by life in a raw state'. For Edward Lucie-Smith (born 1933), 'a middle-class product of a scholarship mill', working as an education officer in the RAF was 'the revelation of another England'. He was 'shattered to discover how poorly most [men] had been taught' as schoolboys. Ears were opened to unfamiliar accents: 'Geordie, Scouse, Mancunian, Brummie, Jock, Cockney'. Les Wiles (born 1936) came from Wool-wich. As far as he was concerned, Geordie 'could just as well have been [the language] of an obscure Mongolian tribe, for all [he] understood of it'. Joining the Army after four years at art school, Mel Calman encountered men who 'spoke a language that said "cunt" instead of "woman" and "fuck" instead of "love".' On his first day in the RAF one National Serviceman counted in disbelief as an airman uttered the same seven-letter swearword 111 times in the course of a single hour. Servicemen's minds were expanded by 'lurid' images illustrating 'sores as big as saucers, tips of pricks rotting off'. When they went on leave they were issued with condoms or 'sports gear', as they were jocularly known. National Service left at least a semi-permanent mark: one former National Service officer, who went on to Cambridge to read English, found it took a long time to get out of the habit of looking at the landscape with a tactician's eye for cover and sight lines.

Getting married

Sex, even procreative sex sanctified by marriage, remained a delicate subject. It was considered indecorous to draw attention to the pregnancy of a respectable married woman. In 1947 when Lady Tweedsmuir (born 1915) attended the House of Commons visibly pregnant, colleagues remarked on her 'bonniness'. Many couples, looking back, remember that they did not 'sleep together properly' before they married, although 'a lot of exciting cuddling went on'. Joe Ashton, who did his courting in Sheffield, thought it was 'a miracle that anyone ever got to a shotgun wedding', couples had so little privacy. Bernard Palmer recalled his fellow National Servicemen who 'went on leave to girlfriends of their schooldays who would not mind the occasional hand up their knickers but who switched the light on the moment you tried to get your tongue between their cherry-red lips'. At the end of the 1940s Prue Marshall, an old girl of Cheltenham Ladies' College, and Julian Critchley (born 1930) an old boy of Shrewsbury, enjoyed 'necking': 'passionate embraces, much french-kissing, breast-baring and happy backseat fumbling'. In a hotel, they 'lay together naked save for our knickers', prevented from 'going all the way' by their mothers' admonitions. When in the 1940s couples talked about 'sleeping together in the same bed as each other', they probably meant just that. Such caution was understandable. Birth control clinics were still 'strictly reserved for *bona fide* married women' and those who could convince the clinic that they were shortly to achieve that status. Accidents happened. Late in 1947 Hilly Bardwell (born 1929) discovered that she was pregnant. Her lover Kingsley Amis (born 1922) tracked down an abortionist and contrived to borrow 100 guineas

(£110). Then he talked to a friend of a friend, a doctor who painted quite a different picture. 'There was perhaps 1 chance in 20 that Hilly would have a haemorrhage afterwards and die of it, that there was a much greater chance still that being deprived of her child would make her (a) bitter and (b) bitter towards me'. They 'agreed that it would be best to get married'. And they did. Even in the most bohemian circles pregnancy prompted marriages. Minors under 21 used a coming child to persuade reluctant or hostile parents to consent to their wedding. But 40 per cent of babies born outside marriage had parents who lived together, often passing as husband and wife – because only the 'innocent' partner could petition for divorce.

Faced with a pregnancy that, for one reason or another would not end in marriage, the grandmothers-to-be stepped into the breach. In the Essex village of Elmdon neighbours were generally sympathetic – 'There but for the grace of God . . .' was a common response. Women who concealed their pregnancies from their families, or whose parents were implacably hostile, resorted to mother-and-baby homes, most of them run by churches. Sometimes the regime was punitive. Unsupported mothers were pressed to give their babies up for adoption, by this time seen as the most appropriate solution to involuntary childlessness: in the mid-1950s, about 1000 babies were adopted each year. Adoptive parents, generally older, middle-class couples, required 'high quality' babies. Children with disabilities and children of mixed race were difficult to place.

Between the wars two children had been the suburban norm. After 1945 the two-child family was the generally accepted ideal. Wives who had been to college were inclined to have three or four children, a brood big enough to justify a 'career' of domesticity. In 1958 the Church of England gave its blessing to the use of artificial contraception – within marriage. The Roman Catholic establishment withheld its approval. Family planning clinics, pioneers of contraceptive advice, continued to favour the cap advocated by their founder Marie Stopes. Caps had some fans. Lella Florence, who had moved with her academic husband from Cambridge to Birmingham, produced a *Progress Report on Birth Control*, based on research done in 1948. She quoted the woman who wrote to ask her 'Dear Friends' at the clinic for their advice: 'I have not had a period for over 12 months now, must I still use my dear old cap, or can I say good-bye to my old friend?' Many women in Florence's sample (and beyond) were put off by the cost of scientific birth control – husbands expected them to pay for caps and other paraphernalia out of their 'wages', their housekeeping budgets. Lella Florence discovered that *coitus interruptus* was 'so common that many women think of it not as a contraceptive but as a normal part of sexual intercourse'. Frustration was the price of withdrawal. But the cap was not a passport to the joy of sex. Phyllis Willmott described 'the Dutch cap . . . shaped like a doll's bowler hat, with a hard rim of black rubber. When I put it in I felt like a stuffed chicken'. Little wonder that Lella Florence came to the conclusion that 'a safe and acceptable alternative to the cap is urgently needed'. The introduction of 'the pill' in the 1960s appeared to be an answer to her prayer.

Legal abortions were rare, though the number obtained on psychiatric grounds grew. Those able to couch their requests in appropriate terms (generally speaking, the more privileged and sophisticated) were the most likely to benefit from this loophole in the law. Terminations were available on a black market in which qualified medics and informally trained abortionists operated side by side. The motivation of practitioners varied. Greed coexisted with compassion. Illegal operations were often squalid and medically risky. When Susana Walton (born 1926), wife of the composer William Walton, found herself unintentionally pregnant in the late 1940s, her GP refused to help. She found an abortionist 'through friends of friends'. Following instructions, she went to a block of flats in Chelsea. 'In one [flat] I had to leave £80 on a ledge; in another I was shown a kitchen table and met a nameless man in a doctor's mask and gown'. When Peregrine Worsthorne's lover haemorrhaged after an illegal operation, he dialled 999: 'Not only did the ambulance arrive . . . so did the police'. The prospect of prosecution was real. But attitudes were shifting. The thousands of signatures collected in support of GPs with working-class practices who were imprisoned and struck off the Medical Register for carrying out illegal abortions on married women with more children than they could cope with demonstrated popular support for the liberalisation of the law. The fairly rapid reinstatement of some doctors convicted as abortionists indicated a shift in the position of the medical establishment.

Involuntary childlessness was assumed, by the majority of the medical profession, to be a female problem. Treatment was not available on the NHS. Artificial insemination using a donor's sperm (usually obtained from a medical or dental student) was discreetly practised by a small number of doctors.

We have descriptions of richly fulfilling marriages sustained and enriched by shared preoccupations. Frances Partridge (born 1900), an architect's daughter educated at Newnham, Cambridge, celebrated 'the pleasure of leading two lives instead of one, and one of them male'. 'We are like two mutually supporting creepers, each propping the other up and at the same time drawing sustenance and stimulation from the other's sap'. The Partridges were literati, Bloomsburies, pacifists. Prudence Rutherford (born 1916), the sporty daughter of an MP – she played lacrosse for England – married John Napier, a medic who had changed tack and became an authority on primates. As their children grew up, she became involved in her husband's projects as his secretary and lab assistant, 'her sons well remember returning home to find the house smelling of boiling monkey bones'. Mrs Napier became an authority on primates, first as her husband's collaborator, later in her own right. Collaboration of this kind was rare. As we have seen, married women were expected to immerse themselves in home and family until their children were off their hands. In suburban England a housewife's job title had not yet acquired the diminishing prefix 'only'. Wives employed at home enjoyed being their own 'bosses'. In traditional working-class communities, married women with children entered a largely female society, rich in kin and mutual aid. Social scientists investigating family and kinship in Bethnal Green recorded a spontaneous observation made by one of their small sons. 'The teacher asked us to draw pictures of our family. I did one of you and Mummy and Mickey and me, but isn't it funny, the others were putting in their Nannas and aunties and uncles and all sorts of people like that'.

Accounts of working-class marriages are often bleak. Jeremy Seabrook observed the shoe workers of Northampton: 'their lives seemed to us no lives at all, but austere sketches of living . . . astringent and without joy'. In the mining communities of the West Riding of Yorkshire, public displays of affection between husband and wife were unknown. The 'row' was an institution. Sexual relationships were inhibited by fear of unwanted pregnancies. It was widely considered – and not just in Yorkshire – that a 'lucky woman' was one whose husband 'didn't bother her often'. Wives were prepared to tolerate 'fancy women' so long as the extramarital relationship was discreet. In working-class Oxford, neighbours were aware of infidelities: 'He's one of the men that's twice married. He stays with one wife on Mondays and Tuesdays and the rest of the week with the other'. Adultery was not a male preserve: 'I know cases where they weren't all their father's children'. In Northamptonshire Jeremy Seabrook's father went 'whore-hopping all over Wellingborough'. Infidelity was far from his only shortcoming. Left in charge of his wife's butchery business in the days of meat rationing, he 'sold his allocation by Wednesday', and then went out and stole 'two sheep, a pig and numberless fowl and rabbits' to restock the shop. Carolyn Steedman (born 1947) remembered that 'in the mid-1950s' her father 'started to live in the attic, treated the place like a hotel'. He came home at six, collected phone messages connected with his job dealing with burst boilers, 'made a mug of tea, washed, went out to his other life'. In all classes, women with adulterous and otherwise unsatisfactory husbands put up with them for the sake of their children. Angela Fox (born 1912), wife of a stage-struck lawyer, speaks for them: 'preserving paternal stability for my boys was perhaps as important to me, if not more so, than keeping my husband'. Money was another reason for holding on to an errant husband. As the National Assistance Board expressed it,

> If a husband's earnings or other resources are not enough to maintain, besides himself, both his wife (with her children, if any) and the paramour (with her children, if any) the defect has got to be met at one point or other by assistance . . . Respect for the marriage tie suggests that it should be given to the legal wife who should be the prior charge on the husband's income.

It was 'easier to enforce the maintenance of those with whom the man is living than those from whom he has parted'.

Divorce and remarriage

Jane McIntire (born 1928) and Geoffrey Grigson (born 1905) set up home together in the mid-1950s but they were unable to marry for two decades. Jane McIntire formally changed her name to her partner's: it was as Jane Grigson that she built her reputation. The argument that the irretrievable breakdown of a marriage should be grounds for its dissolution gained strength from the rising number of such stable, overtly respectable but illicit families. Many couples carried their secret to the grave. Carolyn Steedman (born 1947) discovered her parents' story only after her father's death in 1977. He had deserted his wife and child and moved to London to make an ultimately unhappy new life with Steedman's mother. They passed as husband and wife not only before the neighbours but before statutory authority too. Steedman and her sister, as she explained, 'have proper birth certificates, because my mother must have told a simple lie to the registrar, a discovery about the verisimilitude of documents that worries me a lot as a historian'. Other lies were bolder. Nancy Brooker Spain's son Tom (born 1952) was registered as the son of Paul and Anne Brooker Seyler. Paul Seyler was almost certainly dead and Anne Brooker never existed. Like Carolyn Steedman, Tom Seyler eventually discovered his true parentage – his biological father was Pip Youngman Carter who had had 'kids v. car' arguments with his wife Margery Allingham in the 1930s.

In 1946 Michael Holroyd (born 1935) was the only boy in his prep school whose parents had divorced. An aura of 'rather daring wickedness' hung about him as a result. The end of the war led to what was a spate of divorces, terminating relationships fractured by prolonged separation and adultery. In the late 1940s and 1950s 'discreet' divorces became increasingly common but the 'guilty' could be given a hard time in court and afterwards, in the press and by their peers. In 1953 J. B. Priestley, the popular broadcaster and novelist, heard himself condemned from the Bench as 'mean', 'contemptible' and a liar. Readers of the *News of the World* (or 'the Screws', as it was nicknamed) frankly relished a juicy scandal. Readers of the 'quality' papers turned to the Law Reports. Francis Meynell and Alix Kilroy, in their own eyes husband and wife since 1933, found themselves at last in a position to marry in 1946 when Meynell's second wife Vera agreed to sue him for divorce. Alix Kilroy wished to be cited as co-respondent, 'for this I had to consult my employers' – she was a senior official in the Board of Trade. Her superiors raised no objection but, as a consequence of the divorce, Francis Meynell, the guilty party, was dropped from the invitation list to royal garden parties. The following year two judges, who had omitted divorces from their entries in *Who's Who*, suffered a similar fate when their matrimonial histories came to the Lord Chamberlain's notice.

Many divorces and the remarriages that prompted them passed off quietly. The radio personality Norman Hackforth (born 1908) lived with his future wife Mrs Pamela Buchanan for several years. As he recalled: 'Everybody, in fact, apart from our very closest friends, thought we were married'. When they were free to marry, they did so as quietly as possible. Hackforth found the staff of the register office both sympathetic and practised. The publication of the notice of the marriage and the ceremony itself were carefully timed to foil the journalists and photographers who fed the public appetite for scandal.

So far, divorce has been the focus of our attention. Two high-profile cases demonstrate that it was not divorce but remarriage in the lifetime of a former partner that the churches of England and of Rome condemned. Anthony Eden (born 1897) divorced his wife on the grounds of desertion. Several years later, in 1952, when Eden, now Foreign Secretary, remarried, the *Church Times* called for his resignation. News of the romance between the Queen's sister, Princess

Margaret (born 1930), and Group Captain Peter Townsend (born 1914) broke in the month of the Coronation. Townsend had been the 'innocent party' in a divorce. To allow things to cool down, he was dispatched to Brussels to serve as air attaché at the embassy. The Princess's twenty-fifth birthday revived interest in the relationship. In October 1955, 'mindful of the Church's teaching that Christian marriage is indissoluble, and conscious of [her] duty to the commonwealth', the Princess announced that the marriage would not take place. *Daily Mirror* readers voted roughly 68,000 to 2000 in favour of the match.

Old age

Old people were among the groups to attract the attention of sociologists in post-war London. The social scientist Peter Townsend published his classic *The Family Life of Old People* in the mid-1950s. In working-class Bethnal Green men and women who had been born towards the end of Queen Victoria's reign, who had worked all their lives at physically demanding tasks and lived through two world wars and the great slump that came between, often saw themselves as 'old' in their sixties. Intellectuals like E. M. Forster (born 1879) shared this malaise. In July 1948 Forster noted in his Commonplace Book that 'My mouth keeps dropping open today and reminds me of the long-intended note on my physical decay. Age 69 years, 6 months.' He itemised trouble with his toenails, left ankle, left shin, farts, arsehole, piss, belly, ears, eyes, moustache, hair and teeth.

As Townsend discovered, men and women experienced old age differently. For working men retirement spelled the loss of status and identity as well as a drop in income. (Around a quarter of old age pensioners relied on means-tested supplements.) Husbands were not welcome at home where they got under their wives' feet. 'Voluntary retirement was rare in Bethnal Green'. Many women moved seamlessly from having their youngest – and almost inevitably favourite child – at home to having the special first grandchild to dote on. They remained active members of a female network, in daily contact with daughters and grandchildren living no more than a few minutes' walk away. Mothers and daughters exchanged services. One daughter, helped by her children, did her mother's shopping, cleaning and washing, walked her dog and had her round for Sunday dinner. The other six days of the week granny cooked their midday dinners for them. Another woman, arthritic, deaf and incontinent, was, all the same, able to help her daughter with the cooking, washing and childminding. She was still an expert baby bather. In these close-knit families a child might explain to a visitor, 'I live with my Nan and go upstairs to my Mummy to sleep'.

Townsend stressed particularity within these broad patterns. Some of the old people were clubbable and enjoyed a coach trip and a 'knees-up'. Others saw organised entertainment as an assault on their independence.

> You are pushed on a bus at such and such a time. You get pushed into dinner and tea. It's like a Sunday school outing . . . If I want to go to Brighton, it's my day out. I'm free and I've got money in my pocket and I can do what I like.

A 70-year-old man and his 78-year-old aunt, brought up together as children, took themselves out every Saturday to see a show. This habit was unusual enough for Townsend to describe their relationship as 'almost a courtship'. Old married couples did not often go out together in spite of the lack of home entertainment – by 1955 only one in five of his sample had television sets. Mrs Bassy gave a grim account of her marriage: We don't sleep together, we don't. He has his room and I have mine. He hasn't spoken to me for more than a fortnight'. Other relationships mellowed with age as man and wife found a 'new serenity and affection'.

Distinguished men were feted in old age. The celebrated playwright G. B. Shaw reached his ninetieth birthday in 1946. Penguin published ten of his works in editions of 100,000: the 'Shaw Million'. The National Book League put on an exhibition. The Poet Laureate produced a birthday poem. A renewed interest in folksong brought old countrymen and women into the spotlight: Granny Thorn of Preston Candover in Hampshire was 93 when she came to the collectors' notice.

Frail old people beyond coping on their own were taken into residential care; they were generally the oldest, unmarried, widowed and childless. Benevolent societies cared for former gardeners, governesses, members of the National Union of Teachers, theatricals, cinematographic workers and past members of many other callings in homes concentrated in the home counties and on the south coast. By 1957 the south coast was 'one long geriatric belt, full of widows'; more lavender water was sold there than anywhere else in the UK. In the industrial north the Roman Catholic Church was an important provider of care for the old. And there were proprietary residential and nursing homes to accommodate those with the personal or family means to pay their fees.

Although Aneurin Bevan (born 1897) had abolished union workhouses, feared and hated since they were set up under the New Poor Law of 1834, their buildings still housed the old and needy. Some of the surviving workhouses were huge: Luxborough Lodge in London had a population of over a thousand. In unmodernised institutions, wards slept forty. In the worst, old people were deprived of personal possessions: they had no clothes of their own, no family photographs were allowed; birthdays went unmarked. The wards stank of urine. Ruth Richardson recalled that

> As a child in the mid-1950s in London's Notting Hill, I can clearly remember the local belief that the chimney of a nearby hospital (an old workhouse infirmary) belched the smoke of human fuel. In my school playground small children nodded knowingly, and told each other that those who went in never came out . . . People associated hopelessness, coercion, death, and unspeakable *post-mortem* treatment with the bleak exterior of the old workhouse.

Death

Excused National Service as a conscientious objector, David Hockney (born 1937) worked as a hospital orderly in the late 1950s. Looking back, he was aware of a seasonal pattern of mortality:

It happened to be in the winter . . . and a lot of people in Bradford, especially in those days, suffered with bronchitis: old people who had got bronchitis just came in and died, and there were always lots of people dying in that way . . . They were mostly near seventy-five or eighty.

In rural Suffolk in the 1950s, the professional services of the undertaker had not finally displaced the homely care of the newly dead: George Ewart Evans helped his neighbour Priscilla Savage lay out her husband, his friend Robert. Following her instructions, he placed the old man's hands by his sides 'so that he would lie quite naturally. He was still quite warm when [they] had finished and he looked very peaceful'. Old mourning customs persisted. In Cumberland in the 1950s funeral guests were still served with special biscuits and rum butter. George Orwell (died 1950), scourge of the establishment, opted for an Anglican service for his funeral and a country churchyard for his grave. But the means of disposing of the dead were changing. In 1950 one in six was cremated, ten years later one in three was. The Sussex countryman and singer Jim Copper (born 1882) explained his wish to be cremated to his son Bob (born 1915): 'When I die, boy, have me burnt and then you take my cinders up on the hill and shake 'em round that old boundstone near Blind Pit', a 'favourite spot' since his childhood.

The casualties of National Service were buried with military honours. But they were mourned as sons and sweethearts too. Paul Skeaping (born 1929), the son of a distinguished sculptor, was killed in a flying accident. 'Only his charred and unrecognisable remains' were found. His father John made a seven-foot crucifix from the branches of a cedar tree: 'instead of carving', he 'burned the wood away with a powerful blow-lamp'. 'It had real meaning'.

Like old people, widows came under the sociologists' scrutiny in the 1950s. Dead husbands often remained a strong 'presence' in the homes they had shared. Some were comforted by the sound of his voice and footsteps; other found the manifestations unbearable. 'I used to hear his key in the door and the swish of his coat along the balcony. I just couldn't stand it.' Widows with young children had strong reservations about remarriage. As one explained, 'It would be a good idea for myself . . . For the children, no!' These women embraced the whole burden of parenting, as their mothers or grandmothers might have done, turning to male relatives, more often hers than his, for help with the man's jobs about the house and garden. Older widows were reluctant to give up their homes and move in with a married child. They valued their privacy and their independence and were acutely aware of the potential for conflict with sons- and daughters-in-law. All the same, some women who had been confined for decades to the domestic sphere were defeated by 'even the smallest practical problem' beyond that frontier – such widows' unmarried children were under pressure to stay that way. In working-class families, these home-mates, male or female, 'took the place of the husband as wage earner' and were not 'expected to do much in the home'. Older widows without children were particularly hard hit, one confided: 'I get so lonely I could fill up the teapot with tears'.

Reading

Banham, Mary and Hillier, Bevis (eds), *A Tonic to the Nation: the Festival of Britain, 1951* (Thames and Hudson, 1976).

Baxter, David, *Two Years to Do* (The Hague Press, 1959).

Beadle, Muriel, *These Ruins are Inhabited* (Robert Hale, 1963).

Berkeley, Humphry, *The Life and Death of Rochester Sneath: a youthful frivolity* (Davis-Poynter, 1965).

Bowlby, John, *Maternal Care and Mental Health: a report prepared on behalf of the World Health Organisation as a contribution to the United Nation's programme for the welfare of homeless children* (World Health Organisation, 1951).

Bowlby, John, *Childcare and the Growth of Love* (Penguin, 1965).

Cecil, Hugh and Cecil, Mirabel, *Clever Hearts: Desmond and Molly MacCarthy – a biography* (Gollancz, 1990).

Critchley, Julian, *A Bag of Boiled Sweets: an autobiography* (Faber & Faber, 1994).

Curl, James Stevens, *The Cutteslowe Walls: a study in social class* (Faber & Faber, 1963).

David, Elizabeth, *A Book of Mediterranean Food* (John Lehmann, 1950).

Dennis, Norman *et al.*, *Coal is our Life: an analysis of a Yorkshire mining community* (Eyre & Spottiswoode, 1956).

Evans, George Ewart, *The Strength of the Hills: an autobiography* (Faber & Faber, 1983).

Faulkner, Lucy (ed.), *The Light of Other Days – oral history from Wisbech* (Fenland Oral History Project, University of Cambridge, Board of Continuing Education, 1998).

Fitzgibbon, Theodora, *Love Lies a Loss: an autobiography, 1946–1959* (Century, 1985).

Glass, Ruth, *Newcomers: the West Indians in London* (Centre for Urban Studies/George Allen & Unwin, 1960).

Gosling, Ray, *Personal Copy: a memoir of the sixties* (Faber & Faber, 1980).

Gould, Tony, *A Summer Plague: polio and its survivors* (Yale University Press, 1995).

Gray, Patience and Boyd, Primrose, *Plats du Jour* (Penguin, 1957).

Harris, John, *No Voice from the Hall: early memories of a country house snooper* (John Murray, 1998).

Hennessy, Peter, *Never Again: Britain 1945–1951* (Cape, 1992).

Kerr, Madeline, *The People of Ship Street* (Routledge, 1958).

Leader, Zachary (ed.), *The Letters of Kingsley Amis* (HarperCollins, 2000).

Longford, Elizabeth, *Points for Parents* (Weidenfeld & Nicolson, 1954).

MacBeth, George, *A Child of the War* (Cape, 1987).

Marris, Peter, *Widows and their Families* (Routledge & Kegan Paul, 1958).

Meynell, Alix, *Public Servant, Private Woman: an autobiography* (Gollancz, 1988).

Mogey, J. M., *Family and Neighbourhood: two studies in Oxford* (Oxford University Press, 1956).

Opie, Iona and Opie, Peter, *The Lore and Language of School Children* (Clarendon Press, 1959).

Partridge, Frances, *Everything to Lose: diaries 1945–60* (Gollancz, 1985).

Patterson, Sheila, *Dark Strangers: a sociological study of the absorption of a recent West Indian migrant group in Brixton, South London* (Tavistock, 1963).

Pottle, Mark (ed.), *Daring to Hope: the diaries and letters of Violet Bonham Carter, 1946–1969* (Weidenfeld & Nicolson, 2000).

Royle, Trevor, *The Best Years of their Lives: the National Service experience, 1945–1963* (John Murray, 1986).

Seabrook, Jeremy, *Mother and Son: an autobiography* (Gollancz, 1979).

Spock, Benjamin, *Baby and Child Care* (Bodley Head, 1955).

Steedman, Carolyn, *Landscape for a Good Woman: a story of two lives* (Virago, 1986).

Strathern, Marilyn, *Kinship at the Core: an anthropology of Elmdon, a village in north-west Essex in the nineteen-sixties* (Cambridge University Press, 1981).

Summers, Dorothy, *The East Coast Floods* (David & Charles, 1978).

Swift, Rebecca (ed.), *Letters from Margaret: correspondence between Bernard Shaw and Margaret Wheeler, 1945–1950* (Chatto & Windus, 1992).

Townsend, Peter, *The Family Life of Old People: an inquiry in East London* (Routledge & Kegan Paul, 1957).

Wildeblood, Peter, *Against the Law* (Weidenfeld & Nicolson, 1955).

Willans, Geoffrey, *Down with Skool* (Max Parrish, 1953).

Willmott, Peter and Young, Michael, *Family and Class in a London Suburb* (Routledge & Kegan Paul, 1960).

Willmott, Phyllis, *Joys and Sorrows: fragments from the post-war years* (Peter Owen, 1995).

Winfield, Pamela, *Bye Bye Baby: the story of the children the GIs left behind* (Bloomsbury, 1992).

Young, Michael and Willmott, Peter, *Family and Kinship in East London* (Routledge & Kegan Paul, 1957).

5   Runaway world, 1960–1979

A world under threat

The tense relationship between Russia and the West fuelled a fear that the end of the world might be at hand. The Campaign for Nuclear Disarmament (CND) was launched in 1958. The writer J. B. Priestley (born 1894); the philosopher Bertrand Russell (born 1872); Kingsley Martin (born 1897), editor of the *New Statesman*; and Canon John Collins (born 1905) were founder members. The 1960s are remembered as the decade of 'youthquake' but, at the start, middle-aged and elderly radicals were in the vanguard. The young were not far behind, however. The overwhelming majority of those who marched in protest against nuclear weapons were in their teens and early twenties; many were students.

A sense of loss was pervasive. In *Cider with Rosie*, published in 1959 after a long gestation, Laurie Lee (born 1914) pictured the lost world of country life before the buses ran. *Rosie*'s illustrator, John Ward, sketched dream cottages with jam jars full of wild flowers by the kitchen sink and old china 'some of it even perfect' on the mantleshelf. Published in 1963, Rachel Carson's *Silent Spring* denounced the 'reckless and irresponsible poisoning' caused by farmers' use of pesticides. Carson (born 1907) was American. Sir Julian Huxley (born 1887), a distinguished scientist known to the listening public as a member of the BBC Brains Trust, supplied evidence of devastation close to home in his introduction to the English edition:

> From the royal estate at Sandringham in Norfolk the list of dead birds included pheasants, red-legged partridges, wood pigeons and stock doves, greenfinches, chaffinches, blackbirds, song thrushes, skylarks, moorhens, bramblings, tree sparrows, house sparrows, jays, yellowhammers, hedge sparrows, carrion crows, hooded crows, goldfinches and sparrowhawks. Peregrines had largely disappeared from the south of England. Cuckoos had become 'quite scarce', many kinds of butterflies had virtually disappeared.
>
> Country hedgerows and road verges are losing their familiar flowers. In fact, as my brother Aldous said, after reading Rachel Carson's book, we are losing half the subject matter of English poetry.

Thirty-five years earlier Aldous Huxley (born 1894) had drawn attention to the rising consumption of finite resources in his novel *Point Counter Point*. Huxley had the scientific amateur Lord Edward Tantamount deplore the 'real good guzzle' of fossil fuels: 'Take coal, for example. Man's using a hundred and ten times as much as he used in 1800. But the population is only two and a half times what it was'.

Richard Mabey's *Food for Free: A guide to the edible wild plants* [and shellfish] *of Britain* came out in 1972. His goal was to introduce his readers to the hundreds of 'wild food products' to be found in the British Isles, '130 of which are common'. His haul included nuts, fungi, horseradish and other roots, watercress, samphire, herbs, spices, flowers and fruit. *Vole*, launched in October 1977, campaigned for 'real life'. The *Vole* reader was cosily 'fond of good beer, good bread, good cheese, good books, good bikes, and old buildings and mushrooms and blue-tits and canals and railways and shove-ha'penny boards'. In 1979, in anticipation of the election, *Vole* published 'Green' and 'Groan' lists of candidates.

The appetite for cheap food prevailed. Barley barons built up their acreages, hedgerows were grubbed up, stock was driven off the land and the 'factory farm' was conceived. Pigs were packed in a thousand to the acre; hens kept as egg-layers were confined to cages for ten months and sold on to the soup canners; birds intended for the 'fried chicken trade' were raised in broiler sheds. 'Chicken', reserved for high days and holidays in the 1950s, became an everyday dish.

Everyday things

Profound, sometimes disorienting changes affected everyday life. Railway branch lines had been closing since the 1920s. In the 1950s, the number of private cars doubled; new fleets of lorries and coaches poached freight and passengers. By the 1960s it was hardly more expensive for business people to fly between London and Manchester or Glasgow – and a good deal more glamorous. Dr Richard Beeching (born 1913), chaired the British Railways Board between 1963 and 1965. His axe cut fast and deep: more than 2000 stations, 5000 miles of track and 70,000 staff were pruned. In 1965 the old telephone numbers – WHItehall 1212 was Scotland Yard's – were replaced by all-figure codes. Local government was reorganised. The county of Rutland, lauded by W. G. Hoskins (born 1908) as 'that small part of England as it used to be before the Industrial Revolution – unspoiled, clean, full of fine buildings, of country smell and sounds' was reduced to a district council.

Inflation and decimalisation combined to rob people of the history in their pockets, not just the familiar denominations but the gallery of bas-relief portraits of kings and queens, the oldest displaying the wear and patina conferred by more than a century in circulation. On 15 February 1971 £ s d, which echoed the ancient Roman 'librum, solidus, denarius', were discarded. The old penny (twelve to the shilling) disappeared and the shilling (twenty to the pound) became the 5 pence piece. Metrication of weight, capacity, length and area began in 1974. The sole survivors of the old imperial regime were to be the pint, for draught beer, cider and bottled milk; on the roads, the mile. And time. The calendar with its leap years and uneven months, 60-minute hours and 60-second minutes was unaffected. Not even the 'ages of man' were exempt from the winds of change blowing through England. In 1970 the age of majority was reduced from 21: an 18–year-old could now vote and marry without seeking permission. A curious generation gap opened up in the 1960s and 1970s. At the end of the century many older people still thought in inches, feet and yards, measured ingredients in pounds and ounces and used the Fahrenheit scale for temperatures.

A new society?

The journal *New Society* first appeared in October 1962. Its opening words, taken from Sean O'Casey's play *Juno and the Paycock*, were: 'The whole world is in a terrible state of chassis [chaos]'. Principles that had governed English society and English families time out of mind were called in question. The Peerage Act 1963 allowed hereditary members of the House of Lords to renounce their birthright. Few did. Among them were two reluctant heirs whose peerages had been thrust upon them. Viscount Stansgate, the Act's principal advocate, returned to the Commons as Anthony Wedgwood Benn. (He shed 'Wedgwood' in 1972.) Viscount Hailsham (born 1907), whose political ambitions had been dashed by his father's elevation to the peerage in 1929, resumed life as Quintin Hogg. The fourteenth Earl of Home renounced his title to lead a shortlived Conservative administration. Both Hogg and Home returned to the Lords as life peers.

   The history of England was rewritten – very largely by men and women working outside the university mainstream. In 1963 Edward Thompson (born 1924), a tutor used to enthusing 'evening classes of working people, trades unionists, white-collar people, teachers', published *The Making of the English Working Class*. Thompson's object was to rescue 'the poor stockinger, the Luddite cropper, the "obsolete" hand-loom weaver' and 'the "utopian" artisan' 'from the enormous condescension of posterity'. History Workshop was Raphael Samuel's brainchild, 'an attempt to replace the hierarchical relationship of tutor and pupil by one of comradeship in which each became, in some sort, co-learners'. Comrades could be female: in 1970 History Workshop set up a national women's conference, the first conference of the Women's Movement held in England. The periodical, *History Workshop*, launched in 1976, was subtitled 'a journal of socialist and feminist historians'.

Topical lions

There were new stars in the social firmament. The celebrity was not a novel feature of the social scene. Victorian High Society had issued 'strictly temporary tickets of admission' to 'topical "lions" belonging to all races and vocations'. The Great Train Robbery of August 1963 – a thriller played in real time – caught the popular imagination. The impudent and almost victimless crime, the gaol breaks and the years on the run lent the robbers a spurious but enduring glamour. David Bailey's *Box of Pin-ups* (1965) contained images of actors – Michael Caine (born 1933) and Terence Stamp (born 1938); an advertising man – David Puttnam (born 1941); an artist – David Hockney (born 1937); a dancer – Rudolf Nureyev (born 1939); a decorator – David Hicks (born 1929); East End gangsters – the Kray brothers; a hairdresser – Vidal Sassoon (born 1928); photographers – Cecil Beaton (born 1904), Lord Snowdon (born 1930), Terence Donovan (born 1936); and popular musicians – John Lennon (born 1940) and Paul McCartney (born 1942) of the Beatles and Mick Jagger (born 1943) of the Rolling Stones. Lower-middle-class grammar school boys were prominent. Beaton (Charterhouse and Cambridge), Snowdon (Eton and Cambridge) and Hicks (Charterhouse), who were, not by chance, the oldest of the pinups, represented the public schools. Forty years on, the survivors were still 'lions'. Sporting heroes came into money: until 1961 footballers' earnings had been on a par with miners or long-distance lorry drivers. With the end of the lifetime contract and the maximum wage, stars were paid as stars. In 1969 George Best (born 1946), the son of a shipyard worker from Northern Ireland, was earning £5000 *a week* from the sport. For years virtually every amateur gentleman who was a serious cricketer had depended on the game for his living. Players who were paid a wage by their counties were accommodated in separate, usually inferior dressing rooms and third class railway carriages (while the amateurs travelled first class); their sandwiches were spread with margarine (not butter). The distinction ended in 1963.

Canny politicians recognised the importance of being ordinary. Harold Wilson, who became prime minister in 1964, was born (in 1916) into a solid, if unglamorous, middle-class family. Son of an industrial chemist, Wilson was brought up in a *Guardian*-reading, motorised household, with the *Children's Encyclopaedia* on the shelf and a Hornby train to play with. When his father was unemployed for nearly two years in the early 1930s, the family was able to scrape by on his savings. Wilson was an Oxford graduate. Yet he preferred to portray himself as a plain Yorkshireman, proud of his homely provincial ways. In 1962 he told the *Daily Express* that if he 'had the choice between smoked salmon and tinned salmon, I'd have it tinned. With vinegar. I prefer beer to wine and if I get the chance to go home I have a North Country high tea – without wine'. While members of the old cultural elite still boasted that they had never been 'poor enough to own a television set', Harold Wilson identified *Coronation Street* as his favourite programme: 'The people in it seem to be real'. In 1975 Margaret Thatcher (born 1926), daughter of a provincial shopkeeper, another Oxford graduate, equally determined to assert her modest social origins, when it suited her, would became the first female party leader. She emerged from the general election of 1979 as prime minister.

The 'liberal hour'

Roy Jenkins (born 1920) was an Oxford man of an older type, a poshocrat by adoption and a liberal on social questions, among them several that affected family life. Jenkins became Home Secretary in December 1965. He had published *Is Britain Civilised?* in the run-up to the 1959 election. The 'ghastly apparatus of the gallows' had been effectively demolished by the time Jenkins took office. In 1967 flogging was removed from the penal code; the 'brutal and unfair' laws 'relating to homosexuality' were relaxed; the 'harsh and archaic abortion laws' were replaced. The power of 'absolute censorship', which the Lord Chamberlain had possessed 'over all the public theatres of London', was revoked in 1968. The divorce laws, cause of much distress and undetected perjury, were rewritten in 1969.

There were radicals in the established church too; Michael Ramsey (born 1904), Archbishop of Canterbury from 1961 to 1974, endorsed the liberal agenda. His father was a nonconformist mathematics lecturer at Cambridge; his mother an Oxford graduate, a campaigner for women's suffrage and a Labour Party activist. Ramsey lived up to his pedigree. He was against the death penalty. He accepted the irretrievable breakdown of marriage as a ground for divorce, and rape, risk to the mother's life, mental or physical health and likelihood that a child might be born with severe disabilities as grounds for abortion. In church affairs he was equally audacious. He loosened the ties between church and state. His instincts were ecumenical: he advocated reunion with the Methodists. He met the Pope. He acquiesced in the ordination of women in Hong Kong. John Robinson's million-selling *Honest to God* came out in 1963. Robinson (born 1919), Bishop of Woolwich, argued that there was no obligation on a Christian to believe that Jesus was 'the son of a Supernatural Being sent from heaven'. By exposing academic debate to the public gaze, Robinson dented the unquestioning faith of unsophisticated laymen and women. During these decades the Church of England was in retreat: theological colleges closed, churches were declared redundant. Fewer babies were baptised. Fewer couples chose to be married in church. The distressed and despairing turned elsewhere for succour – the Samaritans, active in London since 1953, set up branches across the country. Alternative spiritualities, mind-expanding drugs and practices attracted some young people. What came to be called retail therapy was a palliative for more.

It's different for girls

The 1960s was a man's decade: David Bailey's only female pin-ups were models. At the start of the 1960s organised feminists were a negligible force. To her son Anthony Wedgwood Benn, Lady Stansgate (born 1897) and her fellow advocates of women's ordination appeared 'rather an ageing crowd'. Germaine Greer's *The Female Eunuch*, published in 1970, helped to make women's liberation a hot issue for a minority of mostly young, mostly metropolitan women. Greer (born 1939) argued that when the Victorian and Edwardian opponents of female suffrage

> lamented that women's emancipation would mean an end of marriage, morality and the state; their extremism was more clear-sighted that the woolly benevolence of liberals and humanists, who thought that giving women a measure of freedom would not upset anything. When we reap the harvest, which the unwitting suffragettes sowed, we shall see that the anti-feminists were after all right.

At the start of the twenty-first century, Greer's words have a prophetic ring.

Equal pay, equal opportunities for education and employment, free contraception, abortion on demand, free 24-hour nurseries were on to the agenda of the women's movement – so was sexual fulfilment. The chant 'What do we want? Everything.' 'When do we want it? Now.' summarised the radical manifesto. Veteran campaigners for women's rights were appalled by its naivety. Contempt for men was an article of faith for many newly politicised women, ignorant of or indifferent to the part male feminists had played in extending women's rights and opportunities over the preceding century. 'Women need men like fish need bicycles' was a favourite slogan. It is worth remembering that the Equal Pay Act 1970 and the Sex Discrimination Act 1975 were sponsored by governments and passed through Houses of Commons and Lords that were overwhelmingly male. Prompted by the campaign to liberate women from their traditional burdens, a minority of men argued that the roles and responsibilities they were traditionally expected to shoulder oppressed them too.

A combination of hormones and surgery made it possible though painful, expensive and socially difficult to 'change sex'. Some gender shifts were carried through with discretion. A sentence printed opposite the title page of *The Pleasures of a Tangled Life*, which was published in 1989, identifies the author as 'Jan Morris, who was born in 1926, lived and wrote as James Morris until 1972, when she completed a change of sexual role'. Though the registration of Morris's birth could not be amended, official bodies like the Department of Health and Social Security and the Passport Office 'responded with an unexpected flexibility'. At Cambridge University Library a cataloguer carefully tippexed 'James' to read 'Jan'. The Morrises' marriage came to an end but, as Jan Morris explained, she and Elizabeth were 'locked' in their friendship 'more absolutely than ever'. Mark, the eldest of their children, 'read every word of *Conundrum* (1974)', Jan Morris's auto-biographical reflections, 'in its successive drafts'. In an epilogue written for a new edition of the book published in 1986, Morris reported that 'Elizabeth, my children and I are all living happily ever after'. Other families found the road hard.

Immigration

Immigration from Cyprus, the Caribbean and the Indian sub-continent was a feature of the 1960s. Very often, the first-comers saw themselves as expatriates, sending money home, going back eventually. The security of a familiar culture and the reserve and suspicion of host communities encouraged incomers to keep themselves to themselves, to work with and for compatriots. Corner shops, takeaways and small restaurants were enterprises that suited families – a rota of reliable workers made it possible to open all hours; today's takings paid for tomorrow's stock. Pioneers acted as agents for brothers, nephews, cousins and neighbours. Women and children followed. Serial migration caused problems for families. Children found themselves reunited with parents they hardly recognised: a face might 'ring a bell' but be hard to place. Integration proved difficult. Old stereotypes persisted. Robinson's the jam-makers were still using a golliwog as their trademark at the end of the 1960s. In 1969 Julie Burchill (born 1959) borrowed a costume from the firm to wear in a fancy dress competition; 'a red satin jacket, striped satin trousers (blue and yellow), an Afro wig'. Politicians played the race card. In 1964 Peter Griffiths, Tory candidate for Smethwick, fought under the banner 'If you want a nigger for a neighbour, vote Labour'. In 1968, the Conservative MP Enoch Powell prophesied race war. The Race Relations Act 1968 outlawed discrimination in employment and housing.

Public decency, private morality

In print and performance, the bounds of public decency were breached. The Chatterley trial of 1960 is a landmark in the history of propriety. *Lady Chatterley's Lover* had been available to the chattering classes since the 1930s. Penguin now proposed to publish it in paperback. The novel offended on several grounds. Lady Chatterley's adultery with her husband's gamekeeper – an uncouth man who talked of his "ut' – betrayed an officer disabled in the First World War and turned the conventional model of liaisons between male aristocrat and female servant on its head. There were explicit descriptions of sexual acts expressed in four-letter words. As a later literary critic put it, 'Lady C was fucked, sucked, buggered and blown'. The prosecution appealed to social prejudice and patriarchy: this was not a suitable book for factory girls, 'your wife or your servants'. Most of the witnesses called for the defence – among them C. Day Lewis (born 1904), appointed Poet Laureate in 1968; the novelist E. M. Forster (born 1879); the film critic Dilys Powell (born 1901); the historian Veronica Wedgwood (born 1910) – belonged, by birth or adoption, to the servant-keeping classes. Richard Hoggart (born 1918), who saw himself 'cast' by the defence as 'the northern working-class provincial', was perhaps its most effective witness. The jury sided with Hoggart. And the book sold like hot cakes. A student at Durham University bought his mother a copy: 'She disappeared off into the sitting room for two days'. Her verdict was: 'It's just like real life'. For other first-time readers, *Lady Chatterley's Lover* was a revelation. The journalist Mary Stott (born 1907), the daughter of journalists, had grown up 'with only childish euphemisms for urination and defecation'; 'no one had given [her] even a childish word for penis'. Until 1960 she 'had no idea what f——— meant'; none of the men she knew 'would have dreamed of using it' in front of her. She had never heard of oral sex. She believed that married women rarely, if indeed ever, experienced orgasm. Censorship was not dead: in 1963 Sheffield purged its libraries of *Fanny Hill*.

The Profumo 'volcano', which erupted in 1961, exposed the seamy side of the London high life. John Profumo (born 1915) was only one of a number of members of the Macmillan government identified as associates of prostitutes and active homosexuals. *Private Eye*, rightly credited with a major part in fanning the flames, was a metropolitan organ. The late night Saturday television show *That Was the Week That Was* (TW3) reached parts of Britain that *Private Eye* did not. To the New Zealander Bryan Gould (born 1939), *TW3* conveyed 'the almost palpable sense of a society on the move'. The BBC dropped the programme in December 1963. But the family's new 'friend' from the 1950s continued to bring subversive visitors into the nation's living rooms. Mary Whitehouse (born 1910) spearheaded a campaign to clean up television. She claimed to have counted 103 'bloodies' in one episode of *Till Death Us Do Part*, a comedy series launched in 1964, before she gave up. In 1965 the critic and journalist Kenneth Tynan (born 1927) said 'fuck' live on television. 'Julian' and 'Sandy', camp characters in the radio comedy series *Round the Home*, broadcast between 1965 and 1969, introduced gay 'palare' to the home audience. BBC plays brought home issues like homelessness and abortion.

Playwrights and directors pushed back the boundaries of the permissible. Drawing on the vulgar tradition of the music hall, *Oh! What a Lovely War* burlesqued and undermined the establishment version of the First World War, a central theme in the private histories of many English families. In the 'lovely war', upper-class, silly-ass generals sent working-class lions over the top to be slaughtered. According to its director, Joan Littlewood (born 1914), the show awakened its audience's 'race memory'. 'At the end of each performance people would come up on stage bringing memories and mementoes'. Although the Lord Chamberlain's jurisdiction over London theatres persisted until 1968, stage societies had been putting on private Sunday-night performances for decades. And the censors were evidently infected by the liberalising tendency. Joe Orton (born 1933) originally called the three-star brothel in *Loot* (1967) 'Consummatum est'. Unsurprisingly, the Lord Chamberlain's office vetoed the proposal – these were after all the words attributed to the dying Christ in the Latin version of the New Testament. 'Kingdom Come' was the alternative suggested. The last prosecution brought by the Lord Chamberlain's office, in February 1966, was prompted by the representation not of sex but of violence – the stoning to death of a baby in Edward Bond's *Saved*. Permissiveness was pervasive. Late in the 1960s the Customs Service returned a magazine to David Hockney it had intercepted endorsed 'nudes: semi-erect'. The tabloid press took full advantage of the new climate: the first bare-breasted Page Three Girls appeared in the *Sun*.

In 1971 Penguin, a publishing house with its finger on the nation's cultural pulse, brought out Lucy Mair's survey of *Marriage*. Looked at in a global context, the current English ideal – 'marriage for love' – was, as Mair pointed out, 'exceptional'. Sentimental and sexual satisfaction were not the institution's prime purposes. Nor were husbands 'necessary'. In African townships and in the Caribbean, unmarried women brought children up, though 'often under great difficulty'. Mair drew attention to the Zambian Ngonis' concept of a 'poorly fixed' marriage, a relationship entered into without formal preliminaries. A relationship that lasted 'fixed' itself. In 1971 the publishers expected readers to find these ideas 'new'. Thirty years later single mothers and couples who had set up home without benefit of ceremony were to be found in almost every street in England.

Biographical writing was of unprecedented frankness. Homosexuality was a powerful new theme. Duncan Grant (born 1885) was shocked when he was shown the draft of Michael Holroyd's biography of Lytton Strachey, published in 1967–68. In old age Quentin Crisp nominated himself a 'stately homo'. His work as a life model in art schools provided the title for his autobiography *The Naked Civil*

Servant, which came out in 1968. Impersonated by John Hurt (born 1940), Crisp strutted into the nation's living room in 1975. In *Kathleen and Frank* (1972), his biography of his parents, Christopher Isherwood (born 1904) publicly declared his own homosexuality: 'Society can afford to overlook the deviant behaviour of an elderly, otherwise respectable, literary man who has sufficient savings in the bank'. The following year Nigel Nicolson (born 1917) published *Portrait of a Marriage*, which revealed his parents' bisexuality. Its reception was mixed: 'A few of my parents' friends expressed misgivings but most confirmed my growing conviction that in the 1970s an experience of this kind need no longer be regarded as shameful and unmentionable'.

The privacy of more ordinary people was breached when adopted children were given the right to obtain information about their parents' identity.

'The Winter of Discontent'

The 1970s ended in disillusion and disarray. 'The Winter of Discontent' (1978–79) was ushered in by demands for big pay rises, backed up by strikes and threats of strikes. Car workers, fire-fighters, bakers, television technicians (who could now face a family Christmas with a blacked-out screen?), tanker and lorry drivers won substantial increases. Their success provoked action by low-paid workers in the public services. Schools and hospitals were hit, roads went ungritted, rubbish piled up in the streets. Liverpool gravediggers refused to bury the dead. The Tory slogan 'Labour isn't working' struck home.

Family economics

Fewer boys took up their father's trades. By the late 1960s, fieldworkers in the Suffolk village of Akenfield were mostly on the 'wrong side' of 50: bad pay and poor housing had driven younger men off the land. In 1962, when anthropology students first came to study Elmdon, an Essex village fourteen miles from Cambridge, it was a farming community with 'kinship at the core' – there were ten households with the surname Hammond. In 1979 only one remained. Mechanical sorting, made possible by the new system of national postcodes, meant an end to the dynasties of postal workers who handed down their 'skill and craft' father to son.

In the early 1960s, the spending power of many families went up as wage rises outpaced price rises. More households headed by an earning couple. Four out of ten married women in their forties and fifties – women whose children were off their hands – were in paid work. So were 2 million women with children of school age. Statutory maternity leave was introduced in 1976 – a move which signalled a shift in attitudes to working mothers. The cost of satisfactory childcare, the disapproval of grandmothers, who believed that a mother's place was in the home, and the pleasure that many women took in their babies, meant a large number of mothers opted out of employment in the short term. Few couples swapped roles.

Double incomes boosted spending. By the early 1960s advertisements occupied between a third and a half of the column inches in daily newspapers, women's magazines and weekly journals like *The Economist*, the *New Statesman* and the *Spectator*. The comfortably placed exponents of 'Conspicuous Waste' vied with partisans of 'Conspicuous Thrift'. The popular BBC situation comedy *The Good Life*, first screened in 1975, juxtaposed the Goods, who had opted out of the 'rat race' and into suburban self-sufficiency, and their next-door neighbours, the Leadbetters, unrepentant big spenders. Newly affluent families did not necessarily mimic the traditional behaviour of middle-class professionals. In Luton well-paid workers were generally more inclined to spend than save or invest in private education for their children. They bought refrigerators, fitted carpets and television sets (they were avid viewers) that they paid for by instalments. They ate well: bacon and eggs for breakfast; steak for dinner. They dressed well. And they took holidays abroad.

Prosperity was by no means universal. In the 1960s and 1970s, there were urban families so poor that they could not 'afford jumble sales'. In 1979 Penguin published Peter Townsend's monumental account of *Poverty in the United Kingdom*. An Oldham couple who took part in Townsend's survey lived, in their own words, 'from hand to mouth'. Mr Nelson had served his time as a painter and decorator; Mrs Nelson had worked in a cotton mill and as an office cleaner. By 1968, though still only in their thirties, they had been forced out of work by disability. Mr Nelson suffered from severe epilepsy; Mrs Nelson from bronchitis and rheumatism. They and their three boys existed on benefit. A fieldworker paid a follow-up visit in 1972. Mrs Nelson explained that 'everything' in their council flat 'except the TV, which we rent, has been given to us'. In spite of ill health and privations, short of money for food and heat and clothes, the researcher described the Nelson family as 'full of respect . . . and affection'.

> Perhaps the answer to a question about holidays was the most telling of all. Had the family had a summer holiday recently? 'Oh yes', said Mrs Nelson immediately, 'we saved and saved for weeks. We put the money in that pot up there. Mind you, we had to take it out sometimes, but we managed to put it back. Then the time came, and we really did go together to see *The Sound of Music*. Oh, it was lovely – that opening scene when she was dancing on the mountains and all free. The children each had an ice-cream, and when we left we walked up the High Street and you know that wallpaper shop, well, we saw that picture, there above our fireplace. We counted up our money. If we walked home we would just have enough for it. So the next morning I walked down and bought it, and there it's been ever since. When you're fed up you can look at it and it reminds you of *The Sound of Music*.

Mrs Hanniman, a Manchester woman whose husband was on a government training scheme, provided the research team with another vivid image of deprivation.

On the day we saw her in 1972, she was visited by two men from a local shop who came to examine a loaf in which she had found a maggot. She was told that she could visit the shop to replace the bread and 'choose a nice cake' in addition. Our interview was interjected with remarks like 'Fancy a nice cake on Tuesday. He did say that, didn't he? You heard him, didn't you? The kids [she had four] will be that excited.' Excitement at having a cake on Tuesday could fairly be regarded as symptomatic of a state of poverty.

Habitat

By the start of the 1960s, homes 'reminiscent of the slums of an earlier era' with newspaper on the table and a pervasive smell of urine were much rarer than they had been between the wars. All the same, many urban families, especially those with young children shared bathrooms and lavatories with other households. In the mid-1960s, in Paddington, a single room was home to a labourer, his wife and their twin sons. And, as the volume of traffic rose, the street life that urban women and children had enjoyed died out. The clearance of substandard properties continued. In the cities, flats scraped ever nearer the sky. By 1968 Islington boasted a twenty-seven-storey tower. That same year a block called Ronan Point collapsed, killing four people. But even before this disaster, professional enthusiasm for tower blocks had waned. Everything looked fine on paper. After sharing with five other families tenants were delighted to have a kitchen, bathroom and lavatory of their own. But high-rise estates proved hard to manage. Rubbish-strewn public spaces, vandalism and muggings changed the tenants' minds.

Tower blocks were a phenomenon of the inner city. Most newly built council houses were 'cottages' with a front door and a garden. In her suburban council house, the mother with small children had 'both bathroom and lavatory upstairs where before she washed the children in the kitchen sink and took them across the yard in the day time, using a bucket at night'.

By the end of the 1950s, the garage had become a standard appurtenance of houses built for sale; central heating had not. The 'Mrs 1970' campaign, launched in September 1959, made the case for it. It is hard for people brought up in warm houses to comprehend the force of pictures that showed Mrs 1970 playing with a naked baby in a bedroom or chatting on the phone draped in a bath sheet. Central heating was not an unmixed blessing. In the past vermin had been associated with poverty but 'fleas appreciate central heating, soft furry rugs, and cosseted domestic pets quite as much as the middle classes.'

The evacuation of working-class families from houses built for the Victorian middle classes opened the way for the 'gentrification' of rundown areas like Notting Hill in London. Young couples sanded the floors of their flats and painted furniture from junk shops bright colours. The opening of Habitat in 1964 'took the guessing out of good taste'. Terence Conran (born 1931) offered 'toned-down modernism' combined with 'a somewhat spurious peasant style'. Bernard and Laura Ashley, who had retreated from London to print textiles in 'rustic' colours' and 'Victorian' patterns, catered for the nostalgic taste. Redundant items of domestic technology – the treadle sewing machine and the mangle – came to be prized as decorative objects.

Liberated by the car, sections of the middle classes colonised villages within commuting distance of work. (In most households men were the drivers, women the passengers.) Charles Moseley and wife moved twelve-odd miles from Cambridge to Reach in the early 1960s. When they arrived, Reach men were still cutting peat from the fen to burn on their fires. 'Johnny Call Weekly' supplied the Moseleys' new neighbours with tinned food, matches, candles, wicks for oil lamps, nails, screws, tools, string, needles, thread, rubber rings to seal preserving jars, coal shovels, galvanised buckets, soap, scrubbing brushes, brooms, paraffin for heating and lighting. The village was served by a travelling butcher's shop. In rural communities like this septic tanks were relative novelties: buckets were the norm. A survey of old people's housing in the rural West Midlands revealed that most had neither flushing lavatory nor fixed bath. Yet nine out of ten wanted to stay where they were.

Incomers took up much more room than their labouring predecessors: the Trade union leader Clive Jenkins (born 1926) and his family of four occupied four old cottages knocked together – forty years earlier they had been home to forty-one men, women and children. Settlers set out to expose and restore 'period features': the Akenfield blacksmith had shut up shop in 1930. His grandson, born three or four years later, reopened the forge. By the late 1960s, he was making a handsome living. His work was not cheap – 'You can buy a pound of nails for 9d but mine cost 4½d each' – but there was a powerful appetite for 'art-and-craft' work, door furniture and the wherewithal of the open hearth. Settlers' gardens, stocked from garden centres, looked 'like shopping' to the native countrydweller.

Reacting against what they saw as the 'tyranny' of the nuclear families in which they had been reared, couples and individual men and women set out to establish communal households free from the hazards of traditional family life: 'there will be no orphans . . . no widows and widowers. No child will be subject to the whim of a particular parent'. A communal household was 'a family but with people I have chosen' or, as one satisfied communard put it, 'a splendid guddle in a vast Elizabethan house in Gloucestershire'. An advertisement in *The Times* in October 1975 combined idealism with hard-headed approach to the money side of collective life:

> Five couples planning to buy a country estate 22 miles from London to set up a commune need three more interested couples. Our interests are wanting to live together in a larger social unit, women's lib., alternative technology, community involvement and alternative education. Most of us are lecturers, teachers or artists. Capital or earning power required.

Solvency was not the only challenge – tensions between community and privacy; difficulties in coming to collective decisions, reconfigured sexual relationships led to the break up of many of these consensual households.

CRADLE TO GRAVE

Birth and infancy

In the late 1950s and early 1960s a generation of, at first inexplicably, damaged babies with vestigial arms and legs was born. Thalidomide, prescribed to deal with 'morning sickness' in pregnancy, was eventually exposed as the cause. The mysterious epidemic cast a shadow over what was a bewildering experience for many women. Professionals rarely explained the point of their instructions: Victoria Glendinning (born 1937), preparing to give birth at home in 1962, was

> given a long list of necessary equipment by the midwife which included clean, empty fish-paste pots. We didn't eat fish-paste and had to buy some specially. I could not think what purpose they might serve. In the event they were just for standing thermometers and clean spoons in.

For most women, in the early 1960s, labour began unpleasantly with an enema and the shaving of the mother's private parts. The procedure was perceived as an assault. As Hugo Williams (born 1942) remembered,

> When the nurse came to shave [his wife Hermine] there was nothing I could do to save her from defilement. The razor-blade packet had a little blue bird printed on it . . . Did the NHS have a contract, we asked, with this little obscure brand of blunt razor blade? The nurse didn't answer. The blue bird was put away for the scrapbook.

In 1965 *Nova*, which advertised itself as 'A New Kind of Magazine for a New Kind of Woman', carried a picture story culminating in a shot of a baby's head being born. To the 'old kind of woman', brought up at a time when it was thought appropriate to describe pregnancy as 'bonniness', images like this, whether published in *Nova* or taken for the family album, were revolting, even pornographic. The new kind of woman who was prepared to be photographed in labour, wanted to be in control of the process. Breathing exercises learnt during pregnancy were designed to help, so was her husband's company. The father's admission to the labour ward was a welcome innovation. Three-quarters of the women the sociologist Ann Oakley (born 1944) interviewed in the mid-1970s had their husbands' company – that was 'the best bit' of what was still 'a smelly horrible experience in a smelly horrible room'. The doctors came in for criticism: they behaved 'as though you weren't there'. Many births were induced. Almost all the mothers in Oakley's sample needed stitches. Only one in five saw her baby born; those who did not felt cheated.

The academic psychologists John and Elizabeth Newson, a husband and wife team, undertook a pioneering study of a cohort of Nottingham children, in infancy, at 4 and at 7 years old. Writing at the start of the 1960s the Newsons were 'primarily interested in ordinary family situations. For this reason we deliberately excluded from our sample . . . all illegitimate children . . . children whose parents were immigrants'. It is improbable that the Newsons succeeded in screening out the many illegitimate children whose parents 'passed' as married. All the same, their definition is an indication of how the notion of what constitutes 'an ordinary family' changed in Britain in the last decades of the twentieth century.

The Newsons saw a clear divide between middle and working-class practice. Working-class women soon gave up breastfeeding because they found it 'dirty', messy and embarrassing. Middle-class women were more likely to persist. Being caught with feeding bottles and dummies was what embarrassed them. Most of the mostly middle-class mothers who talked to Ann Oakley had tried to breastfeed; more than half of them kept it up for a month and nearly two in five were still breastfeeding four months later. Breastfeeding had a strong appeal for environmentally conscious parents. In 1978 *Vole* called it 'the nicest contraceptive in the world'.

In the 1960s, unless they were standing in for mothers on shift work, few fathers took much part in baby care. Changing nappies was their least favourite job. As flat-dwelling and car-owning became commoner, the big old-fashioned sprung baby carriage fell from favour. Light 'carry cots' which slotted into wheeled frames catered for the new-born; the child who could sit up graduated to a folding pushchair. The Maclaren buggy, patented in 1965, revolutionised baby transport: more men were willing to push buggies than prams. Bathing the baby, changing his nappy, pushing the buggy provide only a crude and gauge of paternal engagement. One father, observed in the 1970s, did none of these things but he constantly talked to his child, played games to stimulate the infant and kept a journal logging the baby's development.

New styles of baby clothes came in. When Chrissie and David Lytton Cobbold brought their baby son Henry (born 1962) back to his family's country house at Knebworth, David Lytton's old nanny carried the little boy off. 'His American cotton jump-suits were regarded with horror, and out came David's old Viyella nighties, matinee jackets and boottees'.

The differences between working and middle-class routines persisted as children grew up. At 4, the middle-class Nottingham child was more likely to be reasoned with, talked to at meal times, told bedtime stories. At 7, the middle-class child was more likely to get help with homework; to read and write and paint and draw at home; to have a train set and constructional toys like Lego and Meccano; to own books and borrow them from the public library; to be taken to the cinema, the theatre, concerts, museums and galleries; to have music or dancing lessons. Although very few Nottingham parents never smacked, those 'at the upper end of the social scale are more inclined *on principle*, to use democratically-based, highly verbal means of control'. While 'in the unskilled group, parents chose, *on principle*, to use highly authoritarian, mainly non-verbal means of control, in which words are used to threaten and bamboozle the child into obedience'. The Newsons concluded that 'the child born into the lowest social bracket has everything stacked against him *including his parents' principles of child upbringing*'. Walk through the streets at the start of the twenty-first century and the evidence of the tenacity of these two contrasting cultures, characterised by negotiation and smacking, will be before you.

At one end of the scale, a smack could be the physical equivalent of a mild verbal reproof. At the other, it could result in grievous bodily harm. During the 1960s medical professionals identified the 'battered baby syndrome'. The case of Maria Colwell (born January 1966) horrified the public. Maria had been cared for by her aunt for five years. A wrong-headed insistence on the bond between natural mother and child led to Maria being handed back against the little girl's wishes. In spite of persuasive evidence that the child was both miserable and at risk of serious physical and emotional harm, the authorities failed to intervene. Maria died at her stepfather's hands in January 1973. Despite the outcry that followed her death, similar scandals occurred later in the decade.

For working mothers, there was no simple solution to the problem of childcare. Nursery schools and play groups generally catered for children whose mothers were at home; indeed, many play groups were run by the mothers of the children who attended. Grandmothers and aunts remained the preferred mother substitutes. Sometimes parents were able to work complementary shifts. At Peek Frean's biscuit factory in Bermondsey the mothers of young children worked in the evenings, leaving their husbands to cope with the bedtime routine. In Suffolk women doing seasonal work on the land took their children along and parked them and their toys in giant playpens made out of 'moveable cattle fences'. While she worked as a potato picker in the Fens, Peggy Brittain's son (born 1965) was minded by the wife of the farmer who employed her.

Many children were left with paid caretakers. At one extreme was the old-fashioned nanny ensconced in her nursery. Among the comfortably-off, au-pairs, young women from continental Europe, in England to learn the language, were a popular source of help with children. The au-pair suited working mothers whose children were at school. Local authorities licensed childminders. From 1948 anyone who took on more than three children faced inspection by the fire and health services. In 1968 the regulations were extended to cover anyone paid for looking after any unrelated child for more than two hours a day. One licensed minder interviewed in the early 1970s was a professional engineer's wife who had taken on two paying playmates for her own under-5 child. They had expensive wooden toys – 'You don't have to worry about children swallowing nasty plastic bits' – a paddling pool, outings in the family car. 'She talked constantly to the children, asking questions, listening, explaining. The room was full of toys, well-used but neatly stored, a shelf bursting with books; paper and crayons on the table'. For a single father, childminding was a 'business proposition'. He had trained as a play-group leader, invested in educational toys and turned his garden into a playground equipped with a slide, a swing and a sandpit. Only the well-off could afford care like this. Sometimes children in the care of the cheaper unregistered childminders had nothing to play with. Investigators found toddlers who spent the whole day in their pushchairs, children tied to chairs with nylon stockings or left along for 'long hours lying in an upstairs cot staring at the blank ceiling and bare walls'.

The number of children brought up without a resident father was growing. On average, these children were disadvantaged. For one thing, they were likely to be significantly poorer than their peers in two-parent households. For another, lone mothers found their children harder to manage – the codes of behaviour they laid down were often more extreme than the neighbourhood norm.

Unsurprisingly children started school with widely different experiences and skills. Reception classes in Huddersfield took in children from homes in which 'the pulse of another culture [beat] strongly': Chinese, Italian, Jamaican, Pakistani, Ugandan Asian. There were children who had 'highly developed finger skills', who had already learned to distinguish objects 'by colour, shape, size weight, number and texture' and children who had had none of experiences that would have enabled them to develop this sort of understanding of the world.

Education

The Plowden Report of 1967 came out against the rote learning and drill that Eva Figes remembered from her time at an elementary school in London during the war. It condemned corporal punishment: the committee that produced the report did not 'believe you are going to make a child nicer by beating it'. The Labour Party saw the elimination of the tripartite system of secondary modern, technical and grammar schools as the key to achieving equal educational opportunities for all. Anthony Crosland (born 1918), Secretary of State for Education between 1965 and 1967, memorably declared, 'If it's the last thing I do I'm going to destroy every fucking Grammar School'. The old divisive system would be replaced by comprehensive schools catering for the whole range of ability. In keeping with the government's egalitarian project, the first B[achelor of] Ed[ucation] courses were launched in 1965. Up to that time, certificated teachers had served the primary and secondary modern schools, while academic specialists, graduates, often without vocational training, staffed the grammar schools. A school-leaving qualification for less academic children, the Certificate of Secondary Education (CSE), was introduced in 1965. In 1972 the school-leaving age finally went up to 16.

Comprehensive schools were not an invention of the 1960s. The pioneer authorities included the new towns and cities like London and Coventry that had lost schools to enemy action during the war. By 1970, one in three and, by 1980, nine in ten of the population of state secondary schools went to 'comprehensives'. But the 'comprehensive' picture was complicated. Some schools catered for the whole range of 11 to 18 year olds; others competed with surviving grammar schools. Some authorities provided junior, middle and senior schools; others set up separate sixth form colleges. There were mixed and single-sex schools and denominational schools. Some schools were purpose-built; more often old buildings were utilised. The Labour government lacked the courage to tackle the independent sector with the result that Crosland's project was undermined by the decision of most direct grant schools to 'go private'. Many maintained their local reputation and filled their places, thus pushing up the population of fee-paying pupils.

When it came to planning their sons' education, upper-class fathers were inclined to follow tradition. The Lytton Cobbolds had embraced the idea of a day preparatory school for their eldest son but, in the end, in 1970, he went off to board just as his father had done before him. In 1960 virtually all public schools were single-sex (Bedales remained the conspicuous exception). In boys' schools in particular, life was regimented. The standard rubric ran 'the hair must not cover the ears or touch the collar'. Twice-daily chapel and membership of the Combined Cadet Force (CCF) were compulsory. In the late 1960s a guerrilla war erupted between boys and masters. Hair was a big issue. Chapel services provided opportunities for collective displays of 'dumb insolence'. Marlborough was among the first to relax its regime. In 1968 CCF and weekday chapel were made optional; the first girls – all masters' daughters or boys' sisters – were admitted to the sixth form; outsiders followed in 1969. By 1979 nearly a third of the old boys' public schools were fully coeducational. Classics, the defining curriculum of public and grammar schools since the sixteenth century, lost favour. Up to the mid-1960s scholars at Westminster specialised in Latin and Greek almost to a man; by 1980 science and mathematics had become the conventional choice.

Prep schools changed too. In the late 1960s, boys still used the Latin command 'cave', pronounced 'cave-ee' in the old-fashioned way, as a warning signal. That tradition soon disappeared. Others followed. 'What really determined' the head of St John's College School in Cambridge at the start of the 1970s 'that our boys must have Christian names was standing in the Boot Room one day and hearing Ian Farbon say to his brother Paul Farbon, "Hurry up, Farbon, we're late"'.

Youth

In 1960 most young people left school at the earliest opportunity. The end of National Service increased the number of working teenagers with no responsibilities 'other than giving Mum something towards their keep'. The young workers had money to burn. Clothes and music were their chief indulgences. Reflecting on the new youth culture in the late 1960s, Edmund Leach (born 1910), a Cambridge anthropologist, saw it as an 'attack on English class values'. Working-class teenagers set the pace as consumers, but there was a powerful current of ageism too. The visual signals clothes transmitted might have been designed to enrage the old and irascible.

Beatlemania hit England in 1963. The Beatles started out as 'total Teds' – greasy-haired, leather-jacketed, winkle-picker-shod. Later smart, if unconventional, collarless jackets and mop heads became their, much imitated, trademarks – the Beatle fringe could cover a eruption of acne. The Rolling Stones remained unpolished. The 1960s was the decade of the dolly bird. Shockingly short skirts and thick black stockings were among Mary Quant's contributions. For Bazaar, her shop in Chelsea, Quant (born 1934) had mannequins specially sculpted with 'long lean legs' indecorously 'wide apart'. In Carnaby Street and in the Portobello Road guardsmen's tunics, 'granny' specs and shoes, kaftans – the contents of a posh child's dressing-up box – filled the boutiques; among the most famous was *Granny Takes a Trip*. The irreverent use of military uniforms and the regalia of old age aggravated the tensions between young and old. Almost anything went. Laura Ashley (born 1925) countered the 'mini' with skirts that came down to the ankles. Clothes and hairstyles, traditional gender markers, converged to produce 'unisex' styles. Hippies adopted long hair, exotic impractical clothes, drugs, music and mysticism as their badges – and as a way of 'waving [their] fingers' at the respectable families from which they mostly sprang. When 'punk' came in in the mid-1970s, 'suddenly fashion was about wearing rags, safety pins and bin-liners'.

Young people's speech characterised by lost consonants was both an annoyance and a barrier to communication with their elders. George Melly heard a puzzling account of the Rolling Stones' Free Concert in Hyde Park in 1969 from a 14-year-old. Apparently Mick Jagger had read a poem by 'Che' in memory of Brian Jones. 'I was perplexed by this in that as far as I knew [Che] Guevara had never written a poem. The next day I read that the poem was in fact by Shelley'. An Indian-born Oxford graduate, who returned to the city in the mid-1970s, was surprised to hear 'all around him . . . young men and women speaking with regional dialects and above all with a grammar, lexicon and accent that he felt to be uneducated'. It was in fact the patois of middle-class students who 'had reacted against their parents' speech'.

The disapproval provoked by teenage clothes and music fuelled a 'moral panic' in the spring of 1964. There was disorder at Clacton and then in other run-down seaside resorts, Margate, Great Yarmouth, Brighton, Weston-super-Mare. The press sensationalised scuffles and episodes of vandalism. Words like 'siege', 'riot', phrases such as 'orgy of destruction' peppered reports. Sentences meted out by magistrates exaggerated the incidents' gravity. But some of those born too soon for the new freedom felt left out. In her poem, which begins 'When I am an old woman, I shall wear purple', (1975), Jenny Joseph (born 1932) catalogued the ways in which, freed from the responsibilities of parenthood she would 'make up for the sobriety of my youth'.

Higher education

The number of students in higher education doubled between 1960 and 1970. New universities were launched – Aston, Bath, Bradford, Brunel, City (in London), East Anglia (just outside Norwich), Essex (near Colchester), Kent (near Canterbury), Lancaster, Loughborough, Salford, Surrey, Sussex (near Brighton), Warwick, York – some, like Salford, developed from existing institutions. The 'green-field' foundations were linked to historic towns and to holiday resorts that provided a useful supply of off-campus lodgings – Essex could look to Clacton, Kent to Herne Bay and Whitstable, Lancaster to Morecambe, Warwick, well inland, to Leamington Spa. Only Essex opted for co-residence on campus – male and female students lived on alternate floors of its tower blocks. For many families, sending someone to university was a new experience. One woman remembered how her grandfather, learning that she was going to study sociology and philosophy, asked her to write it down 'so that I can tell people'. The number of women students rose significantly, the number of young people from working-class families did not. To increase the supply of technical expertise, thirty polytechnics were designated in 1966. Over time the polytechnics' curriculum drifted in the direction of the universities'; in 1992 the constitutional distinction was abolished.

For decades, private correspondence colleges like Wolsey Hall had prepared external candidates for London University's degree examinations. The Open University – the 'University of the Air' – 'autonomous, independent, free-standing . . . like the other new universities' was Harold Wilson's idea. Virtually the whole academic establishment, radicals and conservatives alike, was hostile and, in Jennie Lee's words, 'tried to kill off' the 'little bastard'. But the demand was there: teachers without degrees, men and women with family responsibilities, disabled people, members of the Armed Forces, people in prison were keen to enrol. The Open University (OU) abandoned the old harvest-driven academic calendar and admitted its first part-time undergraduates in January 1971. Thanks to credit awarded for past learning, the first cohort of OU students graduated in 1973.

Like the public schools, the face-to-face universities faced a challenge from those 'in statu pupillari'. Enoch Powell, a hated figure among student radicals, faced hostile demonstrations at Bath, Cambridge, Exeter and Reading; at Essex his car was attacked; the University of Birmingham withdrew an invitation to speak. Like racism, Vietnam was a big issue. In 1970 six Cambridge undergraduates were sent to prison and two to Borstal for riotous and unlawful assembly after a demonstration against the Greek regime got out of hand. Students also protested about their tutors, lecture theatres, lodgings. They argued for changes to the curriculum and – more successfully – for representation on university committees and the relaxation of rules governing their conduct during term. At the ancient universities, undergraduates were required to wear gowns on the street after dark. The debate between undergraduate radicals and conservative dons was bitter. The senior tutor of a Cambridge college allegedly invited students unhappy with college regulations to take themselves off to 'red-brick' universities 'where they could sleep with twenty black women a night and smoke pot till they were blue in the face'.

Like the public schools, the men's colleges at Oxford and Cambridge began to admit women: at Cambridge the first became mixed in 1972; the last capitulated fifteen years later.

Sex before marriage

The expansion of higher education in the 1960s meant that more young, middle-class men and women lived away from home during term. When they got their first jobs, the children of men who commuted from the suburbs opted to set themselves up in shared flats, unsupervised by a landlady. All the same, at the start of the 1960s, sex before marriage remained a hazardous activity. The moral conviction, ignorance and fear that had prevented so many of their parents' generation from 'going all the way' inclined young people to stop short of full sexual intercourse. Contraceptive advice and prescriptions, still provided under the label 'family planning', were for married couples. Pregnancies, planned and unplanned, prompted weddings as they had for centuries. Of the Nottingham women interviewed by the Newsons, one in five was pregnant when she married. Parents still felt and expressed disappointment. Brides 'in the pudding club' were expected to avoid wearing virginal white on their wedding day. Births outside marriage were concealed. Many illegitimate children lived in otherwise conventional households, with both parents. Unmarried mothers-to-be without the support of parents or a partner – ten or eleven thousand of them a year in the late 1960s, mostly never-married, young, pregnant for the first time – sought refuge in 'homes' run by local authorities and voluntary organisations. They were expected to give their babies up for adoption and generally they did.

In 1975 thousands of adopted adults were given access to their original birth certificates and thus information about their natural mother that provided the first clue to her whereabouts. By no means every woman welcomed the reappearance of the child she had given up. Adoptive parents were hurt by what seemed to some, an act of betrayal.

The Brook Clinic was the first to offer contraceptive advice (very discreetly) to unmarried women. Public opinion was divided. A London *Evening Standard* poll of 1971, which asked its female readers whether they were in favour of making the pill available to unmarried women, revealed a generation gap: three-quarters of the younger women who voted were in favour, three-quarters of those over 65 were against. By the mid-1970s the Bursar of Goldsmiths College in London claimed that he could calculate the number of students' lovers squatting in the halls of residence 'by the amount of toilet paper used'. 'Living together' was becoming a common prelude to marriage. In the 1970s, contrary to the expectations of those who drafted the new divorce law, the number of babies born to unmarried mothers rose: many fewer were given up for adoption.

Marriage and babies

At the start of the 1960s, women expected to marry young. Between the wars first-time brides were generally 25 or so, first-time grooms around 28. Their children, marrying in the 1960s, were three or four years younger. Ann Oakley (born 1944) was among the minority who went to university. The only child of academic parents, she had hoped for a First. 'On learning that I had "only" got a second-class degree, I wrote on the back of an envelope, which I've kept: "People who don't get Firsts have babies" – a First might have provided a passport to a masculine career path, a justification to do different.' For her, a second-class degree 'without a husband to go with it' was 'an empty achievement'. Marriage meant babies: the first-time mother of 28 or 29 was regarded as an 'elderly' primagravida. By the age of 25 Ann Oakley 'had done the only four things [she] had wanted to do – viz. get a university degree, a husband, a house and two children'. The description 'housewife and mother' applied to her and to the majority of her contemporaries. By the end of the 1970s women were putting off motherhood. A childless marriage was no longer 'socially suspect', having a baby involved 'difficult joint-decision making' for many couples.

New technologies changed contraceptive practice. Many women disliked the diaphragm advocated by Marie Stopes. 'The pill' was introduced in the early 1960s to popular acclaim. Women who took part in a trial in Birmingham were reported to be 'absolutely delighted with the freedom from contraceptive measures related to coital acts'. Users' accounts were less clinical. Unlike the sheath, which 'spoils it', the cap, which was 'messy' and 'the thing their mothers used', the pill was seen as 'absolutely safe and no fiddling about – so natural', 'you simply can't get caught'. The pill was neither universally available nor universally welcomed. The Family Planning Act 1967 empowered local authorities to provide free contraceptive advice, devices and pharmaceutical preparations. Most confined the service to married people. The publication in 1968 of the papal encyclical *Humanae Vitae*, which flatly condemned artificial means of contraception, came as a shock. It ran counter to the recommendations of a papal commission set up to look at the issue – and to the practice of many devout lay people too. The medical establishment continued to express reservations about easy access to contraception: as the 1960s ended, an editorial in the *Lancet* deplored the prospect of a 'generation which does not cherish chastity': the pill, which removed the fear of pregnancy, offered no protection against sexually transmitted diseases. Other professional bodies were chary too. Only in the 1970s did the Pharmaceutical Society sanction the display of contraceptives in chemists' shops. Even then firms like Boots took their time. Enthusiasm for the pill declined following reports, published in the *Lancet* in 1977, of an increased risk of thrombosis among long-term users. The popularity of the sheath revived.

By the mid-1960s, it was reckoned that perhaps as many as 100,000 illegal abortions were taking place every year. 'Back-street' terminations were so common that doctors often assumed that a natural miscarriage was the result of an attempt 'to get rid of the baby'. The Abortion Act 1967 legalised termination provided that two doctors agreed that the pregnancy threatened the mother's life or her physical or mental health or that of her existing children, or would result in the birth of a gravely damaged baby. Women had the right to ask for a termination; the authority to grant it lay with the medics. Fathers had no legal say over the fate of their unborn children. Medics' assessments of 'threat' varied. As the journalist Katharine Whitehorn (born 1928) observed, 'You can get [an abortion] at the drop of a hat in Tower Hamlets' but 'only at the drop of a cheque in the oh-so-moral Midlands'. By the mid-1970s, there was a test for Down's syndrome. More than half the pregnancies of married women in their forties were terminated, often to prevent the birth of a baby with Down's syndrome or spina bifida. Genetic counselling contributed to the rising number of terminations.

By the end of the 1970s, technology was widely used to assist conception. Artificial insemination was a well established, though apparently little used, procedure. Louise Brown, the first 'test-tube baby', conceived outside her mother's body, was born in 1978. Her parents, John and Lesley, had been 'trying for a baby' for fifteen years. Louise's younger sister, Natalie, was also conceived *in vitro*. Neither the NHS nor private health insurance schemes were prepared to meet the cost of the expensive and frequently unsuccessful treatment.

Only a housewife

In some great country houses old-fashioned protocols survived. As a new bride at Cliveden in 1960, Bronwen Astor was astonished to discover that it was her maid's job to squeeze toothpaste on to her brush. At Grimsthorpe as late as 1977 the maids were ironing lavatory paper and laying it out in fans. But by the end of the decade, even when she had guests, the Dowager Duchess of Buccleuch, 'nearly eighty, the grandest of the grand', was stacking plates between courses and wheeling them 'on a trolley into the kitchenette' in her apartment in the family seat at Boughton in Northamptonshire.

Outside the aristocratic time-warp housework was transformed. The modern conveniences that Beveridge had looked forward to in the 1940s – 'clean cooking, refrigerators, mechanical washers for clothes' – became facts of life for a majority of families. In 1960 the designers of council housing still regarded a socket in every room as a novelty. By the end of the decade a letter in *The Times*, bemoaning the consequences of a strike of workers in electrical supply industry listed a string of appliances – which could easily have been extended: 'The radio is dead. The television is dead. The electrical heaters are dead. The kettle is dead. The fridge is dead. My iron is dead.' As technology took over, old skills of the housewife became redundant. To the traditional housewife, a 'line of washing blowing' had been a source of pride. Of course, when it rained and in the winter, her family was condemned to live under canopies of shirts and sheets hoisted up on poles to dry – just as their forebears had. In the 1960s scrubbing boards and hand-turned mangles gave way to top-loaded washing machines with electric wringers, spin-driers and machines that washed and tumbled dry. At first families were fascinated, 'we all sat around and watched our clothes going around and around through the glass porthole at the front'. Firms that collected dirty laundry and delivered clean became thinner on the ground; launderettes were the new urban alternative to home washing. 'Easy-care' fabrics reduced the pile of ironing. Open fires demanded a series of skilled, time-consuming, dirty and often heavy chores. With central heating, fewer sparks, less dust and more money, home decorators opted for pale fitted carpets and upholstery. Warm bedrooms and the proliferation of television and radio sets and record players ate into the family's fireside circle of listeners and viewers.

For families above the breadline, McDonald's, which opened its first English branch in London in 1974, offered a home-from-home: children were welcome – there was even a high chair for the baby. Kentucky Fried Chicken, pizza parlours, curry palaces and Chinese restaurants broadened the popular palate and undermined the tradition of family meals. At the same time, for those with the time and funds to spare, cooking provided opportunities for self-expression and showing-off. Arabella Boxer's *First Slice your Cook-book* (1964) provided the inexperienced 'cook-hostess' with a simple and witty kit. Recipes were colour-coded: blue for light dishes (gazpacho); lentil green for filling (boiled bacon with haricot beans); red for rich (profiteroles). The book was literally in three horizontal slices – 'Soups, Hors d'oeuvres'; 'Main'; 'Sweets, Savouries' – to help the cook-hostess perm three courses into balanced menus. There was 'reliable and expert' advice on wines to complement the main dishes. Katharine Whitehorn's *Cooking in a Bedsitter* (1961), aimed at the young, single, self-catering student and worker, was more down to earth. She pointed out that her readers had a 'natural kinship' with Italian peasants 'eking out three shrimps and a lump of cheese with half a cartload of spaghetti'. Marinades were 'the poor man's fridge'; salads eliminated the chore of cooking vegetables. Aubergines, garlic, green peppers, chillies and zucchinis, now better known as courgettes, were novelties. In 1972, Yasmin Alibhai remembered, 'you could not buy an aubergine in Oxford'.

The traditional values of the house-proud came under attack, first from writers who asserted that there were better ways of spending time and, later, the principled arguments of the women's liberation movement. Throughout the 1960s the *Observer* journalist Katharine Whitehorn assumed the role of the self-declared sluts' advocate, the defender of the anti-housewife who did not manage to get 'the mess off the stairs' before her guests arrived or to shop early for Christmas. Shirley Conran (born 1932) published the ironically titled best-seller *Superwoman: Every Woman's Book of Household Management* (another nod in Mrs Beeton's direction) in 1975. 'No one should waste her life on the treadmill of housework' was Superwoman's mission statement. Women should be 'constructively selfish': replace sheets and blankets with 'continental quilts'; give up tablecloths and napkins; leave dishes to dry themselves. 'It's amazing how much better a room looks if you *don't clean it at all*, but simply tidy it up'. Liberationists saw domesticity as a prison sentence. Housewives spent 'long hours of working banged up in a solitary cell'. Wages for housework might dignify the role but 'nobody should have a housewife' was the fundamental conviction.

Husband and wife

Conditioning in girlhood, the tendency for men at all social levels to earn more, the fact that women bore and generally raised children meant that most wives were ready to subordinate their career ambitions to their husbands'. More equal relationships did exist. Some at least of the 'partnering husbands' had been brought up by parents who were themselves unusually egalitarian. Tony Benn's mother had declared in the 1920s: 'I want my boys to grow up in a world in which the churches will give women equal spiritual status'. Benn was the first male politician to make his support for women's liberation public. His diaries demonstrate that his commitment extended to the kitchen sink. In December 1963 he saw his wife and children off to a Christmas concert and stayed behind to wash up after a meal for sixteen; in 1965, when his son Hilary had scarlet fever, he postponed an official visit. Another Labour Party activist Audrey Wise (born 1935) came from a less privileged background – she had started her working life as a shorthand typist. In 1970 she told the National Women's Liberation Conference that, 'When we run out of toilet paper in our house, *either* my husband *or* I go out and buy some more. We both work, we both bring up the children and we both share the shopping and the cooking and the cleaning'. Her hearers were open-mouthed.

During the 1960s and 1970s women's developed expectations of marriage rose. Ann Oakley and her sister wives-and-mothers were not content to look out at the world with their hands in the kitchen sink. A letter published in the *Guardian* in 1960 led to the foundation of the National Housewives' Register designed to put 'housebound housewives with liberal interests and a desire to remain individuals' in touch with 'like-minded friends'. 'Liberal interests' did not exclude domesticity – the association used 'Tupperware parties', opportunities to buy plastic containers in another woman's home, in its 'getting-to-know-you' schemes on new suburban estates. A graduate student, wife and mother, Hannah Gavron (born 1936) surveyed a sample of her middle- and working-class peers. Gavron's study, published in 1966 under the telling title, *The Captive Wife*, argued that young wives wanted to retain their own identities. From their husbands, they expected emotional satisfaction and physical respect.

Mary Grant, the 'agony aunt' of *Woman's Own*, a mass-circulation weekly magazine, recognised that, by the late 1970s, marriage was 'more about needs and feelings than about the rules, rights and duties of being a husband and wife'. People began to own up to conduct that earlier generations had concealed. 'Open marriage', defined by its accommodation of physical and emotional relationships with third parties, was debated in principle and recorded as a fact of middle-class life. Jill Tweedie (born 1936) was among those who argued that it was better to confess to and accept infidelity than to live a lie. Reports of 'wife-swapping' parties suggest that – in some circles – the assumption that lust might legitimately be separated from love, companionship and family responsibilities was spreading. Middle-aged and securely married, Richard Hoggart (born 1918) found the notion of wife-swapping 'hardly credible' – 'probably it's an urban myth', he concluded.

The longstanding presumption that marriage conferred on the husband the conjugal right to penetrate his wife without her consent came under fire. In January 1972 Jill Tweedie shared with *Guardian* readers her perception that there were 'thousands of households across the country where rape will be committed tonight, carefully camouflaged by the sacraments of marriage'. Chiswick Women's Aid, set up as a community centre in 1971, evolved into a refuge for battered wives and their children. Women from every social class and ethnic group sought help in person and by telephone – by May 1973 the centre was receiving nearly a hundred calls a day. Refuges modelled on Chiswick appeared elsewhere. From 1976 a violent husband could be legally barred from the vicinity of his wife's home. Those who fled violence did not necessarily escape it: battered women were sometimes battering mothers; boys brought up in violence were often aggressive.

Housewives described themselves as 'prisoners at home', 'cooped up', trapped', 'existing not living', 'at a dead end with nothing to look forward to', 'cabbages'. Men reported that their housebound wives were bored, boring, demanding and resentful of their husbands' friends and pastimes. Wives who had been to college had qualifications that they could use as exit visas: teaching was a common destination. Any employment conferred identity: 'I'd rather describe myself as a shrink wrapper than a housewife', a woman confessed in 1976. The pace of change was uneven. In rural Akenfield late in the 1960s young brides were still surrendering to frumpy middle age; at 45 many could be mistaken for their husbands' mothers.

Divorce and remarriage

The Divorce Reform Act 1969, which came into force in 1971, revolutionised the law of marriage by allowing the 'guilty' party to petition for divorce. 'Irretrievable breakdown' was the new formula – in future divorce would simply register the death of a marriage. The main purpose of the change was to legitimise children born to parents unable to marry because an 'innocent', 'paper' spouse refused to petition for divorce. Five years' separation was recognised as adequate evidence that reconciliation was impossible. Legal change did not, of course, eliminate hurt, jealousy and bitterness or put an end to wrangles. Nor did it put an end to legal fault. Divorce by agreement required two years' separation. Adultery and other forms of 'intolerable' behaviour remained common grounds. Men and women with children, anxious for a speedy resolution, were inclined to cite fault. Parents in conflict over custody or access found the charge of unreasonable behaviour particularly attractive. It gave the petitioner scope to wound – one husband described his wife's allegations as 'like something out of the Nuremberg Trials'. Lawyers trained in an adversarial tradition honed the weapons. In 1971 all divorce petitions were heard in open court. Undefended cases were rattled through with unseemly haste – but at considerable cost in legal fees. The lack of decorum offended judges; the cost to the Treasury, which picked up the tab for petitioners eligible for legal aid, concerned the government. By 1977 no undefended petition was heard in open court. And as divorce became commoner, only sensational cases attracted press attention.

An increasing number of men, women and children lived with the financial and emotional consequences of divorce and remarriage. They could be enduring: Julian Critchley, divorced in 1965, was still paying alimony thirty years later. Stepfamilies multiplied. Brenda Maddox's *The Half Parent* (1975) was one of the first books to focus on what she called 'mended broken homes', 'remade families'. Despite optimistic claims by liberal-minded metropolitans like Jill Tweedie that 'divorce creates an underground family that only needs to be stripped of its coverings, its shame, its inherent drama to produce . . . a natural extended family', the mends remained visible. Maddox pointed to the sources of tensions – a stepchild was a constant reminder of the departed wife or husband, the 'ghost' that haunted the new marriage; to the child, the step-parent was the usurper. The end of a marriage often signalled not only the loss of contact with the departing parent (generally the father) but with grandparents, aunts, uncles and cousins on that side of the family too. The number of lone parents, the majority mothers, soared. Some women were reincorporated into their parents' household. Many preferred to keep their independence in spite of isolation and poverty. If they depended on state benefits and were found guilty of cohabiting, they ran the risk of losing their income. The state did little to prepare women to go back to work when their days of full-time parenting were over. The charity Gingerbread, launched in 1970, provided lone parents and their children with support and companionship and campaigned on their behalf.

Old age

More people than ever before lived long enough to see their great-grandchildren – the four-generation family was becoming usual. Many pensioners found that time dragged – they sought ways of killing it. In the early 1960s, only a minority of elderly people surveyed in Bristol had telephones. They were cut off from children who had moved away. They did not encourage familiarity in their neighbours. Television was a solace. In spite of the hard work involved in washing by hand, the television took priority over the washing machine in households short of money. As you got older, people's attitudes changed: in his late sixties Laurie Lee (born 1914), who had been exceptionally attractive to women in his younger days, confessed that he had 'become invisible . . . young girls simply look[ed] through' him.

Families marked milestone birthdays and, in the case of public figures, so did a wider community. At 79, Francis Meynell (born 1891) was still playing ping-pong in the 'lovely twilight' of his life. As a conscientious objector who had gone on hunger strike during the First World War, he was recognised as an important historical source and interviewed for the Imperial War Museum. Meynell's career in design was celebrated by an exhibition at Wolverhampton Polytechnic. Cambridge University Library acquired his papers. His eightieth birthday celebrations 'extended over weeks'. Arnold Toynbee (born 1889) observed that 'ever since 1915' he 'had been surprised at being still alive'. As an eminent old boy he was honoured by Winchester in 1974 with a welcome speech 'ad portas' (at the college gate), in Latin. Toynbee responded in kind, speaking for fifteen minutes and adding a Greek postcript. He used his time, as other old men did when they were given the floor, to 'commemorate . . . schoolfellows' killed in the First World War – at Gallipoli, in Babylon, and in the trenches. (Winchester had made a heroic contribution to the war effort: of the 539 boys who left between 1909 and1915, 531 had volunteered.) In his eighties, the illustrator E. H. Shepard (born 1879) wrote two volumes of autobiography and then went on to produce his first stories for children. He was in his nineties when he added colour to the drawings he had made for *Winnie-the-Pooh* and *The House at Pooh Corner* more than forty years earlier and devised, apparently for his own entertainment, 'a Pooh Orchestra' featuring Piglet on triangle and double bass.

The disabilities of old age were at the forefront of other writers' minds: 'the plight of those of us who have nothing ahead but the increasing obscenity of old age'. Frailty drove the scholar Nora Chadwick (born 1891) from the home she had shared with her husband first to a small flat and then, in 1970 to a nursing home, she hated the feeling that she was a prisoner there. Early in the 1960s Violet Bonham-Carter (born 1887) contemplated two men dear to her: her husband Maurice (born 1880) was reduced to a physical shell; her old friend Winston Churchill seemed 'very far away'. As a widow, she embarked on the adventure of a solitary expedition to the theatre and home 'by Tube'. Though their views are in the public domain, the experience of isolation and loss of autonomy was not, of course, confined to these socially privileged and articulate women.

Death

Attitudes to death were changing. In 1960 suicide was a criminal offence and hanging was still the statutory penalty for murder. Coming round after a suicide attempt, Al Alvarez found policemen sitting 'heavily but rather sympathetically on my bed and asked me questions they clearly didn't want me to answer. When I tried to explain, they shushed me politely. "It was an accident, wasn't it, sir?"' In 1961 suicide was decriminalised. The view that an individual had the right to choose the time and means of death became commoner, as the dramatic rise in the membership of the Voluntary Euthanasia Society during the 1970s suggests. The death penalty was effectively abolished in 1965. A cluster of cases had undermined public confidence in capital punishment. The impossibility of turning the clock back was underlined when the execution of Timothy Evans was revealed as a miscarriage of justice. Nevertheless, the gut reaction of a popular majority continued to assert that 'hanging was too good' for the likes of the Moors Murderers.

Medical technology was beginning to challenge death itself. Fred West, the first recipient of a heart transplanted in Britain, in May 1968, survived 45 days. Other early attempts were equally unsuccessful in prolonging life and the operation did not become routine until a decade later.

The management of natural death was gradually changing too. E. P. Thompson recalled his experience of 'a huge round ward like a panopticon' (a nineteenth-century contrivance to make constant surveillance easy) in what had been a Poor Law hospital.

> I remember one [dying man] who, with the self-effacing courtesy of some elderly working men, was clearly embarrassed by the concern he was causing to his mates on each side. I think he might, out of some sense of modesty, have preferred to have died in a private ward. I think it is likely that his next-of-kin (who, until the last few hours, were confined to normal visiting hours) would have preferred to have been with him there.

Hospices, promoted by Cicely Saunders (born 1918), were a reaction against this way of death. In essence, they were a specialised kind of commune where terminally ill people could be treated, not as patients, but as men, women and children capable of enjoying the last stage of their lives. Provided that physical distress could be avoided, they could still take pleasure in 'a good night', a 'good meal', a family celebration, a hairdo, an outing.

In spite of a decline in religious observance, the churches came into their own when families had a death to deal with. Ted Castle died on Boxing Day 1979. He was not a practising Anglican but his funeral service was held at 'the local church' which he and his wife Barbara had supported financially, believing that it was 'as much a part of rural life as the country pub'. In villages like 'Akenfield' in Suffolk, graves were still tended but, across the nation, this was a custom in decline. The dispersal of families made the regular pilgrimage to the loved one's grave an unrealisable ideal. The Catholic Church ended its ban on cremation in 1966 and in the following year cremations exceeded burials for the first time. By the middle 1960s most people lived within half an hour's drive of a crematorium. Burials took up space – 'Save the land for the living' was the Cremation Society's motto. Ashes could be scattered in a place significant for the deceased or for the whole family.

Reading

Arnott, Paul, *A Good Likeness: a personal story of adoption* (Little, Brown, 2000).

Bailey, David, *David Bailey's Box of Pin-ups* (Weidenfeld & Nicolson, 1965).

Benn, Tony, *Out of the Wilderness: diaries 1963–67* (Hutchinson, 1987).

Benn, Tony, *Office without Power: diaries 1968–72* (Hitchinson, 1988).

Blythe, Ronald, *Akenfield: portrait of an English village* (Allen Lane, 1969).

Boxer, Arabella, *First Slice your Cook-book* (Nelson, 1964).

Campbell, John, *Roy Jenkins: a biography* (Weidenfeld & Nicolson, 1983).

Carson, Rachel, *Silent Spring* (Hamish Hamilton, 1963).

Chadwick, Owen, *Michael Ramsey: a life* (Clarendon Press, 1990).

Conran, Shirley, *Superwoman* (Sidgwick & Jackson, 1975).

Crisp, Quentin, *The Naked Civil Servant* (Jonathan Cape, 1968).

Crosland, Susan, *Tony Crosland* (Jonathan Cape, 1982).

Du Boulay, Shirley, *Cicely Saunders: founder of the modern hospice movement* (Hodder & Stoughton, 1984).

Edwards, D. L. (ed.), *The 'Honest to God' Debate: some reaction to the book Honest to God* (SCM (Student Christian Movement), 1963).

Faulkner, Lucy (ed.), *The Light of Other Days – oral history from Wisbech* (Fenland Oral History Project, University of Cambridge, Board of Continuing Education, 1998).

Gavron, Hannah, *The Captive Wife* (Routledge & Kegan Paul, 1966).

Glendinning, Victoria, *Vita: the life of V. Sackville-West* (Weidenfeld & Nicolson, 1983).

Green, Jonathan, *All Dressed Up: the Sixties and counter culture* (Jonathan Cape, 1998).

Greer, Germaine, *The Female Eunuch* (MacGibbon & Kee, 1970).

Hollis, Patricia, *Jennie Lee: a life* (Oxford University Press, 1997).

Isherwood, Christopher, *Kathleen and Frank* (Methuen, 1971).

Jackson, Brian, *Streaming: an education system in miniature* (Routledge & Kegan Paul, 1964).

Jackson, Brian, *Childminder: a study in action research* (Routledge & Kegan Paul, 1979).

Joseph, Jenny, *Selected Poems* (Bloodaxe, 1992).

Lee, Laurie, *Cider with Rosie* (Hogarth Press, 1959).

Lees-Milne, James, *Harold Nicolson: a biography* (Chatto & Windus, 1980–81).

Littlewood, Joan, *Joan's Book: Joan Littlewood's peculiar history as she tells it* (Methuen, 1994).

Luard, Elizabeth, *Family Life: birth, death and the whole damn thing* (Bantam, 1996).

Maddox, Brenda, *The Half-parent: living with other people's children* (André Deutsch, 1975).

Mair, Lucy, *Marriage* (Penguin, 1971).

Marwick, Arthur, *The Sixties: cultural revolution in Britain, France, Italy and the United States c.1958–c.1974* (Oxford University Press, 1998).

Morris, Jan, *Conundrum* (Faber & Faber, 1974).

Morris, Jan, *Pleasures of a Tangled Life* (Barrie & Jenkins, 1989).

Moseley, Charles, *A Field Full of Folk: a village elegy* (Aurum, 1995).

Newson, John and Newson, Elizabeth, *Infant Care in an Urban Community* (Allen & Unwin, 1963).

Newson, John and Newson, Elizabeth, *Four Years Old in an Urban Community* (Allen & Unwin, 1968).

Newson, John and Newson, Elizabeth, *Seven Years Old in the Home Environment* (Allen & Unwin, 1976).

Nicolson, Nigel, *Portrait of a Marriage* (Weidenfeld & Nicolson, 1973).

Nicolson, Nigel, *Long Life* (Weidenfeld & Nicolson, 1997).

Oakley, Ann, *Housewife* (Allen Lane, 1974).

Opie, Iona, *The People in the Playground* (Oxford University Press, 1993).

Parker, Tony, *The People of Providence* (Hutchinson, 1983).

Pimlott, Ben, *Harold Wilson* (HarperCollins, 1992).

Pizzey, Erin, *Scream Quietly or the Neighbours will Hear* (Pelican, 1974).

Roberts, John Stuart, *Siegfried Sassoon* (Richard Cohen, 1999).

Robin, Jean, *Elmdon: continuity and change in a north-west Essex village, 1861–1964* (Cambridge University Press, 1980).

Rolph, C. H. (ed.), *The Trial of Lady Chatterley: Regina v Penguin Books Limited. The transcript of the trial* (Penguin, 1961).

Seabrook, Jeremy, *The Way We Are: old people talk about themselves. Conversations with Jeremy Seabrook* (Age Concern England, 1980).

Sebba, Anne, *Laura Ashley: a life by design* (Weidenfeld & Nicolson, 1990).

Spalding, Frances, *Duncan Grant* (Chatto & Windus, 1997).

Stott, Mary, *Forgetting's No Excuse* (Faber & Faber, 1973).

Strathern, Marilyn, *Kinship at the Core: an anthropology of a village in north-west Essex in the nineteen-sixties* (Cambridge University Press, 1981).

Sunday Times Insight Team, *Suffer the Children: the story of thalidomide* (André Deutsch, 1979).

Thompson, E. P., *The Making of the English Working Class* (Gollancz, 1963).

Tomalin, Nicholas, *Nicholas Tomalin Reporting* (André Deutsch, 1975).

Townsend, Peter, *Poverty in the United Kingdom: a survey of household resources and standards of life* (Allen Lane, 1979).

Whitehorn, Katharine, *Cooking in a Bedsitter* (MacGibbon & Kee, 1961).

6 A decadent, undisciplined society? 1980–1990

THE THATCHER YEARS

The 1980s were the Thatcher years. Born in 1925, Margaret Thatcher (née Roberts) was a provincial grammar school girl who had gone on to Oxford. Elocution lessons had eliminated her Lincolnshire accent (though the occasional dialect word escaped in moments of excitement – 'frit' for frightened is the famous example). From childhood, 'I wasn't lucky, I deserved it' was her watchword. Proof against poshocratic lures, Margaret Roberts nevertheless left Grantham and her family behind. Since her marriage to Denis Thatcher in 1951 she had enjoyed the benefit of a wealthy husband. As she acknowledged, she could not have made her political mark without the support of 'a first-class nanny-housekeeper'. Once prime minister, however, she promulgated the petty-bourgeois values inculcated by her father Alderman Alfred Roberts, the Grantham grocer: hard work, thrift, initiative, self-reliance. In an interview for *Woman's Own* in October 1987, Mrs Thatcher was to assert that 'There is no such thing as society. There are individual men and women, and there are families'. Labour voters surveyed in March 1986 said much the same: 'It's nice to have a social conscience but it's your family that counts'.

Margaret Thatcher entered Parliament in 1959. At this stage in her career she had a good deal in common with the wives of rich Victorians who, released from home duties, acted as 'housekeepers to the city' or 'the nation'. Indeed colleagues remarked on her resemblance to women active in their own constituencies – but 'writ hideously large'. Twenty years after she was first elected, still one of only nineteen female MPs, Margaret Thatcher became Prime Minister. Given her age, upbringing and political convictions, feminist collectivism was, not surprisingly, alien to her. She prided herself on being 'the best man' in her administration. Other people agreed: during the 1983 election campaign the psychologist Anthony Clare (born 1942) described the Conservative leader as 'a woman who looked like a woman, talked and walked like a woman but behaved with the ruthlessness and confidence which had hitherto been assumed to be the prerogative of men'.

Poshocrats saw her as fair game. The political grandees (who dominated her first cabinet) found her hard to stomach. The words with which she launched her premiership, 'Where there is discord, may we bring harmony', were to prove strikingly unapt. To Ian Gilmour (born 1926), an Old Etonian who had married the Duke of Buccleuch's daughter, the sentiment was both hypocritical and 'appropriately . . . spurious', not a prayer composed by St Francis of Assisi but 'a nineteenth-century pastiche'. In R. A. Butler's view, in electing her as leader the party had 'gone suburban'. Tam Dalyell (born 1932), the Old Etonian Labour MP, described her as 'a bounder'. During the 1983 election campaign the fathers and mothers of History Workshop 'took issue' with her version of 'Victorian values'. The *New Statesman* provided the column inches for their critique and offered a poster representing the prime minister as a vainglorious reincarnation of Victoria, 'Margaret Regina'. In 1985 Oxford dons refused to give her an honorary degree; in 1987 Oxford graduates elected Roy Jenkins – 'poshocrat' by adoption, sponsor of the Labour government's 'liberal hour' – Chancellor of the University. 'Mrs T' was well equipped to stand up for herself: in the phrase of the day, she 'handbagged' her critics.

Martin Wiener, whose frequently cited book *English Culture and the Decline of the Industrial Spirit* was published in 1981, argued that hostility to the 'material rat race', the perception that economic 'success means motorcars and insolence' had suffused the fabric of English cultural life since the nineteenth century. The sons of Victorian industrialists, moulded by the patrician values of their public schools, were inclined to 'let the business slide and [become] country gentlemen'. 'The Gentleman's Club atmosphere in the Board Room' combined with dogged conservatism on the shop floor to made England 'a Luddite paradise', immune to new technology. Wiener's analysis was in line with the new prime minister's instincts. Thatcher favoured self-made men. Cecil Parkinson (born 1931), educated at Lancaster Royal Grammar School and Cambridge, was a student sportsman with Brylcreem good looks who had made a successful career in business. Norman Tebbit (born 1931) had a tough childhood. When his father was thrown out of work in the slump, the family lost everything but the grim determination to keep their heads above water. Mrs Tebbit, who had employed a charwoman, went out cleaning; her husband, famously, 'got on his bike' and found work. Young Norman's earnings as a newspaper delivery boy went into the household budget – and paid for his own first bike. Grammar school and National Service were his passport to prosperity: he learned to fly, joined BOAC (British Overseas Airways Corporation) and, by 1959, had taken out a mortgage on a four-bedroomed house in the new town of Hemel Hempstead. The self-made suburbanite, 'the Essex man', was the archetypal Thatcherite.

The family, sex and marriage

The family, sex and marriage were topics of concern in the 1980s. At the start of the decade, the campaign to find a suitable wife for the Prince of Wales (born 1948) came to an apparently triumphant end. As *Private Eye* had constantly reminded its readers, the choice was restricted for, in spite of an increasingly tolerant attitude to premarital sexual experience, in the wife of the king-to-be, impeccable chastity was a prerequisite. A wave of popular enthusiasm greeted the 'fairytale' royal wedding of 1981; only a tiny minority of cynics and 'women's libbers' took up the slogan 'Don't do it Di'. Diana's elder son, Prince William, was born in 1982. The fairytale, like many romances of the decade, had a sour ending. Feeding an apparently insatiable public appetite for scandal and titillation, the press released ever more powerful demons of voyeurism, sensationalism and innuendo. Celebrities' doorsteps and dustbins yielded 'lucrative detail'. Nigel Dempster's *Social Gazetteer*, published in 1990, collected instances of serial monogamy and extramarital relationships among the subjects of his gossip columns. The Royal Family was not exempt. His heavy hints included the statement that Camilla Parker-Bowles was 'regarded as the closest confidante of the Prince of Wales. By coincidence', Dempster observed incorrectly, 'her great-aunt Violet Trefusis was mistress of his great-great-grandfather King Edward VIII'.

The brouhaha provoked by the revelation, in September 1983, that Sara Keays (born 1948) was pregnant by Cecil Parkinson illuminated a significant shift in attitudes. Miss Keays' affair with Mr Parkinson went back some years. He acknowledged that he had 'told' her of his 'wish to marry her'. Yet, in the end, with her pregnancy in the public domain, having discussed the situation at length with his wife Ann, whom he had married in 1957, and their daughters, Parkinson took the decision that they should 'stay together as a family'. The prime minister, a staunch defender of the traditional family, had apparently pressed him to take this course. Journalists were divided. The *Sunday Times* defended the newer morality: 'There are many in the party and the country who think the more honourable course for Mr Parkinson would have been to have kept his promise, gone for divorce and married his pregnant mistress.' Katharine Whitehorn and Auriol Stevens came to the same conclusion, though they made their case in markedly different terms: 'Mr Parkinson's sin was to give Miss Keays sufficient faith in a secure future to become and remain pregnant – something she had refrained from doing during a long affair – and then welsh on her'. In the view of the *Mail on Sunday*, Miss Keays' predicament was her own responsibility: 'Ambitious and well-off young women of 36 do not have babies by accident. In the age of the Pill and easily available abortion, they choose to have them'.

Writing in the *Sunday Express*, John Junor took much the same line:

> Of course, he has brought it upon himself. Like many another warm-blooded man before him he has been a fool. But will I have Women's Lib and the Equal Opportunities Commission on my back if I ask just one question? In this day and age does any 36-year-old lady become pregnant unless she deliberately chooses?

It is striking that, whether they took Keays' side or Parkinson's, these commentators shared a matter-of-fact acceptance of adultery, abortion and divorce. To the *Daily Telegraph*, however, that proposition that 'a quiet abortion is greatly to be preferred to a scandal . . . hardly seem[ed] a moral advance'.

The family's capacity to harm its members was urged by the comic celebrity John Cleese (born 1939) and his therapist Robin Skinner (born 1922) in *Families and*

How to Survive Them. Published in 1983, the book sold well for the rest of the decade. Practitioner and patient argued that only a therapist's remedial 'parenting' could enable a person to outgrow the damaging 'emotional habits' learned from natural parents.

The 1981 census exposed an unprecedented demographic diversity. This was, in part, a consequence of large-scale immigration from the Commonwealth. In 1951 there had been 75,000 black or Asian people in the UK. Thirty years on there were 2 million. In London, the inner boroughs had concentrations of black and Asian households. Spitalfields was the home of the London Bangladeshi community. Families of south-east Asian origin brought with them the tradition of the arranged marriage – the Immigration Act 1982 was designed to prevent marriages of convenience. Londoners of Caribbean origin settled close to people from their home islands: Jamaicans lived south of the River Thames; settlers from Dominica and St Lucia lived in Notting Hill and Paddington. Stereotypically traditional English families, white married couples with children still at home, clustered in the outer suburbs. In 1987 half the babies born in Lambeth and Southwark were born to unmarried women; in Wokingham in Surrey the incidence of birth outside marriage was one in ten. However, cultural difference was not a straightforwardly ethnic phenomenon: affluent white households in Westminster, Kensington and Chelsea tended to diverge from conventional patterns.

As marital status became murkier, the old prejudices against marriage with 'in-laws' were further eroded. In the early 1980s private Acts of Parliament cleared the way for marriages with a deceased wife's daughter and a deceased husband's son.

Age as well as class influenced habits and attitudes. There were indications that older people's views were generally more conservative. There was a fear that the London Labour Party's 'espousal of the cause of gays and Lesbians' was alienating pensioners. Homosexual relationships between consenting male adults, decriminalised in the 1960s, remained a sensitive subject. An increasing – though by no means universal – toleration of the 'gay scene' had marked the 1970s. The children's book *Jenny Lives with Eric and Martin*, a fictional photo story of gay parenting, translated from the Danish and published by the Gay Men's Press in 1983, provided the press with an opportunity to stir up a storm of homophobia. In 1988 Clause 28 of the Local Government Act outlawed 'promotion of homosexuality as a pretended family relationship'. Other children's books affirmed more traditional values. The Ahlbergs' Burglar Bill (catchphrase: 'I'll have that!') saw 'the error of his ways' and made a fresh start as Bakery Bill, husband and affectionate stepfather.

The first deaths from AIDS occurred early in the 1980s. At first it was seen as a 'gay plague', a self-inflicted disaster affecting promiscuous homosexuals, heroin addicts – and unfortunately also innocent haemophiliacs who had been treated with infected blood products. It was not until 1986 that the government recognised the risk of heterosexual transmission and mounted a national campaign under the banner 'DON'T DIE OF IGNORANCE'. The leaflets dispatched to every household in the UK contained explicit references to semen and vaginal fluid and to oral and anal sex. The message was stark but the language was clinical. The tabloid press supplied human interest – of a sort. The openly gay television personality Russell Harty (born 1934) was a conspicuous victim of the press's systematic hunt for hints of 'sexual indiscretion'. Harty's last illness – he died in 1988 – was made grotesque by journalists, armed with telescopes and disguised as medics, keen to dredge up evidence that he had AIDS. He did not.

The plan to install Cruise nuclear missiles on American bases revitalised the peace movement. In the 1950s the Campaign for Nuclear Disarmament had been spearheaded by elderly 'eggheads', in the 1960s students had taken the lead, now it was the turn of women. In February 1982 the Peace Camp set up at Greenham Common in Berkshire a few months earlier was declared a man-free zone. Some women arrived 'committed as feminists to working collectively'. The Greenham Common women took attention-grabbing non-violent direct action: on April Fool's Day 1983, for instance, women dressed as teddy bears and Easter bunnies picnicked inside the perimeter wire. Their example moved women of all kinds and ages. As the journalist Suzanne Lowry observed,

> There *were* committed feminists and lesbians. There were also intellectuals, librarians, teachers and grandmothers. There was chewed-off short hair, but there were also long silky braids, Queen Elizabeth II perms, expensive bobs and North London worthy tousles.
>
> The first person to greet me on arrival was . . . a shopkeeper from Essex whose three sons were paying for her vigil.

For some, Greenham was a family affair. For one demonstration, Emmy, a resident of the camp, was joined by her mother, her daughter and her sister. The grandmother, frail after a bout of illness, was in a wheelchair with 'several pairs of bolt cutters' hidden 'under her shawl'. 'All the women in my family spanning the ages of 12 to 82 had worked together to fight Cruise', Emmy remembered with pride. Protest boosted women's confidence. It was not only in Downing Street that the female voice rang out with unprecedented force during the 1980s.

Britain and Argentina had a long-running dispute over the South Atlantic territories that Britain called the Falkland Islands and Argentina the Malvinas. Geography favoured the Argentine claim but the population of the 'village on a rock' was of British stock and staunchly loyal to the mother country. On 2 April 1982 an Argentine force occupied the islands. British ships were ordered south to 'teach the Argies a lesson'. The *Sun* led the press assault on 'Johnny Gaucho' with headlines like 'STICK IT UP YOUR JUNTA' (20 April) and, most notorious, 'GOTCHA' (3 May), an ill-judged shout of triumph at the sinking of the *Belgrano*. In spite of significant death toll on both sides, national opinion backed the enterprise and acclaimed the British victory. The prime minister's popularity soared. Sympathy for the families that had suffered as a result of the war was expressed in donations to the South Atlantic Fund. Once again, attitudes to 'the family' were revealed. A representative of the Soldiers, Sailors and Airmen's Families Association was convinced of an unmarried mother's entitlement to be treated as a 'proper widow' only when presented with evidence that the wedding date had been agreed by the vicar and that the dress and cake were ready. 'Controversy and bitterness' were generated by the decision to distribute the fund according to financial need – perhaps the old hatred of the means test played a part but the main provocation seems to have been the assumption that sons were worth less than husbands.

Electronic revolution

In the 1980s the computer came of age. Technology and competition from the developing world wiped out manual jobs in industry and agriculture and increased the demand for technicians and managers that George Orwell had predicted forty years earlier. Prosperity was concentrated in the 'high tech' crescent running south-west from Cambridge to Hampshire and encompassing parts of London. The new town of Milton Keynes in Buckinghamshire proved an outstanding success. From the 1970s, the new Open University was a major employer. In the 1980s, Milton Keynes became the headquarters of other national enterprises: British Telecom, the Trustee Savings Bank. The Abbey National Building Society moved there from Baker Street, London. The town set out to woo Japanese companies; thirty-two were persuaded to establish themselves there. A Japanese boarding school opened. The shopping centre promised 'shopping as it should be'. Parking was easy and free, you could get a meal or a snack, there was 'something for the children', special events were an extra draw. It proved a powerful magnet. Coach companies ran shopping trips to Milton Keynes from as far away as Carlisle. The popular appetite for shopping seemed insatiable. Nevertheless the movement to keep Sunday special successfully resisted the campaign for seven-day opening.

In the affluent metropolitan zones, the 'yuppy' – the young upwardly mobile City worker, earning and spending at a phenomenal pace, was a type of the decade. Journalists coined other 'lifestyle stereotypes' like the 'dinky' (couples with double income, no kids). Everywhere, however, even in Silicon Fen, as wordsmiths dubbed the Cambridge region, technology and takeovers cost jobs. Unemployment became a fact of middle-class life. Blue-collar workers also suffered. In the aerospace industry at Stevenage in Hertfordshire, thousands of jobs disappeared. The higher cost of living in the south-east deterred unemployed people from other parts of the country from taking Norman Tebbit's advice to get on their bikes and look for work; frequently too the specialist skills they had to offer were no longer in demand.

In the 1960s, Liverpool had borrowed glamour from the Beatles. The 1980s were grim years for the city. The port of Liverpool had been declining for decades. Now the city suffered a succession of 'Black Fridays' when redundancy notices came out with factory workers' wage packets. New technologies cut swathes through the labour force. In an automated cigarette factory, for instance, a single technician took the place of 50 workers. Of the 230 youngsters who left a Toxteth comprehensive in 1980, only 36 had permanent jobs to go to. Alan Bleasdale's *Boys from the Blackstuff*, filmed on location in 1981, brought the plight of the city's unemployed men and their families into living rooms across Britain. Yosser

Hughes' refrains 'Gizza a job' and 'I can do that' became national catch-phrases and local football chants. In July 1981 an angry encounter between a black youth and the police sparked serious rioting which lasted for weeks. On 28 July, the eve of the royal wedding, there were fireworks in London's Hyde Park, while in Toxteth, Liverpool torched cars lit up the night sky. In the aftermath of the riots, Mrs Thatcher appointed Michael Heseltine, Secretary of State for the Environment, 'Minister for Merseyside'. He called the report he wrote for his cabinet colleagues *It Took a Riot*. As he explained, 'No sentiment was more frequently expressed to me during the time I spent . . . in Merseyside'. In the eighteen months before Heseltine was moved from the Environment to Defence he made some differences – the river was cleaner and the renovation of the Albert Docks had begun. But in April 1985 70 per cent of the city's population of 16 to 19 year olds were either out of work or on a temporary job-creation scheme.

Heavy industries were in trouble too. In steel towns families had 'set the clock by the shift sirens'. 'At night . . . the sky would light up like a glorious red sunset, and as the slag cooled down so the glow disappeared'. A County Durham man tried – and failed – to picture his home town without its threatened steel works:

> I've thought about it and thought about it and I just can't imagine it. I'm sixty. All my life the works have loomed over this town. My dad worked there; his dad before him. As a kid I went to sleep with the sound of the steel works running. I just can't imagine this town without a steel works.

Corby, the 'industrial oasis in an agricultural desert', the 'Little Scotland' in Northamptonshire, faced a similar shutdown. Like steel, the coal industry was in decline. As households and corporate customers switched to cleaner and more convenient sources of fuel and power, jobs were lost and miners slid down the national league table of earnings. Although a programme of early retirement, voluntary redundancy and transfers to still-viable pits was put in place, the appointment of Ian McGregor (born 1912), 'the Yankee . . . butcher' who had halved the workforce in the steel industry, as chairman of the National Coal Board, was a red rag to militant miners. McGregor's chief adversary was the Yorkshire miners' leader, Arthur Scargill (born 1938). Scargill was the son of a miner and a homemaking mother ('I didn't eat a slice of bought bread until she died', he said). Provoked by the decision to shut the still-viable Cortonwood Colliery, Scargill led his men into a year-long strike in April 1984. A decade earlier the Conservative government had been a casualty of the three-day week brought about by a miners' strike; now large coal stocks and the working miners of the profitable Nottinghamshire pits were insurances against power cuts. As the strike dragged on, the old age pensioners and the long-term unemployed in mining communities began to look well off: 'Shampoo, soap, sanitary towels' became luxuries. Labour councils tolerated arrears of rent. Though their leaders were unpopular in the country at large, there was widespread sympathy for the miners. The comedian Billy Connolly (born 1942) and the jazz singer George Melly (born 1926) put on benefit concerts. Across Britain, moved by the miners' courage, people dropped coins into collecting buckets. At Christmas French miners bought toys for the strikers' children. When the strike ended in defeat for the miners in April 1985, the Durham men laid their banner up in the cathedral as a disbanded regiment might its battle honours. Traditionally miners' wives were homebound. Virtually the only paid work for a woman in a mining community was in the shop and the school. The strike gave an opportunity for women to deploy their organisational skills in the public sphere, leaving their husbands to mind the children and the house. One man is reported to have asked, perhaps tongue in cheek, 'When this strike is over can I have my wife back? Not this one, the other I had before.'

The print trade was the next conspicuous industrial casualty. Fleet Street printers – a formidable dynastic force since the end of the eighteenth century – had accommodated earlier advances in technology: first the steam press then, in the 1890s, Linotype, a process that made the compositor, who set type by hand, superfluous, but thanks to the power of his union, did not put him out of a job. In 1986 the newspaper proprietors, led by Rupert Murdoch (born 1931), overrode the unions' power and brought in electronic typesetting. Many print workers lost their jobs.

'Lifestyle choice' was a phenomenon of the 1980s. The best-off had the longest menu. In 1979 there were 4.4 million people dependent on means-tested benefits; in 1990 there were 7 million. Now, for the first time since the 1930s, beggars became a conspicuous part of the English cityscape. A photograph of homeless people sleeping rough in cardboard boxes under a hoarding advertising Perrier water – fashionable, fizzy, costing more than the price of a loaf – was the telling image chosen for the cover of Frank Field's *Losing Out*, published in 1989. Commentators speculated about the emergence of an 'underclass'. Definitions varied. Those without educational qualifications, young people who had never had a job, the members of big families, old people without occupational pensions, some – but by no means all – single parents and their children were the most commonly identified constituents. Where there was no incentive to get up in the morning, daily life took on different rhythms and routines. With little money to spend, what was there to look forward to? As Jeremy Seabrook observed, 'You always see the first Christmas trees on poor estates'. Defiant deprived families developed what one commentator called 'a "fuck you" mentality'.

Women's work

For married women, paid work had become the norm. Many young women still saw paid employment as a prelude to a spell as a full time wife-and-mother and managed their money accordingly. 'His income always paid the bills, mine paid the one-offs'. Professional women were often reluctant to suspend their careers. Led by the banks, employers developed support systems for working mothers. Professional couples adopted a range of solutions to the dual career dilemma. Janet and Allan Ahlberg made books for children. According to his account, he wrote the words, 'took me about a day', she made the pictures, 'took her about six months'. Their daughter Jessica prompted at least one book when she was 6 or so and wrote 'boredom' on a 'thinks bubble'. Dr Chip Coakley and his wife Sarah shared a post in the Theology Department at the University of Lancaster. (Other academic partners found themselves living apart during the week.) Professional men with wives in paid work tended to help at home. In 1982 the sociologist Ann Oakley (born 1944) shared childcare and cooking with her academic husband; other tasks were divided between them on conventional gendered lines: she cleaned, washed and ironed; he shopped for food (a common arrangement), managed the family's money and domestic machinery. The art critic Tim Hilton (born 1941), working from home, took on the cooking and shopping and looked after his son 'for most of his waking hours'. Many parents of young children committed a large slice of their joint income to meeting the cost of childcare – at home or in a nursery. Less highly qualified married women worked, as they had always done, to buy luxuries or necessities, to get out of the house. The cost of childcare was a problem. One woman minded a child in the afternoon to earn the money to pay another mother to mind hers while she worked in the morning. The state sent out mixed messages to poorer mothers. Lone parents were not obliged to work while they had a child under 16 years of age but family credit, introduced in 1988, favoured working parents.

Where men's jobs disappeared, women's survived: caring, cleaning, serving in shops. Wives whose husbands had little prospect of finding another job, stopped work themselves to protect their family's state benefits. Men responded to long-term unemployment in different ways. Some behaved as though they were on an extended holiday, 'just lounging about, tinkering with the car'. Others cared for children and grandchildren, cooked and cleaned. The bathroom became one older man's 'pride and joy': 'when it's polished, it shines and it's lovely'.

By the end of the 1980s, families who depended on state support were unlikely to be able to meet their children's rising expectations for branded clothes and other goods. Desire to be a 'cutting-edge consumer' was widespread even among young children. The manufacturers of soft drinks, sweets, ice lollies and potato crisps responded to this appetite for novelty. So did the toy industry. Cabbage Patch dolls were the craze in the run-up to Christmas 1983. One old woman denounced the materialism of the modern child. She remembered that she had had 'a doll made from an old gippo's clothes peg and I loved her . . . My granddaughter . . . doesn't know how many dolls she's got, ugly bloody things they are as well, all painted and dressed up like whores'.

The sophistication of the tools used in cooking, washing, cleaning and the electronic armoury of the gardener and the home improver made it more dangerous and thus more difficult for children to enjoy sharing household tasks with their parents. Traffic and the fear that children might be abused or abducted quarantined children in their homes. Junk food and a sedentary life made children fat.

Habitat

The privately owned and occupied country house, a feature of the English landscape since the sixteenth century, was by now a rarity. The Oglanders, who had lived at Nunwell on the Isle of Wight for the better part of nine hundred years, put it up for sale. The Shirleys let their house at Ettington, an estate that had been handed down in an unbroken male line since Domesday. Other houses were converted into apartment buildings.

The tall blocks of council-owned flats championed by architects in the 1950s and 1960s had proved a social calamity. The common spaces, walkways and stairs were vandalised and abused. Canvassing in the lead-up to the Greater London Council elections in 1981, Tony Benn was dismayed to find that 'people were terrified of coming to the door. They just called through the letterbox . . . The state of the stairs was awful'. A Hackney woman, whose brother had emigrated to the United States, reported that, when he came to stay, she got up 'before dawn in order to sneak out and clean the lift' to spare her guests from the human faeces, urine and other noxious debris. Jeremy Seabrook recorded his impressions of Hunslet, Leeds, the district of back-to-back houses where Richard Hoggart had been brought up between the wars. The old houses had been cleared and replaced by

> blocks of prefabricated flats and maisonettes, four storeys high, at right angles to each other, forming symmetrical courtyards with bright squares of grass at the centre . . . The flats themselves are light and spacious, some of them with spectacular views over the changing city skyline.

But

> only a third of those flats are still occupied, because, although only fifteen years old, they are unfit and awaiting demolition. They are damp and structurally unsound . . . The tinned-up doors, pavements and walls are covered with graffiti; there is a choking smell of urine; dogs wild and famished, without owners . . . Plastic containers, silver-foil trays of meals from the takeaway, chicken bones and decaying chips, cartons of washing-up liquid; egg-boxes and kitchen refuse tumbling from a split plastic bag; discarded pieces of furniture – a sofa that has been slashed with a knife . . . there is the shell of a television, and a stripped car-frame. The messages scrawled on the surfaces say Janice had her period here – penny a lick; beat inflation – eat cunt; keep Britain tidy – kill a wog.

In 1980 council tenants were given the 'right to buy' their homes at hefty discounts of up to 60 per cent. The result was a dramatic rise in home ownership. Buyers were delighted: 'If I hadn't voted for Margaret Thatcher, we wouldn't own this house now, would we?' The practice of allocating the better housing stock to 'decent' families and concentrating 'problem' households on 'sink' estates affected the pattern of purchase. The better-off tenants occupied and bought the better property. Regularity and simplicity had been the guiding principles of council house design. The buyers' instinct was to embellish and individualise their property: 'They call it tarting up. It's keeping up with the Joneses'. But it was also an expression of pride: 'I stood and looked at that kitchen ceiling for quarter of an hour last night after I finished it. I know it's silly but it's the satisfaction you get. And I wouldn't feel like that if I didn't own the place'.

At the end of the decade, in the more prosperous south, house prices began to shoot up. Less scrupulous sellers conducted a sort of informal auction after a sale had been agreed but before the exchange of contracts – a sharp practice known as 'gazumping'. Those not already on the home-owning 'ladder' worried that they would never make it. 'Before we bought it house prices were going up every week and we were panicking'. Then, 'virtually the day after we moved in, the house market dropped through the floor'. 'Gazumping' was replaced by 'gazundering' – the term was derived from the euphemism for chamberpot: a chamberpot is a 'gazunder' because it 'gazunder' the bed. A house that had sold for £125,000 now fetched £78,000, an £80,000 house sold for £52,000. Those who had bought at the top of the market found themselves owing more than they could recover by selling their property. 'Negative equity' was the jargon term for their misfortune. The worst affected were first-time buyers in their twenties, often couples in full-time work. One consequence was that plans to start a family were shelved.

CRADLE TO GRAVE

Babies

Though motherhood was often postponed, the ideal of the two-child family, established between the wars, proved tenacious.

By the 1980s it was normal to find fathers in the labour ward. But, while some professionals were sensitive to the father's feelings and might invite him to cut the umbilical cord, he was often treated badly, forced to swamp himself in gown and cap, turned out into the corridor and forgotten. All the same, for many men, watching the birth of a child was an emotional highpoint. The metaphors they chose to convey their reaction came from traditional theatres of masculine endeavour: 'a personal Everest', 'a moon walk'.

Advances in medical technology made it possible to sustain smaller and smaller premature babies. Machines breathed for them and fed them. 'The most expensive end of the business' was how a manager at Chesterfield Hospital described the premature baby unit there in 1989. Many lay people would have echoed Tony Benn's response: 'God! If premature babies are uneconomic units, where the hell are we?' Over the years the scope of the possible was enlarged. The writer Susan Hill (born 1942) recorded the brief life of her daughter Imogen (27 May–20 June 1984) who weighed only 630 grams when she was born after twenty-five weeks' pregnancy. 'She was so unimaginably tiny . . . completely formed and normal – but all in miniature. Her *whole hand* was only as large as the top joint of my thumb'. (Another mother was to describe holding her son as 'like holding a bag of fragile twigs'.) Some babies tinier than Imogen survived, as Susan Hill observed: 'We might have been lucky. A few days before she was born, another baby arrived at 24 weeks' gestation. And weighing 570 grams (60 grams and 1 week less than Imogen)

... she is now a fine, healthy four-year-old.' Many very premature babies suffered grave disabilities, including defects of the heart and brain. The legal judgment in the case of Baby C, born in Yorkshire in 1988, determined that there was no obligation to provide medical treatment for a new-born baby with no 'capacity to interact meaningfully with her surroundings, mentally, socially and physically'. The child should be cared for 'in such a way that she may end her life and die peacefully with the greatest dignity and in the least pain, suffering and distress'.

Medical expertise did not eliminate the impact of home circumstances on the mother and her child. Deaths from 'preventable causes' remained several times higher among the babies of poor parents than among those born to professional men and their partners. Data from the early 1980s indicated that the babies of Bangladeshi-born women were almost twice as likely to die as those whose mothers had been born in England. The sudden, inexplicable death of young children, often called 'cot deaths', devastated families from all social classes. But, by the 1980s, children were routinely immunised against the diseases that had killed their grandparents' contemporaries. Along with tetanus, whooping-cough and diphtheria presented the greatest danger to the new-born who were generally vaccinated against all three in one go. Immunisation against polio, mumps and measles followed. Rubella – or German measles as it used to be known – is a mild childhood illness but one that damages the hearing, sight and hearts of babies infected in the womb. Girls were, therefore, immunised against rubella in early puberty. Of the once familiar diseases of childhood, only chickenpox was allowed to take its course.

Authors of manuals on childcare put an unprecedented emphasis on the father's role in bringing up babies. The veteran Dr Spock (born 1903), sensitised to women's 'crusade for equality and justice', was prepared to argue that 'a father should be willing to cut down to a part-time job' if the mother wished to carry on with her career. For most families this was not a realistic prescription. A father's share in childcare depended as much on the shape of his working life as on his inclination to change a nappy, push a buggy or tote a baby in a sling. The schedules imposed by some occupations were grossly unfriendly to family life. Service couples were subject to prolonged separation. To compensate for the loss of the new mother's earnings, some less well-off men took second jobs. High-powered careers often dictated long hours away from home. The MP Norman Fowler (born 1938) came late to fatherhood: his daughters were born in 1981 and 1984. Diary entries quoted in his memoirs – 'I think Fiona feels like a single parent'; 'I treat the house like a lodging house' – underlined the incompatibility of the standard House of Commons day – 2.30 to 10.30 p.m. – with normal family life. Working hours, along with divorce, contributed to the proliferation of 'weekend fathers'. Penelope Leach (born 1937) was among the writers who wanted babies to be treated in a more 'natural' way. She pointed out the exceptional 'physical separateness' imposed on most western infants. At night, she suggested, breastfed babies, sharing their mother's bed, could 'sleep-feed', 'evolving a timetable' for themselves. Babies should be allowed to suck a dummy, or better still, their thumb, if it gave them comfort; Leach argued in favour of cloth comforters too. It was a mistake, she claimed, to encourage a small child to see toilet training 'as the pinnacle of achievement and the one accomplishment of which his parents truly approve'.

In general, the children of professional and managerial parents stood a greater chance of being breastfed, were more likely to see their parents naked and to have the facts of life explained early. As we observed in Chapter 5, middle-class families divided between those who inclined to the principles of 'conspicuous waste' and those who practised 'conspicuous thrift'. The parents' political principles helped to shape the baby's routine. Some 'Green' parents rejected disposable nappies and opted instead for the old-fashioned towelling square which 'could be reused by subsequent children, passed on to others, recycled into dusters, then floor cloths' and finally rags – handy for such dirty jobs as adjusting a bicycle-chain. Others had reservations about the environmental cost of using washing machines and detergent.

Childhood

Paid employment was widely seen as 'good for mothers, bad for children'. Complications increased as children reached school age. Nurseries were open from morning till evening all the year round. School hours were shorter, there were the long holidays and the intermittent 'Baker Days', set aside for teacher training, to cope with too. The cost of childcare squeezed mothers into less interesting and worse paid jobs or forced them to give up paid work altogether. High-earning parents, concentrated in the south-east, could afford to employ and house nannies: *The Lady*, founded in 1885 remained an important medium for their recruitment. Working parents often stressed the 'quality' of the time they dedicated to their children; less, it was true, than a homebody might have spent with hers a generation earlier but enriched by their outside experience and the spending power it brought. In reality, tired parents and tired children coming together at the end of a long day found 'quality time' elusive. Pressure to conform and to have and wear the same as other children in their peer group made it increasingly hard for parents to preserve and transmit habits and values to the coming generation. Yet some succeeded against the odds.

The fluidity of adult relationships affected children. Couples who split up but maintained a partnership as parents could provide their children with two loving homes, joint holidays and outings. It cost a good deal to achieve such an equilibrium. Money, emotional maturity and the cooperation of the new men and women in the adults' lives were prerequisites. As commentators often observe, stepfamilies were commonplace in traditional English society. Taking the long view, the pattern of 'low illegitimacy, low fertility and long . . . marriage' established between the wars was seen as a 'golden', 'transient conjuncture'. But the stepfamilies of the late twentieth century, the product of broken relationships rather than death, were different in kind. Children of the 1980s might easily go from living with two natural parents to living with a single parent or commuting between their mother's home and their father's, to membership of a stepfamily within a matter of months. Caretaking fathers were in a minority: one lamented that he was the wrong shape to give his children cuddles. Men separated from their children tended to lose touch with them. Generally speaking, the children of one-parent families were poorer than children with two parents at home. Money was not the only challenge. Lone parenthood and step-relationships alike were shaped by what had gone before. For children, separation or divorce could be harder to cope with than the death of a father or mother: a tantalising mirage of reconciliation shimmered on the horizon of their lives.

Composite families varied in their make-up. Step-siblings might be decades apart in age or clustered close together. They might share the same household or live in ignorance of each other's existence. And step-parents faced tricky questions. In what respects did a parent's partner become a parent? Should a step-parent be addressed or referred to as 'dad' or 'mum'? (For a child to adopt a stepfather's surname, that traditional badge of family membership, the natural father's consent was necessary.) Had step-parents the right or responsibility to tell children off or smack them? Parents fell out over any number of things including junk food, clothes and haircuts. A Sheffield United fan bitterly resented it when his former wife's partner took their children to Sheffield Wednesday matches. Keeping in touch with the parents and siblings of a former spouse for the sake of their children demanded a mutual sympathy and patience that many divorced men and women found beyond them. The behaviour of grandparents and other relatives could widen fissures by singling out 'their' children for special favour.

The journalist Alan Brien (born 1925), three times married, saw his children's experiences in a positive light:

> I cannot pretend that this making and breaking of marriages, starting and stopping of families, has not inflicted damage on my children . . . I do not think it is self-deceit to feel that the extended many-parented family does bring rewards and pleasures not found in the tight-knit nuclear unit or the one-parent group – so long as the adults involved give up being childish and the children are taught what it means to be adult. I know my own daughters have all benefited from being able to talk over their fears and worries and pleasures and hopes with stepmothers.

Carol Slater, a working-class woman interviewed for a project led by Ann Oakley, told a bleaker story. Carol Slater had seven children, only one of them living with her and her second husband at the time of the interview; there were twins on the way. Her first child, born when Carol was an unmarried 18 year old, had been adopted; two others had died; a daughter, severely disabled by rubella caught *in utero*, was in residential care; the two remaining children lived with their father, Carol Slater's first husband.

In the later 1980s parliamentary and public concern focused on the damage adults could do to children. Corporal punishment was banned in state schools in 1986. ChildLine, a charity that offered children confidential advice on physical and sexual abuse, was set up in the same year. Some concerns were tragically misplaced. In 1987 92 diagnoses of anal abuse were made in Cleveland in the months of May and June. In the event, it was recognised that the assumption that 'physical signs' were the basis for 'an unequivocal diagnosis' was mistaken. It was for misidentified families a traumatic and damaging instance of moral panic.

Children damaged themselves. The fashion industry's use of waif-like models fed fears of fatness and the incidence of eating disorders such as anorexia and bulimia increased among adolescent girls: 'To become fat means becoming lazy, greedy, selfish, sloppy, stupid, unattractive, uncaring, untidy, disgusting. No price is too great to pay for avoiding gaining weight.' Drug-taking increased. In the late 1980s the use of stimulants like Ecstasy became widespread among young people of all classes.

The boundaries of childhood shifted, rather uncertainly. From an early age children were dressed and presented like miniature adults. They were exposed to many aspects of the adult world through the media and direct experience. Comparing her granddaughter with herself, one upper-class woman concluded that, at 7, she knew 'much more than I did at 17'. Film classifications regulated cinema showings, television companies scheduled programmes deemed unsuitable for children after 9 p.m. but it was the parents' responsibility to regulate viewing at home and more and more children watched unsupervised in their bedrooms.

The authority of a parent over a son or daughter under the age of 16 was challenged by the Gillick case. In 1981 Victoria Gillick objected, in principle, to the possibility that medical professionals might prescribe contraceptives or arrange an abortion for one of her daughters. The courts decided that the 'arbitrariness of birthdays' carried less weight than the perceived competence of the young woman in question. Young people were increasingly involved in decisions about other medical procedures. They were consulted about their preferences when their parents separated or divorced. The Children Act 1989 emphasised parental responsibilities and children's rights. It became possible for a child to disown a parent.

Education

School was the only institution that clearly separated children from adults. As Education Minister in the 1970s, Mrs Thatcher had ended the schoolchild's entitlement to free milk – 'Milk Snatcher' was her first nickname. As prime minister, she presided over cuts in government spending on nursery schools and school meals, economies that hit the poorest families hardest.

The 1980s saw a powerful reaction against the principles that had informed the reorganisation of state education in the 1960s and 1970s. This culminated in the legislation of 1988. The Education Reform Act (ERA) was chosen to signal a new epoch. The Act justified its sponsors' claims. Central government, parents and the heads and governors of popular schools were empowered at the expense of the local educational authorities (LEAs). The Assisted Places Scheme enabled the children of ambitious but less well-off parents to go to independent schools. Where a majority of parents backed the proposal, any state school with a roll of 300 or more could opt out of LEA control. Heads and school governors were made responsible for managing their own budgets. Parents were offered a greater freedom to choose their children's schools: 'parent power' was the new catch-phrase. Head teachers became entrepreneurs, parents consumers. Pushy parents tended to favour well-equipped, small, single-sex schools with predominantly middle-class intakes. House prices and the cost of bus and train fares meant, of course, that parental income was a significant determinant of parental choice. As market forces came into play, the future of less-popular schools was put in jeopardy.

With 'back to basics' as its battle cry, ERA imposed a national curriculum on the compulsory phase of state education. In future, at the ages of 7, 11, 14 and 16 children were to be tested in these subjects against centrally determined targets of attainment: results would be published. Independent schools were exempt. The General Certificate of Secondary Education (GCSE) replaced the GCE and CSE. A grade 1 in CSE had been the equivalent of a pass in the GCE. Only the top three GCSE grades counted as passes for the purpose of university entry. In the 1950s, Ordinary Level, broadly equivalent to the GCE, had been a passport to a range of professional training. By the 1980s, Advanced Levels, degrees, even postgraduate qualifications were required. Examinations were, more than ever, 'a device for rationing opportunity'. Low aspirations made many young people from less privileged families reluctant and generally under-achieving pupils.

The children of the inner cities grew up side by side with youngsters of different cultures and colours. There was friction, even emnity, between black and white – but it was not universal. Jo-Jo, the youngest of seven boys, half-Irish, half-Scots, born and bred in Balsall Heath in the West Midlands, was interviewed in 1986. 'I was brought up by mainly black people,' he said. 'There was always some West Indian granny who would babysit'. As far as Jo-Jo was concerned, Balsall Heath was 'the centre of a melting pot', a place where 'ebony and ivory' lived together in perfect harmony. Certainly many young whites enjoyed Reggae music and, often unconsciously, adopted Jamaican 'patois'. But young whites who 'acted black' encountered hostility from both communities, branded 'wog lovers' by racist whites and resented by their black contemporaries for 'invading areas which those guys didn't want me to invade', as one young man put it. Yet, in spite of persistent evidence of prejudice against black and Asian individuals and communities, by the turn of the century England had the highest proportion of mixed-race couples in the world.

Inner-city schools faced the challenge of children who arrived unable to speak English. The educational experiences and success of children from minority cultures varied. With the backing of ambitious parents, young people from some Asian communities thrived at school. The joke went: 'Question: "What do you call a Patel who doesn't own a paper shop?" Answer: "Doctor".'

Working-class boys began to fall behind in terms of academic achievement and, consequently, earning power. The Youth Opportunities Scheme and its successor the Youth Training Scheme were designed to stop poorly qualified 16 year olds going straight from school to the dole queue. In March 1981 Tony Benn met a group of trainees in his Bristol constituency, 'kids of sixteen and seventeen . . . punk rockers, a black boy with purple hair, guys in sort of Hell's Angels outfits with holes in their trousers'. He summed them up as 'utterly hopeless and demoralised'. Girls with poor prospects of employment saw early motherhood as a means of achieving an adult identity, an income and a home of their own: a baby was 'something that's yours and you can love'.

Higher education

By the mid-1970s, there was a conspicuous dearth of black and Asian social workers and teachers in London. 'Access Courses' were devised, designed to build on 'real life' experience as well as book learning. By the end of the 1980s, in most parts of the country, early leavers, members of ethnic minority communities, women, working-class men, all could use an Access Course as a stepping stone to higher education. Women had come to value themselves as much, or more, for their achievements outside the home as in their traditional domestic sphere. A lack of confidence and self-esteem characterised many of the 'housewives-and-mothers' who joined these courses. Some of these women had the full backing of their partners and children. Others endured sabotage. One man 'flushed essays down the toilet' and 'turned the TV up to full volume' to 'disrupt [his wife's] homework'. There was a world of difference between the experience of a mature student at a city poly and an undergraduate at an ancient university. Stefan Collini, a Cambridge history don, described his university as the venue of 'a long coming-out party for some of the more exam-adept children of the professional and upper-middle classes of, predominantly, South East England'. Brought up among metropolitan sophisticates, Petronella Wyatt was disappointed to find that life at Oxford was 'not at all like *Brideshead Revisited.*'

The marriage go round

The 1980s were marked by a flight from conventional prudence. In many communities the occasion and meaning of marriage were changing. The 'shotgun wedding' was a thing of the past – the options open to unmarried teenagers who found themselves pregnant were, in order of preference, abortion, single mother-hood and, statistically least appealing, marriage. Many fewer babies were available for adoption. In 1980 the Church of England Society received 2500 applications from would-be parents and placed only 156 babies – in the 1960s it had arranged 700 adoptions a year. The evidence of reminiscences, memoirs, biographies and obituaries written in the more permissive present indicates that covert premarital sex was not uncommon in earlier decades. But it was in the 1980s that 'living together' became normal in at least the childless phase of a 'long-term relationship' – a commonly used phrase that implied that short-term sexual relationships were common. Cohabitation came to be accepted as broadly equivalent to formal, certificated marriage. By the end of the decade perhaps getting on for half a million couples were cohabiting (informal unions are hard to track). The high-profile unmarried, child-rearing 'clearly well-established and permanent unit' was a fact of metropolitan life. The language of cohabitation presented problems: 'live-in lover' put too much emphasis on the sexual dimension; 'significant other' not enough;

'posslq[ueue]' [person of opposite sex sharing living quarters] was altogether too coy. 'Partner' emerged as the favoured term – conveniently, it covered gay couples too. Tax relief on mortgages favoured unmarried couples. Employers began to treat cohabiting partners in the same way as couples who had registered their marriages: thus British Rail gave the same travel concessions to both formally and informally attached heterosexual partners in 1981. Yet marriage remained significant. The law of intestacy preserved a clear distinction between a surviving spouse and a surviving cohabitant – to the strong advantage of the formally married. The Department of Health and Social Security took a similar line: members of its staff had a duty to pursue and prosecute lone mothers who were suspected of drawing benefit while living with an employed man. The policy was not justified on moral grounds. It was seen as a matter of equity: a married man was expected to support his wife and stepchildren.

Parenthood

Looking back over her life, Diana Mosley (born 1910), who eloped in the 1930s, observed, 'Marriage as such meant little to me; yet three years after his wife's death we did marry, because we wanted children, and in those days it was supposed to be better for children to be born in wedlock'. By the end of the 1980s the stigma and civil disabilities that had affected children born outside marriage between the wars had virtually disappeared. Among the few heritable privileges confined to a legitimate child were the father's citizenship and hereditary title.

As the differences between married and cohabiting partners diminished, parenthood emerged as a more significant boundary than marriage. The proportion of births that took place outside marriage rose from about one in eight in 1980 to more than one in four in 1990. All the same an unplanned pregnancy or the decision to 'start a family' still prompted weddings. Churches remained a popular setting for marriages even in families that rarely entered a place of worship in the course of their normal life. The dignity of the surroundings and the language helped to make the occasion special. Register offices lacked glamour but from 1995 a variety of spectacular secular sites were licensed for the celebration of marriage – among them the Brighton Pavilion, the Pump Room at Bath and London Zoo. As attitudes to marriage changed, so did wedding cakes. In place of the traditional tiered cake iced in white, couples chose designs that meant something to them. 'A cake in the form of a couple sitting on a settee with the children of their previous partnerships' was one example.

Parenthood was an expensive choice. 'The Tidy House', a story written by three 8 year olds at school, plotted the impact of twin babies. The authors 'called the last part of their story "The Tidy House that is No More a Tidy House"'. And one of them drew a more substantial moral: 'If you never had no children, you'd be well off, wouldn't you? You'd have plenty of money.' Childlessness lost its stigma. The extinction of family lines was one, inevitable, consequence. With less confidence in their posterity, older family-minded people turned their attention to their roots. 'Family history' boomed.

Women – and couples – who wanted children often chose to postpone their first pregnancy. A third of the women born in 1960 went through their twenties without becoming mothers. Those who opted out of early motherhood were haunted by the ticking of 'the biological clock' in their thirties. Failure to conceive could be heartbreaking for them and their partners too. Artificial insemination was a long-established practice – John Hunter, a Scots surgeon, described an insemination he had carried out in 1776. The sperm might come from the mother-to-be's partner (Artificial Insemination by Husband or AIH) or from a donor (AID). *In vitro* fertilisation (IVF), the procedure that produced 'test-tube' babies, was novel, expensive, very rarely available on the NHS and not covered by private health insurance. IVF posed moral dilemmas too. What should be the fate of surplus embryos not implanted in the womb? Should 'commissioning' parents support them indefinitely in rented refrigerated limbo? Agree to their disposal? Donate them to another couple or for medical research? Once a pregnancy had been established, could the practice of 'foetal reduction' (the killing of one or more embryos by a lethal injection through the heart) be justified in the interests of their siblings' improved prospects? The essential question was: when did a foetus become a person? The legal status of a child born as a result of artificial insemination varied according to the identity of the donor and the circumstances of insemination. The law privileged anonymous, medically managed arrangements over do-it-yourself donations between friends.

The tendency for fertility treatments to result in multiple conceptions accounted for a high incidence of very small premature babies, often shortlived: none of the Halton septuplets born in 1987 lived more than 18 days. In many cultures twins had been regarded as an unplanned, exceptional burden. Faced with a multiple birth, one mother exclaimed: 'Why me? I just want to be ordinary and normal'. On top of the exhausting challenge of managing even healthy triplets or quads, parents found themselves being treated as 'social freaks'. Buggies were built for a maximum of two. 'As far as most manufacturers are concerned you have to stay at home if you are on your own with three or more small children'.

Divorce

In the new tolerant climate, fewer couples were prepared to put up with 'monogamous monotony'. Older children often played a part in persuading parents to patch up a shaky marriage – to keep the family together. But, for a significant proportion of the adult population, the obligation to self displaced duty and extinguished the old commitment 'till death us do part'. A desire to remarry frequently prompted divorce – by 1988 more than a third of marriages involved a divorced person. The spectre of the third party goes a good way to explain why, in spite of attempts to make divorce less traumatic, the dissolution of marriages continued to cause distress and bitterness. An uninhibited campaign against an estranged partner could backfire: a spouse unwilling to divorce might find that his or her reaction was interpreted as evidence of the irretrievable breakdown of the marriage.

When home-owning parents divorced, it was usual to give the parent who had custody of the children – usually the mother – possession of the house until the youngest was sixteen or eighteen. Judges recognised that the consequences of the sale of the former matrimonial home at that point could be 'harsh and unsatisfactory' for the children, as much as their mothers, and varied their practice accordingly. The sale and the division of the capital it yielded could be postponed until the woman died or remarried. The end of a marriage did not inevitably spell the death of a family but parents often found the challenge of maintaining the 'charade' and keeping things 'nice' for the children beyond them. The hurt and vindictive had endless scope to do mischief.

Wrangles over chattels were common. Solicitors discovered that some clients were sufficiently embittered to spend £1000 on legal fees to get hold of £100-worth of goods.

Old age

Youthfulness was prized. Men as well as women used dyes and unguents to mask grey hair and wrinkles. Medical technology played a part in making 70 'younger than it was'. Cataract operations restored 'the joys of sight and colour' to those exiled to a 'sepia world'. Hip replacements restored mobility. 'Old age', it was said, 'was becoming a lifestyle choice'. But it was a choice that was open only to those with reasonable health and sufficient cash. The older generations included many whose constitution had been undermined by poor feeding in the hungry 1930s, by polluted air, by smoking. Like the termination of adolescent dependency, the onset of old age varied from person to person.

Retirement from paid work was a significant moment. For the MP Enoch Powell (born 1912), defeat at the polls in 1987, which brought his career at Westminster to an end, was a kind of death. Traditionally the transition had been easier for women, who generally had 'little jobs', insignificant beside their primary role inside the family. During the 1980s, the experience of women and men converged. Jenifer Hart represents the growing number of undomesticated women whose identity was bound up in their work. She reached the retirement age for Oxford academics in 1981. 'Suddenly' her whole way of life was transformed. She was plunged into 'aimless limbo'. Voluntary social work filled 'a gap in [her] life'. In her eighties she wrote her memoirs. Jenifer Hart retired, as Oxford University Statutes required, at 67. Many working men and women found themselves too old at 50.

Meaningful activity kept people going into their seventies and eighties. In 1981 the Cambridge academic Peter Laslett (born 1915) set up the University of the Third Age (U3A). A concept borrowed from France, U3A was designed to make the most of autonomy and leisure – the bonuses of old age – and stave off decrepitude and dependency. Social clubs were set up to cater for ageing members of the Windrush generation of immigrants from the Caribbean. Being needed by family and friends safeguarded older men and women against the bleak fate of 'negative liberty'.

Some occupations offered formally retired people opportunities for continued practice. Professor N. G. L. Hammond (born 1907) retired from the chair of Greek at Bristol University in 1973. As an obituarist observed, 'between 1973 and 1992 . . . he was a visiting professor at 16 universities' and 'books began to flow from him' – the last went off to his publisher shortly before his death in 2001. To the end of her life in 2001, the distinguished embroiderer Beryl Dean (born 1911) worked religious pieces. Barbara Tribe (born 1913) finally gave up teaching at the Penzance School of Art in 1988 but she did not count herself among the retired: 'An artist never retires'. Henrietta Fanshawe was still exhibiting her mosaics in her late eighties. Fred Roy (born 1901), who had been a professional juggler until he was 75, kept his hand in with daily practice and performed for charities. Leslie Edwards (born 1916), a member of the Royal Ballet, left the stage reluctantly at the age of 77. The journalist Bill Deedes (born 1913) went on commuting to work in London more or less fulltime. Brian Johnson (born 1912), best known for his cricket commentaries, worked until he dropped in 1993.

The eminent elderly benefited from a continued or revived interest in their achievements. Writers and politicians found themselves 'pushing up theses'. Landmark birthdays and other anniversaries were publicly celebrated – Alistair Cooke (born 1908) dubbed such events 'state funerals'. John Betjeman received a literary *Garland* on his seventy-fifth birthday. Harold Macmillan's ninetieth birthday, in 1984, prompted him to accept the earldom traditionally offered to former prime ministers. The Queen Mother (born in 1900), was perhaps the best-loved member of the Royal Family. In 1990 her birthday was marked by a parade in London. John Piper was 80 in 1983. His wife Myfanwy, the Queen Mother herself, the sculptor Henry Moore, the poet and performer John Betjeman, the singer Peter Pears and other friends put together a book of greetings and appreciations, including the citation for the award of an Honorary DLitt by the University of Sussex in 1974. Historians' interest in the memories of 'ordinary' men and women helped to give their witnesses a sense of continuing worth. Professionals caring for older people developed reminiscence therapy to keep their clients intellectually and socially active.

But there was a bleaker side to ageing. James Lees-Milne lamented 'the squalors of the septuagenarian body and the anguish of frustrated sexual passion' that left him feeling 'wound up like an old grandfather clock'. Simple tasks became a challenge. Pamela Foster confessed that she could no longer 'open anything'. 'I rush out into the street and ask perfect strangers, "*Would* you be so kind as to open this for me?"' Fear of falling robbed many old people of their independence. Among 'the recreations' John Wolfenden (born 1906) listed in *Who's Who* were 'trying to come to terms with arthritis, bifocals and dentures' (1983) and 'trying to remember' (1984). He died the following year. 'Left alone', the elderly Frederick Ashton (born 1904) 'lapsed quickly into slovenliness, wearing three-day-old soup-stained shirts, dropping cigarette ash on his lap', discarding his false teeth, peeing in the garden because it was too much trouble to go to the lavatory. In his eighties, John Gielgud complained that most of his friends seemed to be 'deaf, dead or living in the wrong part of Kent'. Mental confusion was common. Living with Alzheimer's could be 'like being chained to a corpse', 'a corpse which the undertaker has cruelly forgotten to collect', 'a long bereavement'. Death was not a simple release, however. John Bayley (born 1925), who nursed his wife Iris Murdoch (born 1919) through her long twilight, remarked on 'the gap caring leaves when it stops'.

People aged over 75 occupied half of the beds managed by the NHS. Cut off by the deaths of their contemporaries or their own poverty or disability, forced to give up their homes, old people could find themselves socially redundant, confined to a 'granny farm', dead to the world, even longing for death, but kept going by medical intervention. Generally speaking, life in a hospital or nursing home was not an active life. Gloria Wood and Paul Thompson, who gathered the recollections of men and women in their nineties in the 1990s, observed that: 'The lack of voices from old people's homes is one stark measure of the extent to which institutionalised life saps the confidence of residents in themselves and their ability to speak'. Their witnesses were predominantly female and predominantly middle or upper class. Institutional practices could erode identity to such an extent that only disease or disability remained as a distinguishing mark. Stubbornness, the last vestige of adult independence, made dependent old people hard to manage. By the 1980s the ideal of an all-embracing welfare state, approached in practice in the 1940s, was challenged in principle and seriously eroded in practice. Entitlement to free care in old age was a bastion the popular media were eager to defend. The plight of the old and the sick tugged at the heartstrings but, as both Tory and Labour governments recognised, it was easier to arouse indignation and raise pledges of cash for heroic operations than to increase levels of direct taxation.

Death

By the 1980s, cancer, heart diseases, strokes, pneumonia and bronchitis were the most frequent causes of death in adults. The management of death was overwhelmingly professional and institutional. Experienced staff came to expect the dying to keep to a timetable, not to go 'too soon' or linger too long. We have already noted the high casualty rate among small premature babies, including much-wanted outcomes of medically assisted conceptions. Prompted by parents, nurses and doctors showed a new sensitivity in their treatment of stillborn babies and babies who died soon after birth. They were recognised as individuals and accorded a brief biography: held, named, photographed and given a funeral.

The definition of death exercised medics and others in the 1980s. In the past the absence of a pulse, evidence that the heart had stopped beating, the failure of breath to mist a glass or stir a feather had demonstrated the fact of death. Now technology could maintain the functions of heart and lungs in a brain-dead body. A person in a 'persistent vegetative state' was in limbo, 'alive and not alive'. The decision to switch off the life support system was delicate, often taken in consultation with the next of kin.

The death of a healthy child or adult offered the possibility of 'harvesting' sound organs for transplantation. Perhaps a third of bereaved relatives refused permission: they saw the removal of organs as a violation of the body, they did not want the remains of a loved one cut up or hacked about. The allocation of organs raised further ethical questions. Should they go to the sickest candidate? The healthiest? The one with the greatest family responsibilities? The patient geographically closest to the donor? Organ transplants held out fresh hope to the parents of children with congenital problems. Laura Davies was born with a bowel defect in 1988: an operation saved her life. In May 1992 she was given liver and bowel transplants. When complications ensued, her family, friends and a mass of sympathisers waged a determined campaign for further surgery. In September 1993 she underwent a heroic suite of transplants: liver, stomach, pancreas, small intestine, bowel and kidney. The kidney soon failed. After her death, her father was moved to wonder whether Laura and her family 'might not have been better off' fifty years earlier, before the era of forlorn hopes.

The Falklands War cost 255 British lives. The experience of the 134 widows and the next of kin of the unmarried men illustrated the variety of circumstances in which bereaved families face sudden death. The traditions of the unit and the sensitivity of commanding officers and other key personnel were important factors, so was the place where they lived. The most fortunately placed were probably the SAS (Special Air Services) families who were concentrated in Hereford. They had the support of a close-knit service community and, many of them, family and civilian friends close by.

At Sheffield Wednesday's football ground in April 1989, 96 Liverpool supporters died, crushed or asphyxiated. Unprepared for a disaster of this magnitude, professionals handled the painful process of identification clumsily. Relatives were prevented from touching or holding the bodies of sons, daughters and partners. The defensiveness of the agencies responsible for the spectators' safety (the police above all), the stereotype of the football fan as a drunken lout, press sensationalism, popular voyeurism and the law's delays and obfuscations combined to intensify and prolong the families' distress. In the days following the disaster, the stadiums at Anfield in Liverpool and Hillsborough in Sheffield became the first focus of a great spontaneous floral tribute to the dead. The custom of leaving flowers at the site of an accident that had claimed a life spread – black spots on the roads bloomed.

Tim Parry (born 1980) was one of two boys killed by an IRA bomb in Warrington in March 1993. The blast occurred on 20 March; on 25 March, his parents agreed to switch off the life support system. The consultant described 'how the body could go into spasm and jerk about, perhaps even moving so violently that a leap clear out of bed was possible'. The prospect so horrified his mother that she could not bear to be present when it happened, a decision she was to regret. The nursing staff allowed Tim's father to lie beside him on his bed, hold him in his arms and kiss him goodbye as the machinery was switched off.

Cancer and AIDS killed young and middle-aged people. With notice of their deaths, richer people with AIDS chose where they would die. The gay community made a powerful collective response to the challenge of death by AIDS. They set out to enable those who were open about their condition to die in style. The London Lighthouse, opened in 1988, was fitted out like a luxury hotel – it was the 'Hilton of hospices'.

Hospices still accommodated a tiny fraction of the dying, no more than one in ten at the end of the decade. Hospice staff set out to 'end on a bright note' but, as one doctor confessed, there was 'no dignity in dying, you can't have your bottom wiped with dignity'. Blake Morrison (born 1950) left a graphic description of his father's last illness. The former GP, in his mid-seventies, whose life had been 'a web of little scams', died from bowel cancer. While he was still able to drive, he told his son how he stopped at a Happy Eater 'to dig the shit out by hand'. Later he needed panty-pads and suffered faecal vomiting. He approached 'the great moment of death' like 'a baby in distress'. There were better deaths. Prue Postgate was diagnosed with cancer of the colon in her forties. Her 'unwinnable battle with so much bitter pain and hopelessness' ended 'gently'. Her death was expected and planned for. She was at home with her family. As far as her husband Oliver was concerned, 'there was no unfinished business, nothing left unsaid or unforgiven'; the couple had already shared 'their time of mourning'. Janet Ahlberg (born 1944) liked finding and making presents that suited her family and friends. In 1994 she dealt with her coming death from cancer by choosing the things they would remember her by and writing 'farewell postcards'. Her husband Allan celebrated her life and work in *A memento*, as he described *Janet's Last Book*. *Janet's Last Book* was a patchwork of finished and rough work for their books, birthday cards (for her daughter's tenth she drew Jessica at a party attended by characters from the *Beano*), pictures of presents she had made or decorated for her friends and family. It was a memento originally intended for them but soon shared with the wider circle of her admirers.

Most people were cremated. Services slotted into tight schedules, were often impersonal, conducted by strangers, the 'well-meaning man of God' who had never met the subject of his address. Many mourners, unfamiliar with the rhythms of church services, did not know when to stand up or sit down. Alongside hymns, families chose popular songs to express their feelings: 'I did it my way' and 'You'll never walk alone' were among their favourites. Then, as the service ended, to the accompaniment of 'awful piped music', 'the coffin slid away on a conveyor belt'. 'Someone pressed a button and off he went'. Perhaps alienated by the funeral service, families left the staff of the crematorium to scatter the ashes. Burial was the choice of older people and, often, the parents of babies and children who found some comfort in visiting their graves. Tim Parry was buried in an Everton strip with 'two Everton footballs, donated by the club, cradled in his arms'. What tokens did other people carry to their graves?

The funerals that commemorated their subjects most appropriately were probably those of people who, like Tim Parry and the Falklands War casualties who identified strongly with a team or regiment, those whose families and friends had a developed sense of theatre and those planned well ahead. Enoch Powell devised a complicated ceremonial cycle fifteen years before he died in 1998. The day was to begin with a requiem in Westminster Abbey, attended by his widow, his two daughters and other close relatives. The first public celebration took place in St Margaret's, Westminster, the parish church close by his beloved House of Commons; the second in Warwick, in the church that housed the chapel of Powell's wartime regiment. He chose to be buried in the uniform of a brigadier of the Warwickshires. Less well-known families also organised distinctive funerals. Jane Warman's mother 'couldn't bear those black cars, those po-faced men'. Her family decided on alternative arrangements:

> We took mother in the back of the battered old dormobile with a beautiful Persian carpet draped over the coffin. But the road was very hilly. Every time we went uphill, the coffin slid backwards. We had this awful vision of it slipping out onto the road – and we all laughed. She would have loved it.

Memorial services also allowed for idiosyncratic commemoration. Sir Angus Wilson (born 1913) was a 'stately homo' of the old guard (he recalled that in his long life he had progressed from Nancy Boy to Gay, via Pansy and Queer). At his memorial service his partner Tony Garnett (born 1936) read an epitaph that the architect Sir John Soane had chosen for his wife in 1812. The verse, composed by the Soanes' friend Barbara Hofland, begins

> I did not know thee in that happier hour
> When smiling Youth upon the lap of life
> Sprinkles her gayest flow'rs

After formal goodbyes, the bereaved continued to celebrate the dead in their own ways. In Aldershot before the Falklands War a group of young men from the Parachute Regiment had habitually pooled their small change to buy the last round of drinks in their local. For a while, after the war, a share of the coins were saved and scattered on the graves of comrades who had died, as a kind of libation. Theresa Burt, whose 17-year-old son Jason was killed in the war, followed the fortunes of the Chelsea football team on his behalf and put reports of the matches in his room. The academic Hugh Tinker also lost a son in the South Atlantic. He spent the summer after his death working on *A Message from the Falklands: A life of David through his letters* (1982). 'Through his letters he could reach out and make known how he had come to grasp the meaning of the war'. On 28 May 1982 David Tinker had written

> I cannot think of a single war in Britain's history which has been so pointless . . .
>   To recapture a place which we were going to leave undefended from April, and deprive its residents of British citizenship in October. And to recapture it, having built up *their* forces with the most modern Western arms (not even *we* have the Exocet which is so deadly). And fighting ourselves without the two pre-requisites of naval warfare, air cover and airborne early warning, which have been essential since World War II . . . They really should not send people in the services to study history at university.

Colin Parry, who had kept journals of his sons' childhoods, used the material he had collected as the basis of an affecting biography.

Reading

Ahlberg, Allan, *Janet's Last Book* (Penguin, 1997).

Ahlberg, Allan and Ahlberg, Janet, *Burglar Bill* (Heinemann, 1977).

Bosche, Susanne, *Jenny lives with Eric and Martin* (Gay Men's Press, 1983).

Campbell, John, *Margaret Thatcher: volume 1, The grocer's daughter* (Cape, 2000).

Carr, Jean, *Another Story: women and the Falklands War* (Hamish Hamilton, 1984).

Clapson, Mark *et al.* (eds) *The Best Laid Plans: Milton Keynes since 1967* (University of Luton Press, 1998).

Crick, Michael, *Michael Heseltine: a biography* (Hamish Hamilton, 1997).

Dempster, Nigel, *Nigel Dempster's Address Book: the social gazetteer* (Weidenfeld & Nicolson, 1990).

Diamond, Anne, *A Gift from Sebastian* (Boxtree, 1995).

Field, Frank, *Losing Out: the emergence of an underclass* (Basil Blackwell, 1989).

Garfield, Simon, *The End of Innocence: Britain in the time of AIDS* (Faber & Faber, 1994).

Gillick, Victoria, *A Mother's Tale* (Hodder & Stoughton, 1989).

Hart, Jenifer, *Ask Me No More: an autobiography* (Peter Halban, 1998).

Kavanagh, Julie, *Secret Muses: the life of Frederick Ashton* (Faber & Faber, 1996).

Keating, Jackie, *Counting the Cost: a family in the Miners' Strike* (Wharncliffe, 1991).

Laslett, Peter, *A Fresh Map of Life: the emergence of the third age* (Weidenfeld & Nicolson, 1989).

Leach, Penelope, *Who Cares? A new deal for mothers and their small children* (Penguin, 1979).

Lowry, Suzanne, *The Princess in the Mirror* (Chatto & Windus, 1985).

Morrison, Blake, *And When Did You Last See Your Father?* (Granta, 1993).

Oakley, Ann, *Social Support and Motherhood: the natural history of a research project* (Blackwell, 1992).

O'Conner, Garry, *The Secret Woman: a life of Peggy Ashcroft* (Weidenfeld & Nicolson, 1997).

Parry, Colin and Parry, Wendy, *Tim: an ordinary boy* (Hodder & Stoughton, 1994).

Reiss, Herbert (ed.), *Reproductive Medicine from A–Z* (Oxford University Press, 1998).

Routledge, Paul, *Scargill: the unauthorized biography* (HarperCollins, 1993).

Seabrook, Jeremy, *Landscapes of Poverty* (Blackwell, 1985).

Simpson, Bob, *Changing Families: an ethnographic approach to divorce and separation* (Berg, 1998).

Skynner, Robin and Cleese, John, *Families and How to Survive Them* (Methuen, 1983).

Spock, Benjamin, *Parenting* (Michael Joseph, 1989).

Stanworth, Michelle (ed.), *Reproductive Technologies: gender, motherhood and medicine* (Polity Press, 1987).

Steedman, Carolyn, *The Tidy House: little girls writing* (Virago, 1982).

Tebbit, Norman, *Upwardly Mobile* (Weidenfeld & Nicolson, 1988).

Tinker, Hugh, *A Message from the Falklands: the life and gallant death of David Tinker from his letters and poems* (Junction, 1982).

Widgery, David, *Some Lives! A GP's East End* (Sinclair-Stevenson, 1991).

Wiener, Martin, *English Culture and the Decline of the Industrial Spirit, 1850–1950* (Cambridge University Press, 1981).

Wolfram, Sybil, *In-laws and Outlaws: kinship and marriage in England* (Croom Helm, 1987).

Wood, Gloria and Thompson, Paul, *The Nineties: personal recollections of the twentieth century* (BBC, 1993).

Young, Hugo, *One of Us: a biography of Margaret Thatcher* (Macmillan, 1989).

Conclusion
Prophesies fulfilled?

In poll after poll readers voted J. R. R. Tolkien's *The Lord of the Rings* (published in 1954–55) *the* book of the twentieth century. The struggle of the brave and lucky against evil appealed to Tolkien's contemporaries, who had fought in the First World War, and to their sons, who had fought in the Second. 'The fantastic' in its many manifestations has been identified as the century's 'dominant literary mode'. By the millennium sober predictions and even science fantasies of earlier generations had become realities. In an essay published in 1941 George Orwell foresaw a rising demand for technical experts of all kinds, managers and sales-people – and 'the spread of middle-class ideas and habits' to the working classes. Earlier, in the 1920s, Kegan Paul, Trench, Trubner and Co brought out a run of provocative, prophetic pamphlets. Robert Graves's *Lars Porsena*, which we encountered in Chapter 1 on Cultural Tribes, was among them – in keeping with the high status of the classical tongues, almost all of the little books had titles derived from the ancient world. Many of them grappled with issues of gender and what contemporaries would have thought of as the future of the race. Norman Haire, eugenicist and sexologist, wrote *Hymen or the Future of Marriage* (1927). He calculated that 'only one marriage in four may be judged as even tolerably success-ful, and a very much smaller proportion can fairly be considered as really happy'. His remedy for this sad state of affairs was radical. He advocated 'rational' sex *education* for children and sexual *experience* for young people as they reached physical maturity in their mid-teens: 'unwanted pregnancy will in time disappear, consequent on the increased knowledge of contraception'. He predicted that 'prejudice against the unmarried mother' and her baby would vanish. The state would support children. Easy consensual divorce would be legalised. Speculating on the *Future of Morals* (1925), C. E. M. Joad argued that 'in a purely promiscuous community the livelihood of women would be intolerably insecure. Hence women are the guardians of morality, knowing that it guarantees their bread and butter.' But now

> Birth control has come to stay; it has also knocked the bottom out of what is called sexual morality.
> Economic independence enables [women] to have children without going either to the altar or into the workhouse. The practice of birth control makes it unnecessary even to have the children.

As the clear cut line of demarcation between married and unmarried unions becomes obscured by the increase in the number of the latter, it will no longer be either possible or necessary to put the unmarried mistress so completely beyond the pale of decent society as has been customary in the past.

Robert T. Lewis argued for nursery schools 'to remedy the defects often inherent in the conditions of home life'. They would serve 'as a great instrument of preventative medicine' and free mothers to pursue careers.

In the last quarter of the twentieth century, means of birth control, abortion included, became more readily available. The old rules that women should 'save themselves' sexually until their wedding night and that marriage was a lifetime commitment were openly and widely breached. A substantial segment of decent society had ceased to spurn 'the unmarried mistress'.

In the past, prudent couples had put off 'starting a family', sometimes by means of heroically prolonged engagements, until they had established themselves financially. Now highly qualified women postponed motherhood until they were firmly set on a career path. Parents dedicated to pursuing parallel careers reproduced 'virtual orphans', brought up by mercenary caretakers. A significant proportion of heterosexual couples chose to remain 'childfree'. The qualifying adjective 'heterosexual' acknowledges the unprecedented – if incomplete – frankness about sexual orientation. Homosexual partners no longer passed themselves off as master and man.

The infantilisation of adults

The twentieth century was the age of the teddy bear (born 1903). In her forties, Angela du Maurier (born 1904) recalled that dolls were for best.

> But our bears were our children; I still have the two I was given when a year old. They lie on my bed, very dirty and furless . . .
> I find people of my generation on the whole do cling to the toys of their childhood, far more than our grandparents of the Victorian era did. My brother-in-law's little bear goes everywhere with him accompanied by one of Daphne's; they are known as the boys.

The brother-in-law in question was General 'Boy' Browning (born 1896). The response to an advertisement that the actor Peter Bull placed in the personal column of *The Times* in 1969 revealed the widespread necessity for bears. Pauline Marrian (born 1904) and Mister Bear had been brought up in a nanny-ruled nursery at a time when childish ailments could kill: 'after measles and the whooping cough' Mister Bear endured 'Turkish baths beginning in the oven and ending on the clothes line'. In 1925 Mister Bear and Miss Marrian threw a party for 'the teddy bears we had known in our nursery days. Some of them came all alone by post'. Graham Shepard (born 1907) passed his distinguished bear Growler on to his daughter Minette. John Betjeman's dependence on his bear Archibald Ormsby-

Gore was celebrated in his verse autobiography *Summoned by Bells*, published in 1960: 'He . . . doesn't let me down, never loses his temper . . . He's there whatever happens'. Adults acquired bears. When Amy Johnson (born 1903) flew solo to Cape Town in 1932, she took a bear with her as mascot. A Teddy Bear Museum opened at Stratford-on-Avon in 1988.

Fictional bears abounded. Rupert first appeared in print in 1920. Winnie the Pooh made his debut in 1924 – the illustrator E. H. Shepard used his son Graham's 'magnificent bear' as his model. Biffo occupied the front page of the *Beano* until Dennis the Menace ousted him in 1951. Sooty came on the scene in 1952; Paddington arrived from Peru in 1958. A Latin translation, *Winnie Ille Pooh* (published in 1960) was a best-seller on both sides of the Atlantic – in the melting pot of the United States it was the first foreign-language book to head the list. John Betjeman described Archibald Ormsby-Gore's adventures to his own children in *Archie and the Strict Baptists*. It became public property in the bear-besotted 1970s. Disney democratised Pooh in the 1960s.

In fact and fiction, bears were sex toys for grown-ups. Setting the scene for a seduction in *Crome Yellow* (1921), Aldous Huxley chose to compare the young woman in question to a teddy:

> Her purple pyjamas clothed her with an ampleness that hid the lines of her body; she looked like some large, comfortable, unjointed toy, a sort of Teddy bear – but a Teddy bear with an angel's head, pink cheeks, and hair like a bell of gold.

In John Osborne's *Look Back in Anger* (1956) Jimmy Porter, sweet-stall holder, product of a 'white tile university', and his wife, a colonel's daughter, find refuge from cruel reality in 'their cosy zoo for two': he is the bear and she the squirrel. They have furry animals to match. H. G. Wells and Rebecca West (born 1892) began an affair before the First World War. These literary lovers communicated in jungly baby talk – a variety of the patois Wells called 'idiotic': he was Jaguar, she Panther. Eighty years on the same fantasies coloured the Valentine's Day messages published in the national press.

Peter Pan, first produced in 1904, is another of the twentieth century's defining cultural institutions. Michael and Peter Tomlinson (see pp. 14–15) were among the many boys of their age to be named after characters in the play, their mother's favourite. When the actor who impersonated Nana, the nursemaid dog, went off to serve his country in the Great War, 'he first taught his wife to take his place as the dog till he came home'. The annual revivals provided George Shelton, who played the audience's favourite pirate – Smee – from 1904 to 1929, with what he called his 'old age Pansion'. *Peter Pan* is an anthem in celebration of childishness. Its author J. M. Barrie laid down that 'all the characters, whether grown-ups or babes, must wear a child's outlook as their only adornment'. Mr Darling behaves 'more like a boy and less like a real father'. Wendy Darling is the mothering child who steps into the shoes of lost parents. Her name derived from baby talk: 'friendy', baby for 'friend', became 'wendy' when an infant lisped it. In 1929 Barrie gave the copyright of *Peter Pan* to the Hospital for Sick Children in Great Ormond Street. Fifty-nine years later the House of Lords amended a copyright Bill to secure the royalties for the hospital in perpetuity. And who could grudge the sick children that bonus?

From the outset, the popularity of *Peter Pan* was exploited for gain. Picture postcards were published. Heinemann brought out *Peter Pan's Postbag* with Pauline Chase, the first actress to play Peter, as editor. The intended readership was clearly adult. Letters that displayed 'amusing instances of childish orthography are given as they were written and in some instances it has been thought worthwhile to reproduce them in facsimile'. One was typed on 'dAddy's typewrittere'.

Peter Pan was not the only literary boy of arrested development. The fame of Pooh left Christopher Robin in the shade (where Christopher Milne preferred to be). Like Peter, Christopher Robin is less a boy than a sentimental man's dream of a boy. Richmal Crompton (born 1890), then classics mistress at Bromley High School for Girls, published her first story starring William Brown in 1919. She chronicled his adventures for another fifty years. William is far from fey. Equally he is free of the humdrum preoccupations that traditionally inhibited adults.

In the 1970s infantilism infected the popular press. When the editor of the 'soaraway *Sun*', which had risen, soberly, from the ashes of the left-wing *Daily Herald* in 1964, set out to demonstrate that there was 'more to life than washing up', he indulged the schoolboy in his readers. The bare-breasted Page Three Girl first exposed herself in 1970. Words of three to six letters loomed large in the red-top tabloid text. Old playground crudities (tits, bum) rubbed along with newly coined terms for copulation (bonk, rumpy-pumpy), pet-names promiscuously applied (Queen Mum and Di) and raw manufactured emotion (fear, fury, rage).

In real life, the chief victims of infantile adults who disregarded their traditional obligations as spouses and parents were their children. As adults entered a second childhood, children put on adult dress and habits. By the end of the century, children were rejecting old-fashioned toys. They wanted 'lifestyle accessories'. It was impossible to predict which stunt would pay off. 'No group of consumers has ever changed its tastes as quickly and completely as modern children'.

A new confessional mode

The ingrained habit of keeping friends' and families' secrets was eroded. According to the Old Testament story, more familiar in the 1920s than in the 1990s, when Adam and Eve discovered shame, 'they sewed fig leaves together, and made themselves aprons' to cover their nakedness. By the end of the twentieth century there were many fewer fig leaves in place than there had been in 1920. Barriers of taste and decency were broken in the 1960s and 1970s, when Michael Holroyd opened a window on Bloomsbury, Christopher Isherwood 'came out' in print and Nigel Nicolson published a *Portrait* of his parents' unconventional marriage. By the end of the century revelatory frankness had become almost conventional among individuals with a high public profile. The nature of the disclosures varied, as did the motivation. The griefs and joys of ordinary families were exploited by the press. As Evelyn Waugh observed in *Vile Bodies* (1930): 'People did not really mind whom they read about provided that a kind of vicarious inquisitiveness into the lives of others was satisfied'. It is impossible to tell how far this new confessional mode has displaced the old reticence across the broad sweep of English families.

'Foreign blood', birth outside marriage, illness and thoughtless, unkind acts had been the stuff of traditional family secrets. Now many were brought out into the open.

The Royal Family serves as a useful index of changing patterns of behaviour. When Prince Charles was born in 1948 the prime minister, Mr Attlee, commended the 'example' the Royal Family set in 'private life'. In the mid-1950s the Queen's sister renounced the option of marriage with the divorced man of her choice. In 1992, the year the Queen called her 'annus horribilis' – she was a less competent Latinist than Hugh Dalton (see p. 87) – Andrew Morton brought out *Diana Her True Story*. The fairytale royal wedding of 1981 had a sad, sour sequel. After the Princess's death, Morton revealed that she was his principal source and he had interviewed her 'by proxy'. Tapes of intimate telephone conversations between the Waleses and their lovers entered the public domain. Both broadcast the fact of their infidelity in television interviews. Notorious womanisers like the Tory MPs Alan Clark (born 1928) and Steve Norris (born 1945) were much more economical in their confessions.

Gay men 'came out' in print. *Ruling Passions*, Tom Driberg's raw account of his life as a journalist, MP and promiscuous homosexual was published posthumously, in 1977. Friends who sat with him in the Lords 'told him that if he published', he would be forced to retire from the House. In his seventy-fifth year Lord Montagu of Beaulieu (born 1926), twice charged with homosexual offences in the early 1950s, broke his 'vow of silence'. He wanted his three children (born 1961, 1964 and 1975) and, by the late 1990s, 'beyond the reach of cruel school bullying' to learn 'the truth' about his own sexuality and these painful episodes 'first hand'. The film-maker Derek Jarman (born 1942) published his sexually explicit autobiography *At Your Own Risk* in 1992. He spoke from the perspective of a PWA, a Person With AIDS. His life spanned the gay revolutions of the later twentieth century.

> When I came to University [King's College, London] I was unaware of queer bars and clubs. I wasn't to meet anyone until I was twenty-one who admitted he was queer and he was as old as my father . . . There were very few young people out – mostly old queens.

Biographies that revealed the 'ambisexual lifestyles' of the Bloomsbury group 'broke the secrecy that surrounded us . . . Virginia Woolf was bisexual . . . Maynard Keynes was queer'. Jarman was among the hosts at the great coming out party of the 1960s and 1970s.

> By the early eighties two men having sex was no longer perceived as a trans-gression. HIV changed that . . .
>   'AIDS, AIDS, AIDS', shouted the kids in the playground, 'Arse Injected Death Syndrome'.

But, even among the self-styled liberals of the chattering classes at the close of the century there was a limit to the knowledge and tolerance of gay sexuality. Both Katherine Bucknell, the editor of Christopher Isherwood's account of his *Lost Years*, and Peter Conrad, who reviewed the book for the *Observer*, recognised that 'rimming' would be a practice unfamiliar and distasteful to some of their readers. The editor supplied the definition in a footnote; the reviewer provided a buffer several paragraphs thick and a flag to warn the squeamish.

Where will we go from here?

Demographic trends may be significant. There is no doubt that English society is ageing. The number of people over 80 doubled between 1970 and 2000. The Queen Mother shared her hundredth birthday with a dozen or so women and men. Those of us who will be old in the first decades of the new millennium are already mature adults. The proportion without adequate incomes is likely to present a particular social challenge. Divorced women not entitled to a share in their husbands' occupational pensions will be a significant new group. Among the 'old old' chronic degenerative illnesses, including dementia, are widespread. How big a share of the national purse should be assigned to treating and caring for people with frail bodies and flaky minds? At what point does medical intervention – as opposed to palliative care – amount to a cruel and costly prolongation of the process of death?

Uncertainties surround other vital boundaries. Legally, birth confers identity and rights. The survival of babies born long before their time has highlighted the question of the rights of the foetus. Only the preservation of the mother's life legally justifies the abortion of a foetus capable of life outside the womb but legal intervention to protect the unborn child from maternal abuse or neglect is exceptionally rare. Should this be so?

The right to marry is confined to couples born of opposite sexes. Neither homosexual partnerships nor partnerships involving transsexuals can be legally affirmed by marriage. Should this continue?

Historians interpret the past. They do not predict the future. Fiction writers who do tend to favour dystopic scenarios. In Aldous Huxley's *Brave New World* (1932) genetic technology has been harnessed to produce a rigidly stratified society. The lyrics of a popular song epitomise the regime's strategy for keeping the population happy: 'orgy-porgy' sex and soma, the state-sanctioned narcotic.

After Hiroshima, the threat of the Bomb stimulated visions of a new Dark Age. John Wyndham (born 1903) set *The Chrysalids* (1955) after 'God sent Tribulation' – evidently nuclear doomsday. In *Riddley Walker* (1980), Russell Hoban (born 1925) described in a richly imagined future language 'what came after Bad Time' at the end of the twentieth century. The 'Puter Leat' had got too 'clevver' for their own and other people's good and the '1 Big 1' 'ternt the nite to day'. 'Not many came thru it a live'. Hoban portrayed the hopeless impotence of people suddenly deprived of the sophisticated support systems that they had enjoyed:

There come a man and a woman and a chyld out of a berning town they sheltert in the woodlings and foraging the bes they cud. Starveling wer what they wer doing. Dint have no weapons nor dint know how to make a snare nor nothing. Snow on the groun . . . Crows calling 1 to another waiting for the 3 of them to drop. . . . The man the woman and the chyld digging thru the snow theyy wer eating . . . dead leaves which they vomitit them up again. Freazing col they wer nor dint have nothing to make a fire with to get warm.

Although the United States and the former Soviet Union no longer confront each other, the world is not secure from nuclear disaster. Our vulnerability to the breakdown of the technologies that support our ways of life has increased in the twenty-odd years since *Riddley Walker* was written. In the 1970s computer viruses were dismissed as urban myth. In the 1980s the threat was recognised. Measures were taken to immunise electronic systems of communication. Yet the possibility that essential services might suddenly be ravaged by a high-tech pandemic remains.

Fears of declining fertility have informed the plots of novels set in the near future. P. D. James's *The Children of Men* (1992), a book with strong Christian overtones, is set in 2021. It opens with the violent death of 'the last human being to be born alive on earth' just over a quarter of a century earlier – in 1995: 'Overnight the human race . . . lost its power to breed', even 'frozen sperm . . . lost its potency'. The story ends optimistically with the birth of a boy child. Margaret Atwood's catastrophe has more complex roots. *The Handmaid's Tale* (1985) is set in the United States 'in the near future'. As Atwood (born 1939) has explained, an oppressive patriarchal regime has won power as a consequence of

> the intersection of several trends . . . the rise of right-wing fundamentalism as a political force, the decline in the Caucasian birthrate in North America and northern Europe, and the rise in infertility and birth defects due, some say, to increased chemical pollutant and radiation levels, as well as to sexually-transmitted diseases.

Concern about the future health of the planet has been a theme of environmental debate since the 1970s. Thanks to the accident of geography, the British population is less exposed to natural catastrophes like the earthquakes, cyclones, droughts and floods that periodically lay waste to other parts of the world. The impact of new diseases such as AIDS has proved less devastating in the UK's rich and technologically sophisticated society than in sub-Saharan Africa. That is not to say that medical science will always rise to the challenge of disease.

One other thing is pretty certain. The historian of the family will face a new and challenging pattern of evidence. In the past the letters of famous men and women were treasured by recipients and autograph hunters: like the relics of a literary saint, Charlotte Brontë's account of her sister Anne's funeral, dismembered by her father Patrick, was distributed across six archives. Families and their houses preserved the archives of obscurer people. Alix Meynell based her life of her grandmother, born in 1844, on the diaries that Alice Dowson kept from 1862 until her death in 1927. Along with the family albums, the diaries came into Mrs Meynell's possession when her Uncle Alex died forty years later. Kingsley Amis and Philip Larkin, born in the 1920s, were unusually prolific correspondents. The biographies of eminent men and women who reached the end of their lives in the late twentieth century were increasingly based on the more fragile evidence of memories – the voices of family, friends and colleagues. Mark Girouard has described the challenge that faced him as the biographer of the architect *Big Jim Stirling* who, 'outside his office correspondence never kept letters that were written to him' and 'after the age of sixteen . . . never kept a diary'. In consequence, 'to a large extent' Girouard's biography is 'an orchestration of other people's voices'.

> A portrait of Jim and his work . . . built up as the result of my talking to more and more people, going through files and photograph albums in his home, his office archive and elsewhere, visiting his buildings, looking at his drawings, finding postcards and the occasional letter, and reading everything that I could find published by and about him.

Remember George MacBeth (born 1932). His father died when he was 9, his mother ten years later. In his thirties, MacBeth published *A Child of the War*, a memoir that is in a sense an extended commentary on the collection of small, apparently commonplace, relics of their lives, the souvenirs that linked 'the generations that never met' – his parents and his child.

Nowadays family archives tend to be richer in images and ephemera than in words. Without captions to supply the who, the when, the what, the where, the why, pictures and things decay into quaint montages as memories blur and fade. Make your contribution to the chain of evidence: label your snapshots and your videos. Leave your heirs and successors a family tree. Give them memories of the time before they were born.

Index

Steedman, Carolyn 110–11
steel industry 152
Steen, Marguerite 51
stepfamilies 141, 158–9
Stephen, Leslie 15
Stephens, Robert 47–8
Stevens, Auriol 148
Stone, Willy 23
Stopes, Dr Marie 2, 45–6
Storr, Catherine 10
Stott, Mary 49, 50, 123
Stowe School 40–1, 77
Strachey, Lytton 15
Streatfeild, Noel 104
Street Offences Act (1958) 92
Strong, Roy 61
students 134–5; protests 135
suburbs, housing in 32, 49
suicide 143
Summerson, John 5
Sun, Page Three Girls 124
Sutherland, Helen 20

Taylor, Ann 104
teachers 38, 94, 132, 140
Tebbit, Norman 147
teddy bears 173–4; fictional 174
Teddy Boys 105
teenagers: as consumers 105, 133–4;
 'kicking Daddy' 105, *see also* students
telephone 60; code changes 118
television 96, 138, 142; impact of 89–90
Tennant, 'Bim' 56
Tennyson, Hallam 41
Terry family 18
Thalidomide 129
That Was The Week That Was (TW3)
 123
Thatcher, Margaret 120, 146–7, 150,
 160
Thomas, Irene 6, 42
Thomas, Keith 7
Thompson, E.P. (Edward) 119, 143
Thompson, Valerie 19
Thornhill, Sir Henry 40

thrift: middle class 26, 126, 158, *see also*
 make-do-and-mend
Tickell, Crispin 75
Till Death Us Do Part 124
Tinker, Hugh 170
Tolkien, J.R.R., *Lord of the Rings* 172
Tomalin, Nicholas 37, 43
Tomlinson, Clarence 14–15
Tomlinson, David 14–15
Tomlinson, Michael and Peter 174
Toomey, Leonard 29
Townsend, Group Captain Peter 112
Townsend, Peter (social scientist) 2,
 112, 126
Toxteth 152
Toynbee, Arnold 142
toys 26, 154; wartime 75, 77
transport 118
Tribe, Barbara 166
Turing, Alan, Sara Turing's biography of
 17, 37
Turner, Ernest 33–4
Tweedie, Jill 140
Tweedsmuir, Lady 107
Tynan, Kenneth 124

undertakers 114
unemployment 23, 25, 151–2; long-term
 154; middle class 151, *see also*
 employment; poverty
Unemployment Insurance Scheme
 (1920) 27–8
Universal Aunts 20
universities 41–2, 105; Access Courses
 for 162; new 134–5; in wartime 77,
 see also Cambridge; Oxford
University of the Third Age (U3A) 165
Unsworth, Ellen 22
Unwin, Rayner 29–30
US servicemen (GIs) 79

vandalism, seaside resorts 134
Vaughan, Paul 41
vermin 31, 67, 127
Vesci, Lady 43